Coleen is a much-loved television presenter whose credits include *This Morning*, *Loose Women*, *Dancing on Ice* and *The Secret Guide to Women's Health*. She also writes a popular weekly column for the *Daily Mirror*, and is the author of two novels, *Envy* and *Denial*. Bernie is a celebrated actress of stage and screen, whose credits include *Blood Brothers*, *Brookside*, *The Bill* and *From Pop Star to Opera Star* as well as, most recently, *Calendar Girls*. Maureen and Linda are both well-respected, award-winning West End actresses. They all sang in the famous Nolan Sisters group, which chalked up massive record sales in Britain, Europe and Japan. Amongst their various hits, their single 'I'm In The Mood for Dancing' has become a cult classic loved by millions around the world.

the nolans

Survivors

A Powerful Story of
Secrets, Betrayal, Love and Hope

PAN BOOKS

First published 2011 by Sidgwick & Jackson

First published in paperback 2011 by Pan Books
an imprint of Pan Macmillan, a division of Macmillan Publishers Limited
Pan Macmillan, 20 New Wharf Road, London N1 9RR
Basingstoke and Oxford
Associated companies throughout the world
www.panmacmillan.com

ISBN 978-0-330-53146-7

1 3 5 7 9 8 6 4 2

A CIP catalogue record for this book is available from
the British Library.

Typeset by Ellipsis Digital Limited, Glasgow
Printed and bound by CPI Group (UK) Ltd, Croydon, CR0 4YY

Visit **www.panmacmillan.com** to read more about all our books
and to buy them. You will also find features, author interviews and
news of any author events, and you can sign up for e-newsletters
so that you're always first to hear about our new releases.

Dedications

To Carol, Jane and Vicky, my girls, who got me through the toughest times with laughter, tears and wine. To everyone I've loved and lost along the way who have made me the woman I am today: you will stay in my heart always! To Mum and Dad – I wish you could see all I went on to achieve. I miss you so much.

To my beautiful family, Ray, Shane, Jake and Ciara for loving me no matter what. I love you with every beat of my heart.

To Amanda at Urban for never losing her patience with endless phone calls and emails, I'm definitely going to find you a husband! Last but not least I'd like to dedicate this book to my manager Neil. You found me, you held my hand, you believed in me and because of you I survived!

Coleen

To my wonderful mother, who I've always tried to emulate as a person; she was everything a mum should be and more, my hero. Also my father who, with all his faults, I loved dearly. And finally to the two most important people in my life, Erin and Steve. Erin for being a truly wonderful daughter, all I dreamed she would be. My little ray of sunshine and my inspiration.

Last but by no means least a truly amazing man without whom I couldn't have got through. He has been by my side, my rock and shoulder to lean on literally, every step of the way, caring for me and Erin, holding my hand, holding me and loving me more than I ever dreamed I would be loved. Thank you Steve. Truly my world!

Bernie

To all my family and friends, especially my brothers and sisters – I'm here because of you. To Mum and Dad, I know you would be proud. I love and miss you so much. To Lloyd, Sarah and 'Lucy Lastic', your dad loved you more than life itself, as do I!

But especially for 'my Brian' whose encouragement, support and never-ending love made me the woman I am today. I love and miss you every minute of every day, and I will always be 'your Linda'. Big hugs from Hudson xxx.

Linda

To my family, you are all special people. To all my friends throughout the years – thanks for your love and support. To the newest member of my family, Maddison, and my beautiful grandaughters Ava and Sienna, who enrich my life.

And finally, to the lights of my life, my gorgeous husband Ritchie and my wonderful son Danny. I couldn't exist without you.

Maureen

Thank Yous

From us all: To Alison for telling it as it was. Ingrid, Dusty and all at Pan Macmillan publishers for letting us tell our story. Our management and agents Neil and Amanda for, well, everything actually!

Bernie: And I have to thank Tony Clayman for twenty great years together; Drew Jaymeson for getting me through all those auditions; Frank Wilcox, for Kate and especially Erin; Mark Kissin and Dr Stephen Houston for saving my life and all the nurses and staff at the Royal Surrey Hospital Guildford. If I've missed anybody I owe you a large glass of . . .!

Linda: I have to make special thank yous to clinical nurse specialist in breast care, Sarah Guilfoyle, the best white hankie waver in the business! Dr Jean Brigg, consultant clinical psychologist who had the worst tissues but on many occasions was the reason I survived. The NHS. Long may it survive!

Neil and Amanda, my management and agents, for believing in me/us and letting us live the dream one more time! Yvette Hales and Neil Warnock, my first solo agents and still my friends twenty-five years on. Bill Kenwright, for believing I could be 'Mrs Johnstone', even though my audition was 'crap' – his words!

All my friends, especially Graham and Sue, Amanda, Suzanne, Gillyarta, always there when I needed them. My wonderful sister-in-law Annie, 'my buddy', who sorted the paperwork, did the legwork and generally made it bearable, and my brother-in-law Ray, for being a great friend to my man. Love you both.

Maureen: And thank you to Joe Lewis for believing in us – sadly he is no longer with us. Massive thanks to Alan Ainsworth for sharing his talent in the early days. Thanks to my beautiful sister-in-law Linzie, taken too young aged only twenty-six, for showing me what being a good person is all about. Thanks Mum and Dad for your constant love and support and to all the fans out there, thanks for your loyalty and support in the good but especially in the not-so-good times.

Contents

Contents

1.

Maureen

Our Dublin Home

Maryville Road was teeming with kids from first thing in the morning until darkness fell over the flat, open street. All day girls were skipping and boys kicking footballs, babies were parked up in prams getting the air and toddlers were scrabbling around on the pavement. All you could hear was laughing, shouting and singing. Hardly ever did a car grind past, so the road belonged to us children. It was a time of pure happiness.

'Mum, can we go out to play now?' I'd ask before I'd even finished my porridge in the morning.

It didn't matter if it was winter or summer, red-hot (which was rare) or lashing down with rain (which was a lot less rare). Whatever the weather, us kids from the St Anne's council estate in Dublin would still be playing out until Mum came charging down the street yelling that it was time for bed.

I was the fourth Nolan child to appear and there were still another four waiting to make their appearances after me. Eight kids might sound like a total nightmare to lots of people nowadays, but down our street in those days we were considered quite a small family. The Brennan family two doors down had twenty kids!

1

MAUREEN

Our house was full of music all the time. Dad would be playing his Frank Sinatra records in the front room while Mum would be singing show tunes in the kitchen. Then there were the rest of us kids all over the house, making all sorts of racket with tin lids, spoons and any other implement we could lay our hands on.

No one in Maryville Road had much money, but the terraced houses were scrupulously tidy and the small patches of grass out the front were kept neater than bowling greens. Ours was just the same.

We had two rooms downstairs: the back room, where we lived most of the time, and the 'parlour', which sounded dead posh when Mum said it. There was floral wallpaper on the walls and a floral three-piece suite which almost matched, but not quite! On the floor were Mum's pride and joy, her vinyl tiles. At weekends she would drag us in from the street, tie rags to our shoes and get us to dance around the parlour. We thought it was all great fun. It was only later that I worked out she was actually getting us to polish the floor! She was canny like that, our mum.

Upstairs there were three bedrooms. Mum and Dad had one, the girls slept in another and the boys in the box room. At Christmas we'd all sleep top to toe in the same bed as a special treat, although I can't remember any of us sleeping much at all because we were all so excited.

From the start I was very much a middle child. I always felt very loved by my parents, but by the time I came along everything had been done before by my older brother and sisters, so nothing I did was particularly surprising. Then, after me, came the babies who were doted upon. So I just slotted in somewhere in the middle, pretty much unnoticed a lot of the time.

Middle kids are often fairly uncomplaining and easy to please. I guess I fitted that description. And in a family where you had to shout to make yourself heard, I was very, very quiet. I was a boringly good mouse! But the thing that made me feel really special was sharing the name Maureen with my mother. I liked to think that gave us a closeness that the others didn't have.

My closest ally in the family back then was my brother Brian. He was just a year and five days younger than me and also very quiet, so we got on well. Brian and I played together all the time, although it was usually me having to join in with his boy games. Even though I was desperately quiet, I got to be quite good at making 'pop, pop, pop' machine-gun noises from behind Dad's armchair.

Our family was pretty much divided up into the Boys (Tommy, the eldest, who was born in 1949 and Brian, born 1955), the Girls (Anne, who was born in 1950, Denise, 1952, and me in 1954) and the Kids (Linda, Bernie and Coleen when they turned up). When I wasn't with Brian, I was with my older sisters, Anne and Denise.

Tommy was five years older than me and even when he was probably only around ten, he already seemed like an adult to me. He was the leader of the boys' gang in Maryville Road and I utterly hero-worshipped him from afar. He seemed far too old and cool to have anything to do with me.

Anne was the leader of the girls' gang in our street. She was strong and tomboyish, and would stand up to anyone who bullied the younger kids. She'd climb trees and spit down on people who were causing trouble or jump off really high walls to show she wasn't scared. Once she broke her arm and then broke it another four times afterwards because, just as it was mending, she'd hit someone with her plaster. I adored her.

Denise was always going to be a singer. Even when she was still in a cot, she'd sing that old song 'Oh My Pa-Pa'. She'd sing from the moment she woke up until she went to bed at night. She was also brilliant at practical things and at looking after the younger ones. She virtually brought up Bernie when Mum had all the rest of us to look after.

I felt this incredible pride and sense of security at being part of 'The Nolans'. Dad always said that family came above everything. And, being naturally quiet, it gave me a tremendous confidence to know I belonged to something as big and strong as my family. That's not to say everything was perfect. There were tensions between my mum and dad even then, but I was way too young to realize it.

From the moment they met there were big differences between them, and I guess those were magnified as the years went by. Dad was born in 1926 and was brought up in Clontarf, a suburb of Dublin. Although his family weren't well-off, they were quite middle class. His parents hadn't been particularly musical, but Dad adored big band music and had a fabulous voice. He became known in the city as Dublin's Sinatra! One evening Dad was spotted singing in a nightclub in Dublin and was offered the chance to perform in England. But he was the only son in the family and his mother wouldn't let him go so far from home. His dream was crushed before it had even begun and I think that created a terrible sense of frustration in him which grew and grew.

Dad was quite short and very skinny with dark hair, so he

even looked like Frank Sinatra in his heyday. Most of the time he was very shy, but he could be extremely charming and when he started to sing, women would go weak at the knees. When he'd had a few drinks, his shyness would go and he'd be the life and soul of the party. He was very much a 'lad about town' and he had all the chat, particularly for the ladies!

I would sit at the window waiting for him to come home from work in the evenings. Often he'd bring me a red-and-white striped candy cane and the moment I saw him come round the corner holding it, I'd be running up the road to meet him. 'Ah, you're my gorgeous girl,' he'd say, bending down to pick me up.

Once he said to me: 'Maureen, I'm going to buy you the moon and stars.' For weeks I waited and waited and waited for him to bring that moon and stars home for me. I thought my dad could do anything.

'When are you getting them for me?' I asked one night. The poor man must have been desperately wondering how he was going to talk his way out of that one, but he managed it alright!

I adored my dad, hero-worshipped him even. He could sort out anything, and families would come to him from all over the estate if they were having problems or needed advice.

Mum's background was quite different. She was born in 1926 and was brought up in Inchicore, another suburb of Dublin. Her whole family loved music and her father spent all his spare time singing and putting on shows around Dublin. She had two sisters and a brother and they all had amazing voices.

Mum had a natural talent and the most beautiful voice. She was so good that, at seventeen, she was selected to train as a soprano at the Dublin College of Music. But she didn't go. We were always told it was because she didn't want to be an opera star, she just loved singing, but maybe her family put pressure on her too. Whatever the reason, it meant that neither Mum nor Dad had taken the chance to pursue their talents as far as they could have.

Mum was naturally more outgoing than Dad and didn't need a drink to be able to chat to anyone. She was straight-talking and was never one for hiding her emotions, whether she was laughing like crazy or in a foul temper. She had dark hair and greyish-green eyes and was quite traditionally Irish-looking and very beautiful. I think Denise and Coleen are the sisters who now look most like Mum. Bernie and Anne look more like Dad, and our brother Brian is his spitting image.

Mum had no ego at all and even though she was incredibly talented and very popular in the clubs where she would perform, she never did it for the applause. It was just about the music.

In 1948 Dad was performing in an act with one of his sisters. One night she was ill and couldn't sing and Mum, who was by then singing in bands around the city and at the famous Clery's Ballroom, was the understudy. That was how they met.

They never discussed it with us, but we think that fairly soon after they started going out together, Mum must have fallen pregnant.

I think Dad and his family thought he could do better than my mum and I'm sure he tried to get out of marrying her. He already had all these frustrations that he hadn't gone to work in England and when Mum got pregnant I suppose he resented the fact that he would now be tied down by a wife and kid. That hadn't been what he had dreamt of at all.

Mum's parents were very traditional Irish-Catholic working-class people and they'd have been horrified about their daughter being an unmarried mother, so she ran off to London. The idea was that Dad would follow her a few days later, they'd marry and then start a new life there together.

Except Dad never turned up. Poor Mum stayed in a boarding house in north London waiting for him day after day. She was twenty-one, on her own and pregnant. She must have been going out of her mind with worry.

In the end the lady who ran the boarding house wrote to Mum's parents in secret. When they received the letter, they took the boat over to London and brought her home. When they got back, Dad was told: 'You *will* marry her.' That was how it was in those days, but it can't have been the best start to married life.

I've never seen a photograph of their wedding day in 1948, and I don't know if any were even taken, but there are some pictures of them in those early days and they look happy.

Sadly though, I think my dad felt completely trapped and very frustrated from the word go. And although Mum never talked about it, she must have felt incredibly hurt and betrayed that he'd abandoned her in London. From the very beginning, my mum always adored my dad, but I think my dad always thought he could do better.

Singing brought them together though. On stage they were known as Tommy and Maureen, the Sweethearts of Song. How corny is that?! In the clubs, they would sing duets with one microphone, gazing into each other's eyes. But it was a lot less romantic when, a few hours later, Mum would be up setting and lighting the coal fire and stirring a massive pan of porridge for seven kids. There are even pictures of her performing on stage when she was six months pregnant with me!

Dad worked in accounts and bookkeeping and for a while he worked in a glass shop, but his jobs never lasted very long and there was hardly ever any money to spare. Poor Mum had all those kids, but we had no washing machine. She had to do all the clothes by hand then put them through a mangle in the back garden. But I remember always having clean clothes and the house was spick and span. I don't remember ever feeling poor or hearing Mum complain about our situation. I guess everyone in Maryville Road was in exactly the same boat.

When I was older and asked Mum how on earth she managed to look after all of us with cloth nappies and no washing machine, dishwasher, tumble dryer or any of the other mod cons we have nowadays, she'd just say: 'Tsh, it was fine.' She'd always make that 'Tsh' sound as if she couldn't imagine what I was making such a fuss about!

At five years old I followed my brothers and sisters to St Ita's School at the end of our street. We were taught Gaelic and I can still remember some of it, although when I speak it, it does tend to sound like gobbledegook. I remained very quiet at school and was a solitary child in the playground, preferring to watch what was going on rather than be part of the action. I never really had close friends and my biggest wish at playtime was that my dad would drive by in his car. I'd imagine how I'd be able to wave at him through the fence and how fantastic it would be. I'm sure if I'd told him how much I dreamt of it, he would have driven past every day, but I never revealed my secret wish to anyone. At home and at school, I was happy to disappear into the crowd.

I was five when Mum had Linda in February 1959. I can

remember her being heavily pregnant, with a huge bump, but she was down on her hands and knees scrubbing the kitchen floor. She went into labour a month early, but rather than make a fuss, she simply put her coat on and took the bus up to the hospital. I thought the world of my new baby sister. She was one more addition to our big Nolan family and it made me feel even safer and more secure.

The following year, in October 1960, Bernadette – Bernie – was born. She was tiny and so cute and I loved having her around too. My family meant everything to me. But then, in a flash, for reasons I still don't understand to this day, everything changed. I was suddenly ripped away from my family and home, and my little world was turned totally on its head.

It all began when Mum took Anne and me to our family GP and lots of different tests were carried out on us both. When the results came back, Mum was told that we both had heart weaknesses and needed specialized treatment in hospital.

Apparently, my problem was that I had a slight heart murmur and a high white blood cell count. No one ever explained to me what that actually meant or how serious my condition was, and I still don't know now. No doctor I've seen as an adult has ever found anything wrong with my heart, so the whole thing is a bit of a mystery.

Anne was found to have rheumatic heart disease. The strange thing is, I don't remember either of us being ill, although I suppose something must have made Mum take us to the doctor in the first place.

We were taken to St Gabriel's Convalescent Home in Cabinteely on the outskirts of Dublin. It was a big, fairly modern but quite beautiful building, with large windows overlooking the city.

When we first arrived at the hospital there was an outbreak of chicken pox, so Anne and I were put in twin beds together in an isolation room. Because of that, it wasn't too bad saying goodbye to Mum because I knew Anne was there and she would always look after me. But it was still the first time I'd spent a night away from home and I missed everyone. At that stage, I thought I'd be home in a couple of days – how wrong I was!

We were stuck in that room for two or three weeks, but at least we were together. However, when the chicken pox outbreak died down, Anne and I were separated and put in different wards. I was only six, but was put in a ward with more than twenty other children I'd never seen before. We spent day and night in metal-framed beds lined up neatly against the wall. I hated it.

The nurses would wake us at six o'clock every morning, help us wash and give us breakfast. After that, it was back to bed. I was allowed to get up for just half an hour a day. It couldn't have been more different from the noise and chaos of Maryville Road, which I'd loved so much. The hospital was deathly quiet and I wasn't even supposed to walk anywhere, let alone run around.

Mid-morning, we were given a cup of hot milk, which always had a thick skin on top of it. It was foul, but no one cared about that. 'Drink up, dear,' the nurse would say, thrusting the cup in my direction as I tried not to gag at the thought of it. For years afterwards I couldn't drink milk.

As the weeks turned into months at Cabinteely, a group of girls on my ward started picking on me. They soon made my life a misery. Their favourite trick was to wait until it was pitch-black and then make me get out of bed, walk down the corridor on my own and fetch them each a glass of water.

'Come on, Maureen, where are our drinks?' they'd taunt me. At first I'd pretend to be asleep, but they would just go on and on at me until I did what they said. I'd always hated the dark, but that building, with its high ceilings and long corridors, was petrifying. I was terrified of that long, lonely walk down the ward to the water tap, but I was even more scared of the girls waiting for me in the beds next to mine.

Night after night they'd make me walk up and down the ward, time after time, but after a while they must have found someone else to pick on because it did stop.

But our imprisonment at the hospital went on. I don't know whether the doctors and nurses thought I was just too poorly to return home or whether I was simply forgotten about, but Maryville Road became a distant memory to me.

I remained quite isolated. My only friend was a chubby girl called Gertie who really must have had a heart problem because her skin was tinged with blue. She was an orphan and quiet like me. Then one day this beautiful, glamorous woman came in and took her away. She must have adopted her, and I felt so glad for Gertie that she had gone away with such a kind-looking woman.

Once a week we were supposed to have school lessons, but I soon fell way behind my classmates back at St Ita's. A teacher came to the hospital once and asked me to spell 'up'. I was seven years old, but I didn't have a clue!

At one point while I was there I caught chicken pox and had to be put in a cot in an isolation room away from the ward. Except everyone forgot about me. I'd been told to stay in the cot all day, away from the other children, and I was such a meek and well-behaved child that it would never have occurred to me to not do what I was told. So I stayed there all day without a single thing to eat or drink. It was just me and my own little thoughts.

When evening came I finally began calling to people to come and rescue me. Eventually one of the nurses found me and she went mad at her colleagues for forgetting about me. Even at that age, I was very laid-back, and I wasn't angry or upset that I'd been forgotten about all day. I was just glad I'd finally been found.

In the end, I stayed at the hospital for eighteen months.

Friends have since asked me if I think my parents had actually put me into care and just told me it was a hospital. I honestly don't know. I don't ever remember feeling ill, but each day I was given medication and once a week the doctor came to check on me when he did his ward rounds, so there must have been something wrong with me.

I went into hospital stick thin, but the meals were huge and I wasn't able to run around the way I had at home, so within months I was really chubby.

Mum was only allowed to visit twice a week, but she'd always bring bags of treats and beetroot sandwiches that she'd made at home for me. I hated beetroot, but I'd never have told her that. Mum had to take three different buses to get from our house to the hospital, but every single week she was there to see us, without fail.

I don't remember Dad coming to see us, even though he had a car by then. And children weren't allowed into the hospital, so my brothers and sisters didn't visit at all. I didn't even see Anne very much because she was on a different ward and we weren't allowed to mix much with kids from other parts of the hospital. But for all that, I still don't remember feeling particularly sad; I just did what I was told and got on with it. The only time I cried was one afternoon when Mum came to visit, gave me a big hug and handed me my weekly bag of beetroot sandwiches.

Suddenly Anne announced: 'Why do you keep bringing Maureen beetroot sandwiches? She doesn't even like beetroot.' I was devastated that Anne had let my secret out of the bag and Mum might be upset. I sobbed all night.

We weren't even allowed out of hospital for Christmas. I can't remember whether Mum came to visit us, but maybe she did because I don't have memories of it being a sad time. All I'd ever wanted was a panda bear and that Christmas I got one. It was brilliant.

I made my First Holy Communion in hospital too. It is such a special day for young Catholic girls. One of the nurses sat up for hours with me the night before, curling my hair, and I slept in pink curlers all night. The next morning, she didn't really comb it out, so when my family arrived for the mass, they saw this chubby girl with huge curls. They couldn't understand what had happened to the scrawny, straight-haired girl they'd known before.

Mum and Dad brought all my brothers and sisters to watch the service, but they still weren't allowed to come near me and all I could do was wave at them from a window. They all looked so much older than when I'd last seen them. Afterwards, they went home and I went back to my hospital bed alone.

It must have been lonely, but I can't remember being miserable. I'd always been a very easygoing, laid-back child and wasn't prone to hysterics and tears. The hospital simply became my home, just as it did for most of the other kids there. One girl on my ward was there for seven years! I didn't long to be allowed out because I guess I'd become institutionalized to such an extent that I couldn't imagine it. The best thing I hoped for was that I would be allowed to spend an extra half an hour out of bed each day.

Then one day, when my mum was visiting, she announced that I was going to be leaving. Now that the possibility had been raised, I was beside myself with excitement. Mum explained that the family had decided to move to England and I'd be going with them. But it wasn't all good news: Anne was being left behind. Apparently, her heart condition was still thought to be so serious that she needed to stay in hospital.

It seems incredible that Mum and Dad had decided to move away for a new life in a different country and were leaving their twelve-year-old daughter behind. I think Anne is still shocked by it now. But that's what they did.

I was delighted to be going home to Mum and Dad, but I felt terribly guilty about leaving Anne. I think she was desperately disappointed to be staying in the hospital, particularly as the rest of the family were going to be so far away. But Mum and Dad promised she would be following us soon, after a few more check-ups. It gave her some hope to cling too.

The day I was due to leave hospital I woke up so excited but still not quite able to imagine what it would be like to be back home again. There was a gymkhana on in the fields next to the hospital that morning and all the other girls were chatting about seeing the horses, but all I could think about was that when we got back from the gymkhana I'd be going home. It was a wonderful day and when we came back for lights out at six o'clock, Mum and Dad were waiting for me.

When Dad's car pulled up outside Maryville Road, there were balloons and banners all around the door. All my brothers and sisters were waiting for me and it was wonderful to be back with them. Bernie had really grown up in the time I'd been away and she was toddling around. Mum cooked us a special big dinner, but the best bit for me was sitting around the table with my family again, laughing and chatting in the way that I remembered. I felt happier than I could ever remember.

Anne and I have talked a lot about our time in hospital and why we were there, and we are still not entirely sure. We're both certain though that we would never have allowed our own children to go through such an ordeal. But things were different then and people took the advice of doctors unquestioningly. It was certainiy all very strange.

I was only home a few days before we packed up and made the trip to England. Work in the Dublin clubs had been drying up for Mum and Dad, but one night a man in the audience had introduced himself to Dad as Fred Daly. He said he worked as a concert secretary in Blackpool and that there would be loads of work there during the summer season and also on the northern working men's clubs circuit. I think Dad decided that this time he wasn't going to let another big opportunity pass him by, so he grabbed it and arranged for us all to go.

Dad was leaving the car behind, so we went as foot passengers on the boat, sleeping in bunks, with all our clothes and possessions packed into massive suitcases. It was a terribly rough crossing across the Irish Sea and every single one of us was sick on the boat. Even Mum was sick. It was like one of those films of the Irish fleeing to America during the famine.

When we arrived in Blackpool, Dad took us kids for a walk along the prom. 'But where are all the black pools?' I asked him. I'd imagined we were going to a place surrounded by ponds of black water!

I thought the strangest thing about England was that almost everyone seemed to have a dog. In Ireland, hardly anyone had one; here, they were everywhere. But there were far fewer children and none of them played out in the street like in Maryville Road.

I was still only eight, but I could already tell England was going to be a very different place.

2.

Linda

Life in England

I was just three years old when we stepped off that sick-stained boat in Holyhead in 1962. But I was already desperate to perform.

Back in Dublin, I'd trip up and down Maryville Road like a celebrity in my hee-highls (which was what I called Mum's high-heels). The neighbours got so used to me clip-clopping up and down the street that they'd all be joking: 'Ah, here she comes again in her hee-highls!' I loved being the centre of attention.

The man who had recommended to Dad that we should move to England was called Fred Daly, but to us kids he was simply 'Uncle Fred'. In those days, all your parents' friends were Uncles and Aunts, even when there were no blood ties at all. Uncle Fred was convinced we'd find tons of work in Blackpool as a singing family. The town's entertainment business was booming and it certainly seemed the ideal time to try our luck. Even so, it must have been a terrifying move for Mum and Dad. There they were with seven kids, and the youngest, Bernie, was just two years old. We had no home, no savings and no work lined up.

But, as it turned out, Uncle Fred was right and within a

couple of months Mum and Dad had become firm favourites on the Blackpool club scene. They were still doing their Sweethearts of Song double act, staring adoringly at each other throughout their duets and doing all that romantic stuff. The audiences loved it. Dad was very, very handsome and was always popular with the ladies in the audience. Mum and Dad were soon doing bookings most nights in the clubs around Blackpool and the north-west.

When we first arrived in Blackpool, the whole lot of us moved into Uncle Fred's terraced house at 64 Ascot Road. He was a single man whose marriage had broken up and he'd probably enjoyed living on his own in peace and quiet until he suddenly woke up one day to find a massive, noisy family had descended on him. Goodness knows what he was thinking of, letting us all stay. But Uncle Fred was a kind, gentle man with a warm, open face and he never seemed to mind the noise and chaos. He talked for hours with us kids and introduced us to the excitement of going to Blackpool Football Club. We all loved him.

The house was very small, with just a back yard to play in, but it was fine. And six months later there was another arrival when Mum and Dad sent for Anne and she was finally allowed to leave hospital. When she got to Blackpool, doctors carried out a week of tests on her and found a slight problem with her heart, but nothing too serious. They didn't find anything much wrong with Maureen at all. We were so young it really didn't occur to us kids to wonder why two of our sisters had been in hospital for the best part of two years.

Soon afterwards, Mum's single, younger sister, our Auntie Theresa, also moved over from Ireland. She lived down in London, but would come up at weekends, laden down with presents for us all. If Mum and Dad were out doing shows at weekends, Auntie Theresa would babysit, but Mum would always come and tuck us in and kiss us goodnight, no matter what time she got home from a show. I'd be half asleep but able to smell her panstick foundation, and it was such a comforting smell. It meant she was home and everything was OK.

I adored our mum and thought she was the most beautiful woman alive. If she was getting ready for a show, I'd sit next to her at her dressing table and watch her put on her make-up. She'd dab on one last bit of lipstick and then always say the same thing: 'Now, am I beautiful?'

'Oh yes,' I'd reply.

Soon after arriving in Blackpool, we started going down to the Uncle Peter Webster Show on the Central Pier. It was a talent contest and every time it was on we'd all hurtle in through the doors to grab seats near the front. Each of us sisters would perform different songs. I'd do 'Tonight, Tonight' from *West Side Story*, even though I was still only tiny.

And Bernie was only two years old when she landed first place in the entire competition singing 'Show Me the Way to Go Home'. She won a gold watch, which she sold to Mum for three pence to buy sweets. Mum was pretty wily like that! Maureen and Denise also won a *Daily Mirror* competition singing a duet of the Andy Williams song 'How Wonderful to Know'. They had fabulous voices even then.

We'd been in England a couple of years when Mum fell pregnant with Coleen. She was really sick and couldn't go out singing for a few weeks, so one night Dad took Anne, who was then fourteen, Denise, who was thirteen, and Maureen, who was coming up for eleven. The audience loved the idea of a family who could all sing. Dad realized he was onto something and started taking the older girls to shows with him more and more often.

We'd all sung together at home from when we were tiny and it just seemed entirely natural to do it on stage too. I was about five when I first went on stage with the rest of the family to perform, but it wasn't a big deal. I was desperate to sing all the time; it didn't matter to me who was listening.

During Mum's pregnancy, us kids spent hours arguing over whether the new baby was going to be a boy or a girl and trying to choose names. When someone mentioned Coleen, we all agreed: 'Oh, that's perfect.' She was the only one of us kids born in England and when she arrived, on 12 March 1965, they gave her a good Irish name to make up for it – Coleen Patricia.

Just before Coleen was born we had moved out of Uncle Fred's house (he must have been delighted to get rid of us at last!) and into our own home in Waterloo Road in Blackpool. It was a terraced house with a small garden at the front and a bay window looking out onto the street. There was a rosebush on the path to the front door, which scared me to death every time I left the house, dashing past it as quick as I could before I got attacked by wasps or thorns.

Upstairs there were four bedrooms. Our two brothers had one big double room; Anne, Maureen, Denise and I had the other; Mum was in the back bedroom with Bernie; and Dad slept in the box room. Poor old Coleen started out sleeping in a drawer, as there wasn't even a cot for her. When she was older, she'd snuggle up next to whichever sister or brother she chose for the night. Usually it was Anne, who was like a second mum to her.

It was a squash, but all ten of us lived quite happily at Waterloo Road – with only one bathroom!

There was no television during the day back then, and certainly no computer games, so we made our own entertainment. There was constant noise coming from every room and there was always someone to talk to. I speak loudly anyway, but if you didn't in our house, you would never get heard. Maureen and Coleen were the quiet ones who were never really bothered about pushing themselves forward. Even now people have to stop Bernie and me from talking, so that Maureen and Coleen can get a word in edgeways. But don't be fooled just because they're quiet; give them a chance and they'll talk the hind legs off a donkey!

Bernie and I are only twenty months apart in age and we played together all the time. One year I got a twin doll's pram for Christmas and Bernie got a single one. We'd spend hours taking our babies for walks up the road to the bus shelter, where we'd sit chatting. 'Oh, they kept me awake all night,' I'd grumble to Bernie.

'I think mine wants feeding,' Bernie would fuss, picking up her doll. We loved those babies.

Bernie and I had our own little gang, along with Peter Bond from down the road (who always insisted on being in charge) and Suzanne Fleck from next door, who's still my best friend now. We'd spend hours playing a game of chase in the street, where you had to run to the 'home' before being caught by whoever was 'it'.

We would never have dared to do anything really naughty – Dad would have killed us – but we were once caught stealing apples. Peter and Suzanne had climbed up the trees and were throwing all the apples down to me at the bottom. We thought we'd got away with it and were walking home carrying armfuls of apples when an angry-looking man appeared in front of us. 'Have you just stolen apples from my tree?' he stormed.

'Erm, no, I've just bought them,' I replied, very unconvincingly.

'Clear off and don't do it again,' he said, and we went sprinting down the street so fast I thought my legs would fall off!

Bernie, Suzanne and I also loved playing Miss World on the upstairs landing. We'd raid the older girls' and Mum's wardrobes and take it in turns to be the commentator and the contestants.

'And who are you?' the commentator would boom into a pretend microphone.

'I'm Miss India,' the contestant would reply, walking out onto the landing with a towel wrapped around her head. 'And my ambition is to work with young people.' Hilarious!

I was six years old when *The Sound of Music* came out at the Palladium Cinema, which was over the hill from us, down towards South Shore. We went to see it seventeen times. Yes, seventeen! And it might sound cheesy, but it did make us think: 'Oh, maybe we could do that too. We could be a family that sings together, like the Von Trapps.' I've probably seen that film another twenty-five times as an adult. Every time it comes on the television, I have to sit down and watch it. And I've got the DVD too!

Bernie had started performing with the rest of our family quite regularly before she was three years old and so then it was all nine of us on stage. We became the Singing Nolans and were known in pubs and theatres all over the north-west of England. I loved it. I really did feel like one of the Von Trapp kids.

Usually we performed a couple of times a week. I would be so excited getting in the car to travel to wherever we were performing. On the way, we'd all sing together. It came so naturally and we could harmonize without even thinking about how we were doing it. Anne, Denise and Maureen were in the school choir at St Catharine's by then, so they taught us little ones the songs they'd learnt, like Brahms' *Lullaby*, in German, French and Irish.

When we got to the club where we were performing, we'd usually have to do two hour-long slots in which we'd sing harmony songs from shows like *The Sound of Music* and *Mary Poppins*, then Mum would do some light opera stuff and Dad would do a few Sinatra numbers. Tommy played the drums while the rest of us kids sang a solo. Mine was Shirley Bassey's 'Big Spender'. I was about nine by then and that is a big song for a little girl, but it was just play-acting for me. Originally, Bernie was going to sing 'Big Spender' and so Mum had had this Shirley Bassey-style floor-length evening dress with sequins made for her. But when Bernie came to put it on in the dressing room, she started crying. 'I don't want to wear that,' she sobbed.

'Oh, I will then,' I piped up. Of course, the dress was about six inches too short for me and ended halfway down my legs when I wore it, but I didn't care; I loved it.

Bernie's solo became the Flanagan & Allen song 'Strolling', for which she would wear a little straw boater and a blazer. Maureen did 'These Boots Were Made for Walking' and Denise did the big ballads like 'This Is My Life'. Brian sang 'Let's Go Fly a Kite' in the *Mary Poppins* medley.

At the end of a night, Bernie and I would be playing chase around a crowded, smoky club, waiting for Dad to drive us home. We were still too young to know any different or to feel tired, but I think the night after night of performing became quite gruelling for the older ones. On the way home from a gig, Mum would be like one big pillow on the back seat, with Coleen on her knee and Bernie and me on either side of her. After a while, Dad bought an estate car and Mum would make up a bed in the boot for Bernie and me. We'd fall asleep as soon as Dad turned on the ignition and we wouldn't wake up until we were back at Waterloo Road.

Even when we weren't on stage in the clubs, us kids would still be performing. The older girls – Denise, Anne and Maureen – would put on shows in the garage and I was (usually) allowed to join in. We took it all very seriously and would throw a blanket over the girder in the roof to create a backstage area. Then we'd line up old chairs in rows and drag in our neighbours, Auntie Theresa and any of our parents' friends we could find, charging them tuppence for the privilege! We'd get really nervous before going out on to the stage, even though we were actually performing in front of an old blanket, surrounded by half-empty tins of paint and Dad's tool kit. But we loved it, really loved it.

As the years went by, our family landed more and more gigs, until we were performing almost every night of the week. The whole lot of us would come pouring in the front door from school, bags and blazers flying in all directions. 'What's for tea?' Mum was asked over and over again, until it sent her demented. 'Bees' knees and spiders' ankles' was her stock reply. But when it came to dishing up the food, it would be a big plate of something fantastic, like boiled bacon and cabbage with a mountain of potato.

Then we'd all pile into Dad's Vauxhall Victor estate to perform in one club or another. Often it was the British Legion in Manchester, but we'd also travel over to Leeds and Liverpool for some shows. When we all fell out of the car at the other end, we'd look like the Clampetts from *The Beverly Hillbillies*, with all our bags, cases and bits and pieces we needed to bring with us.

In the long summer holidays or at Easter we would sometimes go up to Scotland for two weeks and do the clubs there. Most of the time I adored it, but there were times when I got fed up because I couldn't just go round to my friends' houses for tea after school like other girls did.

For five years, from when I was ten, we did a summer season at the Brunswick Club in Blackpool. To me, that felt like the height of showbiz. By the time we arrived in the evening, the club was always packed and thick with smoke. There were two small dressing rooms behind the stage where we would sit waiting for our two slots on either side of the bingo.

Then, when I was about twelve, there was a change in the licensing laws and because Bernie and I were still so young, we weren't allowed to perform in the second part of the act, after half past nine. At first I was mad. 'What do you mean, Bernie and I can't stay and sing?' I wailed to Mum. But there was no way around it, so Auntie Theresa, who had got married and moved to Blackpool, or another family friend would offer to come and pick up Bernie and me after our first slot of the night and take us home on the bus. On the way we'd stop for chips and gravy, which was a real treat, and soon I was quite happy that I didn't have to hang around all night at the club.

We were getting noticed by more important people in the music industry and once we were invited to do a show as the Singing Nolans at the Grosvenor House Hotel in London with Sidney Lipton and his orchestra. It was the first time we'd had an orchestra, and that was amazing. Mum and Auntie Theresa made us new yellow dresses with strands of gold running through them which were just beautiful. At the end, some of the showmen put Bernie and me on their shoulders and carried us round. I was so excited. We got £75 for that show, which was a fortune to us. The only problem was that Dad had bought eight Coca-Colas, an orange juice and a pint of beer before the show and it cost him £11. He nearly collapsed!

At the end of each season at the Brunswick Club, we would do our last show then drive straight to Manchester airport and fly off on holiday to Benidorm. We'd stay in a hotel, which was a massive treat.

Then, one summer, we got work performing on a P&O cruise ship. We only had two or three shows and the rest of the time it was just a holiday. There were swimming pools, games rooms, huge tellies and endless food. We had an absolute ball! Bernie was incredibly cute then, with a little pageboy haircut, and one of the passengers took such a shine to her that he gave her a wad of American dollars. Mum persuaded her to swap the lot for a fiver. Another smart move on her part!

The only time we never worked was at Christmas. I think that's why I still love Christmas so much, because it felt very special. Mum and Dad were really into the whole idea of Santa visiting and, even though they never had much money, they made it magical for us kids.

On Christmas Eve Dad would take us little ones into town

in the afternoon. Later we'd go to midnight mass, then pile home, so excited, and all sleep in the same room. Next morning we'd be up by five o'clock. I remember one year getting up just as Mum and Dad were coming up to bed. They must have been up all night getting our presents sorted. They just took one look at us, turned round and came down the stairs again.

On Christmas morning our living room looked like a toyshop. There'd be so much stuff: bikes, doll's prams, train sets and umpteen puzzles and games. 'Santa doesn't wrap presents,' Mum told us. It would have taken her days on end to wrap all those presents!

Even with eight children, I never ever felt left out or jealous of anyone else's presents. I don't know, maybe some of them were second-hand, but we never knew that. We'd also get a new outfit each to wear on the day and our own stocking. And Santa left a letter for us all, telling us what good children we'd been over the year and that here were our presents as a reward.

For lunch, there would be all of us kids, Auntie Theresa and her husband, Uncle Jim, and friends of my parents. There could be twenty of us for a big turkey dinner. Afterwards we'd pull the couch up closer to the fire and all squeeze on and watch a Disney film or a Hollywood musical. In the evening Mum and Dad liked to throw a party and even more people would turn up.

Mum and Dad must have been so busy, with so many kids to look after, but they always made time to make each of us feel special. Once a week they took one of us into town after school on our own. It meant that your turn only came around once every eight weeks, but when it did, you felt like the most important person in the world. Mum would meet me after school and we'd go into town on the bus and meet Dad when he came out of work. We'd walk down the promenade, then go for dinner at one of the Golden Egg restaurants.

Dad had so much enthusiasm and he was fabulous to spend time with. If you told him about something you'd done or were interested in, he would sit and talk to you about it properly, not just try to brush you off with a 'that's nice' like some adults did. Once he took us camping, even though we only drove for five minutes up to Preston New Road and put our tent up there, at a little site. We were thrilled. Other times he'd take us all along the coast to St Anne's, where we'd play rounders on the grass.

Mum was great too, but of course she was always so busy running the house and looking after all of us. She did all the washing, cooking and cleaning, and we didn't lift a finger. She was a typical Irish mother and totally ruined us. All eight of us and Dad would get up from the table at the end of dinner and just leave everything there. Mum would then spend an hour clearing the table and doing the dishes!

When I went round for tea next door at Suzanne's house, her mum would get us to lay the table, then afterwards she'd say, 'Right, one of you wash, the other can dry.' Having to help out was a total novelty, and I quite liked it. It was only when I was older that I thought: 'Why on earth didn't Mum make us all help?'

Even in England, Mum still didn't have an automatic washing machine and had to haul all the clothes in and out of her twin tub, which she filled up with a hose attached to the kitchen tap. Then, after everything had been boiled up, she'd take the clothes out into our tiny garden and put them through the mangle before hanging them out to dry.

For a while there was no central heating at Waterloo Road

either. If we came in after performing in a club at four o'clock in the morning, Mum would still be up at six to start building up the fire with coal, newspaper and firelighters. By the time we came downstairs, the fire would be blazing and our white school blouses and bottle-green skirts would be hanging on chairs all around it, so they were warm for us to put on. Mum would have a massive pan of porridge on the hob and made sure we'd all had a hot breakfast before we left the house. She'd help us get dressed, put our coats on and get us out the door to school. All that, and Dad would still be in bed.

Mum was a brilliant cook. Her food was quite plain, but great. On a Saturday a huge pot of stew would be standing on the hob from first thing in the morning, although she insisted on making it with stewing steak or meatballs, not lamb, which is more usually used in an Irish stew. The boys would be out at football in the afternoon and us girls would be playing with friends, but all day the rich, comforting smell of stew would be getting stronger and stronger. Then Mum would do boiled bacon and cabbage with mashed potato to go with it. Denise would prefer mince to bacon in hers and Tommy would want peas instead of cabbage, but Mum catered for all these demands without a word of complaint. It is only thinking back that I realize how much she ran around after us.

Of course, she had her moments, when she screamed and shouted. We'd be upstairs playing and hear her yelling: 'Maureen, Linda, Bernie . . . come down here NOW.'

But while Mum would scream and shout, we just needed one look from Dad to think: 'Oh God, I'm in trouble now.' Dad was very strict with all of us, but it was particularly tough on the older girls when we were living in Blackpool. They weren't allowed to wear tights until they were fifteen and had to go out in knee-high white socks while their friends were all in micro-miniskirts and high-heeled boots.

I remember the big girls – Denise and Maureen – sneaking out in the evenings when Dad was out somewhere. But one night he must have found out what they'd done and apparently he was on his way home from the pub to sort them out. As they came round the corner of Waterloo Road, Mum was screaming at them: 'Get in here now, your father is on his way home!' They were running down the road like you wouldn't believe!

Dad wouldn't even have allowed us to mention the word 'boyfriend'. He was totally against anything like that. One summer, when I was about twelve and we were working in Scotland, we were performing with Neil Reid, the child singing star who'd won *Opportunity Knocks*. He was the youngest British artist to ever have a number one album, and for a while everyone was talking about him. We were the same age and, after a couple of weeks, we became quite keen on each other. He'd even sing to me in the back of our minibus. I think Mum and Dad knew about it, but it was totally innocent, although very romantic.

Then once, when I was about fourteen, I sneaked out with Suzanne and we met some lads from the boys' school, St Thomas's, in town. All we did was go to the amusement arcade – it couldn't have been more innocent! But it's very hard to keep anything secret in Blackpool and the minute we turned into Waterloo Road, we knew we'd been found out. Suzanne's mum and my mum were both stood at their front doors with faces like thunder, arms folded in fury. 'Get in here now!' Mum yelled with a whack around my ear.

But although they were strict, neither Mum nor Dad were

hugely interested in our education. They weren't great at things like going to parents' evenings, even though I always wished they would. I suppose they were always busy in the evenings. The morning after a parents' evening at my school, St Catharine's, on Preston New Road, the other kids would all be chatting about what each teacher had said, but I had no idea what any of them thought about me.

I was never a high achiever but, like my brothers and sisters, I was OK at English because Dad had always encouraged a love of reading in us. I think Mum and Dad always thought we would be singers and because of that schoolwork didn't really matter. That was a shame really because although I wasn't great academically and I always wanted to sing, it would have been nice to have had some encouragement when it came to school. Maybe there were other things I could have been good at.

Mum and Dad bought us loads of books. We had all the Disney stories (*Cinderella* was my favourite) and then I started reading Enid Blyton's Malory Towers books and became obsessed with the idea of going to boarding school. 'Well, that's fine, you go to boarding school,' Mum would say, 'but don't think it will be all midnight feasts and adventures.'

As I got older, my fascination with boarding school moved on – to Donny Osmond! I adored him. Bernie was more into David Cassidy and our bedroom walls became a battleground as we both tried to pin up the most posters of our competing heroes. I even had a Donny Osmond pillowcase and was a proud member of his fan club. One afternoon I was out in the garden when Mum screamed out: 'Donny Osmond's on the telly.' I pushed the porch door open so hard as I hurtled inside that I put my hand through the glass. I sat watching him on the television as my hand bled all over Mum's carpet!

When the Osmonds came to perform at the Belle Vue arena in Manchester, Mum and her friend Betty took me, Bernie and Suzanne to see him. It was the best night ever! We were at the front of the queue and when the doors opened we went sprinting in. But, overcome by it all, Bernie suddenly fainted. I couldn't believe it! 'If you think I'm waiting here until the St John Ambulance turns up, you've got no hope,' I shouted back to poor old Bernie as Suzanne and I ran off into the crowd.

It was such a great time of my life. I know some of my sisters don't have such fond memories of their teens because they found night after night of performing quite gruelling, but I loved everything about show business. Maybe it was because I shared that passion for singing and showbiz with Dad that we got on so well. There were times when he lost his rag with me, just like he did with all of us, but I don't remember ever being scared of him in the way that some of the others were. I wasn't a particularly rebellious child, but I could stand up for myself. And by the time I came along, Mum and Dad were both much less strict. Dad and I didn't have much to clash about. All I wanted to do was perform.

3.

Maureen

Secrets and Sadness

They called us 'Blackpool's very own Von Trapp family'. They really did! It would be up there for everyone to see, on the posters stuck on the walls of clubs and theatres around Blackpool.

And for years we really thought we could be just like the perfect-sounding, lovely looking kids in our favourite film. We'd even sit around the table at home and sing together; the boys doing one part of the harmony and the girls the other. We all adored *The Sound of Music* and watched it over and over again. It seemed just like our lives – except we didn't live in a mansion in the Austrian alps.

But gradually I think we all became aware that things weren't quite as perfect as they were in the films we saw at the Palladium Cinema at the top of the hill on Waterloo Road.

Perhaps the younger ones were sheltered from it, but as us older kids grew up, we could see more clearly the huge gulf which separated our parents. I don't know whether Dad started drinking more heavily because he felt stuck in an unhappy marriage or because of his unfulfilled dreams, but whatever the reason, it cast a dark shadow over our home.

Like Linda says, ours was a very traditional childhood and

our mum was very Irish. I suppose by that I mean that all her efforts went into looking after her children, waiting on them hand and foot. I don't remember her ever getting down on the floor and playing with us, the way mums do nowadays, but she couldn't possibly have had time – there were eight of us to cook tea for!

In fact, it seemed like she was always in the kitchen. But she liked a laugh while she was slaving away, cutting up the veg for another massive Irish stew. Tommy and Brian could really get her giggling and, although she wouldn't admit it, she liked a dirty joke, my mum.

But when friends came round, it was Dad they wanted to talk to. During the day, when he was sober and in a good mood, he was the best person in the world to be around. He was always interested in whatever any of us had to say. If I told Mum what we'd been learning about at school, it'd be: 'That's lovely, Maureen, now I must get that pie in the oven for our tea.' But if I told Dad, he'd sit down for an hour and discuss it in detail. He would talk about books and music and, even though none of us had a lot of schooling, we learnt a lot from our dad.

If any of us ever had a problem, it was always Dad we turned to – everyone did. Just like when we lived in Ireland, there would often be one of the neighbours knocking at our front door, asking Dad for advice on a financial matter or some family crisis. He was always interested in other people and that made people want to be around him. He had strong opinions on things too, although he didn't like it when they were challenged. He was a complex man because as well as that incredibly caring and exciting side there seemed to be a simmering anger.

Dad must have thought that his life had been thrust upon him. It wasn't what he'd chosen, but it had happened anyway: the kids, the day jobs that never lasted very long, the cramped house in Waterloo Road, the constant racket, mess and chaos and the stress of providing for such a big family. He was still an amazing singer, but by then he must have realized that he was approaching middle age and wasn't going to be the next Sinatra and perform at Madison Square Garden. He was a bookkeeper at a printer's in Blackpool, and that was hard to take. He was besotted with his kids, but he felt trapped, frustrated and very unhappy.

While he was the one who was bitter and upset about the way things had worked out, Mum was the one trying to make things better. It was Mum who would pawn her jewellery and anything else of value that she could find around the house to get enough money together to pay the bills. Back then, as a child, I thought it was Dad who held our family together, but now I realize it was probably Mum all the time.

Dad realized though that there was a potentially big market for a singing family, so he drove us hard to get whatever we could out of it. Like Linda said, Bernie was just a toddler when she started singing and, later, so was Coleen. Looking back, I can't believe Mum and Dad made them do it. Maybe that's not quite fair. They didn't 'make us' perform, but we all grew up knowing what was expected of us. And in the Nolan family you did what was expected of you without asking any questions!

After a while, some local councillors in Blackpool objected to the little ones performing at such a young age. They said we were being exploited. And we were. But obviously we didn't realize that then. When I was fourteen, I was singing in front of an audience every night of the week. A lot of the time I hated it. I quite enjoyed singing, but I wasn't desperate to perform in the way Linda and, later, Bernie were. What I resented most was the relentlessness of it all, going out on stage night after night after night. But, in my mind, there was no way I could have said, 'I don't fancy it tonight, Dad,' or 'Can't I go to the cinema with my friends instead?'

We never tried to get out of a show because, like I said, we knew what was expected of us. Often it wasn't even that I wanted to go out with my friends – that wasn't really allowed anyway, even if we weren't performing. All I really wanted sometimes was to stay at home and watch telly, like all my other classmates at St Kentigern's. Often I would be shattered, but rather than an early night, we'd have to heave ourselves into Dad's Vauxhall Victor estate for a show in Wales.

And Dad was always late for everything. He was an horrendous timekeeper and so we'd be racing to get to a show, and he'd be shouting at us and at Mum, and she'd be yelling back at him. It was chaos. Being a very quiet child, I could get totally lost in all that noise. It was like being in the centre of a tornado! It was only well into my teens that I realized I did have opinions too, just like the others, even if I didn't want to shout about them all the time.

When we arrived at the club where we would be performing, Dad would go for a drink at the bar while the rest of us got ready. From then on, he'd drink pretty steadily throughout the evening, and as we were performing almost every night, he was soon consuming a hell of a lot of alcohol. Dad was only ever really a social drinker; he didn't have a stash of bottles at home or anything. But because we were out most nights, he had the perfect opportunity to drink most nights.

During the years we lived in Waterloo Road, I remember him drinking more and more and more.

After a show, Dad would head straight back to the bar for another drink. He always had plenty of chat and people loved being around him, so while he was there, propping up the bar, he would be the centre of attention. But us kids would be exhausted by then. We'd have been at school all day, travelled for a couple of hours to perform and then had to sit on a dressing-room floor while Dad finished his whiskey. Sometimes the younger ones – Linda and Bernie – were so over-tired they'd be playing manic games of chase around the smoky, crowded club, but mostly I remember us all slumped against each other on the filthy floor of a dingy stock room which was doubling up as our changing room.

'Tommy, these kids are shattered,' Mum would say. 'We've got to get them home.' But he would barely acknowledge her and just carry on drinking.

Often it was two in the morning before Dad would have had his fill at the bar. Usually he drank whiskey, but sometimes it would be brandy too. Then he'd lurch back to the car and drive us all home, so far over the limit that it terrifies me when I think about it now. Often we'd come back from north Wales in the middle of the night, with our dad dead drunk at the wheel. Amazingly, only once did he have an accident, when he'd been drinking and was on his own in the car. I don't know why that didn't go to court and he wasn't jailed. It was never really talked about, but I think he had to pay out to someone for years afterwards because of the crash.

Once or twice I remember Dad couldn't come with us to a gig because he was poorly, so we got a lift with one of his friends. We thought that was brilliant because we'd turn up on time, do our act and leave immediately afterwards. It was so much better.

And then, of course, there was the violence that came with Dad's drinking. Although he could turn his temper on us kids when he was riled, it was Mum who really bore the brunt of it. Saturdays were the worst, of course, because it was footie day. Dad would start drinking early and then go off to Blackpool Football Club. Denise, Anne and I would often go with him and stop off for a drink beforehand at the Blackpool Supporters Club. After the match, us girls would go home for Mum's stew and join the others to sit down and watch a film on the telly. Then Brian and Tommy would get home after having gone to the match with their mates.

But there was a tension in the air all day because we never knew what kind of mood Dad would be in when he finally got home. Sometimes he'd come back in great spirits, but we'd be treading on eggshells because his mood could change at a moment's notice.

When someone drinks that much, it can be anything that sets them off. Dad would wind Mum up and, because she was already up to her eyes with having to look after us kids, she'd lose it with him and then the whole thing would kick off. Mum had an Irish temper and could be quite volatile, and if Dad was having a go at her, she would stand her ground. Us kids would be thinking: 'Oh, Mum, don't answer him back, you're only going to get a whack,' but she would do it anyway. As a kid, I couldn't understand why she didn't just keep quiet and stay away from him, but as an adult I can see that she had every right to stand up for herself if he was being unreasonable.

But, of course, the moment Mum did say anything that

annoyed him, she'd get a backhander. One of the worst fights I can remember them having was over which saucepan Mum should have used to cook dinner. They began yelling at each other and Dad ended up whacking her round the face and then kicked her too. He didn't normally kick or punch; usually it was just an open-handed slap. But that night he kicked out at her and hit a vein in her leg and it started bleeding everywhere. It was terrible. None of us kids made a sound; we were all terrified of winding Dad up even further. I think we felt guilty too. We felt we should be doing something to stop it all, but none of us was brave enough to take on Dad in that mood and we didn't know what else to do.

It didn't happen every day and sometimes weeks would go by and there would be no violence at all, but it was still far too regular for me.

When Dad did slap Mum, it was horrific. Mum would cry, while us kids stood around, utterly helpless and feeling sick inside. I would never have dreamt of trying to stop our dad. If we were upstairs in bed, or in another room, we'd listen, feeling terrified when we heard the rowing start, and then eventually there'd be the loud sound of a slap or a thud.

I'd lie in bed with the covers pulled up to my chin and pray that Mum and Dad would get a divorce so the rowing and fighting would come to an end. But then, when things were so bad between them that I thought they really might split up, that thought terrified me too.

Usually though, when we woke up the morning after a big row, it was like nothing had ever happened and things would trundle on as normal until the next time Dad had too much to drink and the rowing started all over again.

One day Mum decided she'd finally had enough of it all

and packed a suitcase with all her things. 'I'm leaving!' she screamed at Dad.

But she was back later the same day. Mum told me years later that she knew our dad would fight her madly for custody of us kids and she could never leave us. But if she took us with her, where on earth would she go with eight children? So she stayed with Dad. And, despite everything he did to her, I'm convinced Mum always loved him.

Us kids had no idea then that the problems in Mum and Dad's marriage had been going on for years. They were still living in Ireland and Mum was pregnant with Denise when Dad landed a singing job with a dance band in Cork. He was very popular in the clubs there and stayed for a few weeks. Soon afterwards, Mum discovered Dad had been having an affair while he was away.

Mum found out who the other woman was and travelled down to Cork to confront her. But when she got there she had a terrible shock – the other woman was expecting a baby too. And it was Dad's!

Mum stood on the doorstep and said, 'Tommy Nolan is married to me, and this is our baby I'm carrying here, so leave him alone.'

I don't know how the other woman reacted, but soon afterwards she moved to London and Dad returned to Dublin. In Ireland, at that time, being a mistress was very frowned upon and it would have brought great shame on the woman's family, which is why I think she was sent over to England, where she had a baby girl.

It's strange because it means there is another Nolan sister out there somewhere. We know the name of her mum and we'd all love to meet her now to see if she is like us – or if she can sing! But most likely she has absolutely no idea about her real dad and we wouldn't want to do anything that might upset her.

When we were growing up, Mum always had a bit of a thing about Denise. They are quite similar, but whatever Denise did, she could never quite please Mum. Nothing was ever good enough. It was very subtle, but Mum was always stricter with Denise than the rest of us, even though she wasn't a naughty child at all. Denise would say, 'I can't do anything right for Mum!' and we'd laugh about it. But, deep down, that must have really hurt her. Looking back, I'm convinced it was all because of Dad's affair during Mum's pregnancy with Denise.

I'm sure that my dad has other kids out there too. We never knew for certain of any more affairs, but he loved attention from women and I'm sure there were many, many others.

Mum and Dad had moved into separate bedrooms before Mum fell pregnant with Coleen, so I was quite shocked when she announced that there was going to be another baby. I guess they must have found the time to conceive her somehow. After Coleen's birth I don't think they ever slept in the same bed again.

Mum was still only thirty-nine, so it was very young for her to stop having a sexual relationship with her husband, but I think she simply focused all her attention on us kids and she was able to be happy in her own way. But, unbeknown to us, Dad had turned his attention elsewhere in our house – and this became the most shocking secret of our family life.

A few years ago now, Anne sat us all down and told us that Dad had sexually abused her for years. She doesn't remember it happening as a young child, but after she joined us in Blackpool after leaving Cabinteely, he regularly touched her sexually.

Dad was besotted with all of his kids. He truly thought we were all incredible – the boys and the girls.

Family meant everything to Dad and over and over again he'd talk about how, as a family, the Nolans *must* stick together.

Above all, he was obsessed with his daughters. It was slightly different with the boys. Tommy had always been a free spirit and clashed with Dad over everything. And Brian, who adored Dad and desperately wanted to be like him, tended to get a hard time from him for that.

I think it was Dad's obsession with his daughters which made him so strict with us when we hit our teens. He just couldn't or wouldn't bring himself to let us older girls have normal lives, with boyfriends and nights out. Out of all us girls though, it was Anne who he was utterly besotted with. I always knew Anne was his favourite. I could tell by the way he talked to her and listened when she was speaking. I'm sure he really did think they could be a couple and Anne once said that when she was sixteen, he asked her to run away with him. 'Because you know I love you,' he told her.

It must have been so confusing for Anne. When she left school, Dad found her a job at the printer's with him, for £5 a week. She was so good to us younger ones and every week she would buy us a comic each out of her wages. Dad seemed to be almost in awe of Anne, which never made any sense to me at the time because she was always the one who was rowing with him. But now I think he admired her for being so strong. I wonder if she was the person my dad had always wanted to be: brave and fearless.

When Anne talked publicly about the sexual abuse in a book

she wrote after Mum and Dad had died, some people refused to believe her. It caused a lot of upset in the family, but I never doubted what she said. And although it was painful for all of us, I felt Anne should be free to talk about her experience, and I supported her doing it.

Dad wasn't really violent to us kids, although there were a couple of occasions when he lashed out, particularly if he'd been drinking. But usually just one look from him was enough to get us into line because we knew how bad his temper could be. Mum would scream and shout at us if we were mucking about, and she even had a bamboo cane which she'd whack us with if we were really playing her up. But, deep down, we knew she was soft. If she sent us to bed crying, she'd wake us up later to tell us she loved us. Dad was much harder though. One glance from him was all we ever needed to stop whatever it was he didn't like.

Tommy and Anne were the only ones who stood up to him. Tommy was the eldest and when he reached his late teens he became a bit of a rebel. He was into Black Sabbath and heavy metal music, which Dad loathed. Tommy would stay in his room for hours playing his drums, while Dad yelled up the stairs at him to keep the noise down. The pair of them clashed on virtually everything, and Dad hated people disagreeing with him. Although, looking back, I wonder if maybe Dad secretly admired Tommy for knowing his own mind and sticking to his guns.

Brian was very different. He hero-worshipped Dad and tried so hard to be like him. He was a great singer and even looked just like Dad, but instead of Dad being kinder to Brian because of this, he was often far harder on him. Brian was very quiet and Dad would sometimes just ignore him. That was crushing for Brian.

The only time I ever remember Dad being violent to me was years later, after we moved to London and were living in Ilford. I was 22 then and had just got back from a day's work with The Nolans. The whole family and a friend of mine were sitting round the dining table eating one of Mum's amazing meals and talking about the day, but Dad was in a bad mood and concentrating on the TV in the corner of the room. 'Ssshh,' he said, clearly annoyed that he couldn't hear the telly.

'There's a TV in the lounge if you want to watch it,' I replied.

Without hesitating, Dad leant across to where I was sitting at the table and whacked me round the face, tipping up my plate at the same time.

The room went utterly silent.

Then, after what felt like an age, Linda said, 'Maureen, you've got potato in your hair.'

I got up from the table and stormed past Dad, but as I did so he lifted his hand to me in a fist. I don't know whether he would have hit me again; I was already out of the door by then and Mum had rushed over and grabbed him.

I was so shocked that he could do that to me and I cried for hours. I wasn't a kid, I was a grown woman by then, but I still felt utterly powerless. I guess he must have been in a real rage about something because he'd never done it before and he never did it again. My sisters and I laugh about it now though because of Linda's hilarious comment about the potato.

One of the worst nights was when we were still living in Blackpool and Dad punched Anne in the face. We were about to go out to do a show when the pair of them started rowing about something totally silly. But Dad got really mad. 'Don't you dare contradict me!' he shouted at Anne.

But Anne is a very strong person and I think she'd made up her mind that she wasn't giving in to him, and she refused to back down. The row got worse and worse and then Dad punched her twice in the mouth. The rest of us were watching and it was a horrible moment, but Anne didn't cry. Within seconds, Anne's lip had swollen up massively, but she was still determined to go ahead with our show that night and she went on stage with a huge fat lip.

Afterwards I think we were all left with a feeling that we should have done something more to stop it. Our brothers felt that most strongly because, as boys, they thought they should be able to protect their mum and sisters. But, looking back, what could any of us have done? We were kids. And although we adored our Dad, we were very scared of him too.

One night Dad and Tommy had a fearsome argument in the tiny kitchen at Waterloo Road. They were yelling at each other and it looked like they would come to blows. Brian got in between them and was pleading with Tommy to calm down. I think all three of them thought Tommy might lose it with Dad, but eventually Brian talked him round.

Brian had been really brave, but afterwards Dad started yelling at him. 'Get away from me!' Dad shouted at Brian. That was so upsetting for Brian and so horribly unfair. I felt terrible for him. He loved our Dad so much, but he was treated very badly by him.

Most of the time I think there was nothing we could have done to stand up to my Dad, but other times I think we must have been total wimps. There were eight of us and Mum, but we were all totally overpowered by him. I mean that we were all in his power.

Even when I was fifteen and sixteen, we were so banged down in everything. We were hardly ever allowed out with friends. Anne, Denise and I were so straight-laced that when we did go out people would call us 'the Three Wise Virgins'! I'm not sure whether Dad was scared something bad might happen to us in the outside world or whether he was simply jealous that we might have a life away from the family.

Whatever his thinking, Dad needed to have total control over his family – and that was what he got. Everything he loved, we loved: Frank Sinatra, football, black and white movies and books. Everything he hated, we hated: hippies, pop music and heavy metal (apart from Tommy, of course).

And so, despite being terrified of him when he was in a rage, we worshipped him the rest of the time. He could be such a lovely person, and when he was sober he really would talk to us for hours about books or music, in a way that other grown-ups just wouldn't.

I certainly grew up desperate for his approval, and I think my brothers and sisters did too.

As I hit my mid-teens, I found myself getting angrier that I was missing out on normal teenage life because of my Dad's rules and our constant round of performances. Once, when I was sixteen, Mum and Dad wouldn't let me go to a dance on a Sunday night, so I sneaked out when Dad wasn't around. When I got away with it, Anne, Denise and I started to escape whenever we saw Dad nip out for a drink. Soon, almost every night when we weren't working we would go to the Oxford pub, where all our friends hung out. Mum must have known, but turned a blind eye to our disappearances. For us, the thrill of feeling like normal teenagers was worth the risk of being found out by Dad.

As I got older and went out more, I was with Anne and Denise all the time. We'd go everywhere together: the pub, the football and the 007 nightclub, if we could get away with it. The 007 was a classic 1970s disco and we loved it. When us girls went out together, I was still very much the quiet one. Denise was very funny, which the boys loved, and Anne was very cool with any blokes who tried to chat us up. I just stood there and let the others do the talking.

But although we started breaking Dad's rules by sneaking out the house at night, we still knew that taking boyfriends home was a total no-no. I had my first kiss in a club where we were performing when I was fourteen, then had a boyfriend at sixteen, but I never told my parents. Dad would have gone mad at the mere idea.

On one of our cruise ship tours, Anne and I made friends with two of the stewards who worked onboard. The next time they were docked near Blackpool they came to see us perform at the Brunswick Club. At the end of the night Dad was propping up the bar, so the boys offered to walk us home. It was so innocent, but it was lovely. We bought chips and walked along the front before they dropped us home. I was sixteen and Anne was twenty then, but we still slept together in bunk beds, and that night we stayed awake for hours talking about our handsome sailors. The next morning they were leaving from the railway station to rejoin their ship.

'Dad, can we walk down and say goodbye to the stewards?' I asked the next morning.

'No,' was his simple reply.

We knew better than to argue, so we never saw those

boys again. I was so hurt. It was such a simple thing, but Dad wouldn't release his control on us even to let us do something as harmless as that.

But for all Dad's drinking and the violence going on in our house, I still can't say it was an unhappy childhood. Not at all. Waterloo Road was a madhouse. After a while, Mum just gave up trying to keep the cleaning under control and everything needed either repairing or painting or sorting out, but we still hadn't got much money and none of that seemed hugely important. It was a noisy, exciting, great place to be. Our friends always wanted to be at ours and Mum never minded how many mates we brought home, even though she had eight kids of her own. She didn't mind if we were noisy or messy; to her, that was what home was all about.

For me, there was never anywhere else in the world that I wanted to be. I loved being part of that big family. I got lost in the middle of it, and that suited me fine. I felt safe being part of the Nolans.

Christmas was the best time to be part of our family. Mum and Dad would build it up for weeks before, so that we were all beside ourselves with excitement – well into our teens! Like Linda said, Christmas was the one day we never had to work. But then, at Christmas 1973, we were asked to perform at the Cliffs Hotel in Blackpool. A special cabaret was being laid on during the day for a man called Joe Lewis who was managing director of a big firm called Hanover Grand.

'I'm sorry, we don't work at Christmas,' Dad told the manager of the Cliffs.

But they were insistent that we did the gig and kept asking and asking Dad to reconsider.

In the end Dad asked for a silly amount of money – £80!

We'd never earned that for a show before. Dad was convinced they'd tell him to forget it and book someone else, but, incredibly, they agreed. So, for the first time ever, after we'd spent the morning ripping open our amazing presents, we piled into Dad's car and went off to sing carols for the lunch guests at the Cliffs Hotel.

It was the performance that changed our lives.

4.
Linda

Having a Ball!

'You must bring your daughters down to London,' Joe Lewis told Dad. 'These girls are going to be massive stars!'

Joe Lewis was a short, dark-haired man with an incredible sense of energy. He was a cockney boy made good, but what we didn't realize at that first meeting was that Joe Lewis wasn't just any old businessman. He was already one of the most successful people in Britain through his restaurant and night-club business and was to go on to become one of the world's richest men, now living in the Bahamas with a fortune of around $3 billion. Not bad, eh?

Dad was a bit sceptical about the whole idea of moving to London at first. And, looking back now, I can see why he and Mum must have been worried. Where would we live? How would we survive? What would happen when the work dried up?

Dad was also scared that he might lose control of the group, and of his family. Like Maureen said, Dad had always run every-thing in the Nolan family and what he said, went. Now there were all these big men in flash suits taking an interest in us as a business opportunity, and that must have been daunting for him.

The deal was that if we went to London it was just going to be the six girls in the group. Joe Lewis wanted us to perform at his nightclub, the London Room in Drury Lane, but he had also signed us up with the intention of getting us a recording deal. Apparently, all the record companies he approached thought it would be easier to promote just us girls rather than the entire family. But that meant Mum, Dad and our brothers wouldn't be part of the act any more. Mum and Dad understood the way things worked in the record industry, but that must have been hard for them, particularly when they were both so talented. The boys had jobs in Blackpool and so they weren't desperate to go to London with us. They were happy for us and they understood why it had to be just us girls. Tommy was doing really well on his own, anyway, doing solo gigs as a singer and comedian, and Brian had always had a wonderful voice too.

Us girls were desperate to move to London. I'd never really studied particularly hard and had staked everything on a career in show business. I knew this was our big opportunity, which might never come around again. If we didn't grab it, most likely we'd be propping up shop counters for the rest of our lives.

'Please, Mum, pleeeeeease, can we go?' I'd plead with her. Then Bernie would take over the pleading, then Anne, then Denise, and so on until we'd all had a go.

'I'm just not sure,' Mum would reply. 'London's a big place. Where will we live?'

But Joe Lewis had an answer for everything. 'You can stay with me,' he said. 'Bring the whole family.'

So that's what we did. One morning at the start of 1974, Anne, Denise, Maureen, Bernie and I got on the train at

Blackpool station with Mum and set off for our new adventure down south. We were all so excited. But as Dad, Coleen, Tommy, Brian, Auntie Theresa and some of our friends stood on the platform waving goodbye, it was really horrible. Coleen was too young to come with us immediately, so she was staying in Blackpool with our brothers and Auntie Theresa. Dad was going to travel up and down. We managed to keep ourselves under control as we waved at everyone, but as soon as the train pulled out of the station, we all burst into floods of tears.

I wasn't yet fifteen, but I was still very aware that we were leaving that part of our life behind us.

When we turned up at Joe Lewis's house next to the Royal Wentworth Golf Club in Surrey, we could barely speak. We were properly dumbstruck. There were huge iron gates out at the front, then a long drive half the length of Waterloo Road that led up to the house. Oh my God, it was amazing! The word 'house' doesn't really cover what we saw in front of us. It was a mansion really, the sort of thing we'd only seen on telly before. When we walked in through the huge front door and into a hall the size of our front room, I thought I'd died and gone to heaven. There was a swimming pool, a snooker room, tennis courts, a huge garden, a housekeeper, a gardener and a chauffeur.

The previous night we'd been in our Blackpool terraced house, but now Bernie and I were sleeping in a bedroom big enough for our entire family to live in! We couldn't stop giggling. The bed had pillows that our heads sank deep into when we lay down, and when we looked out of our bedroom window all we could see were trees and greenery.

But despite their amazing wealth, Joe Lewis and his family

weren't at all snooty. In fact, they could not have been more welcoming to us. Joe's wife, Esther, was Irish and absolutely lovely. He had a son called Charles and a daughter, Vivienne, who became my friend. It must have been strange for them, having all these people move into their home, but if they ever regretted their offer to let us stay, they never showed it. Esther would sit and chat with us for hours when we got back from performing in the evening. And on Sundays we were invited to join the family for the most incredible roast dinners that were served properly at the table by the housekeeper. We loved it, but we did miss our brothers and Coleen.

Coleen did come down to London with us at the beginning but she was still just nine and I think she liked being at home, out of the spotlight. She went back to Blackpool, just coming down to do occasional shows with us. Dad stayed in Blackpool most of the time, but if he was down in London for a while, Tommy, Brian and Auntie Theresa would look after Coleen.

I think both Mum and Dad desperately missed performing themselves. They were incredibly proud of their girls, but they had been used to going on stage almost every night of their adult lives and it must have been hard for them to be confined to backstage.

The Nolan Sisters performed six nights a week at the London Room, but because I was just fifteen and Bernie was thirteen, we could only do two or three performances a week each because of the licensing laws. On our nights off we would be taken out to see shows or we'd relax in front of the telly, which was fabulous for us. But the routine was pretty relentless for the older girls. At the same time, we were also recording singles with a small label called Target Records which our management had found. It was incredibly exciting going into recording studios, even though we didn't have much success at that stage.

We were also being groomed for television. Dad was still officially our manager, but Joe Lewis had also brought in a guy called Robert Earl to work alongside him. Robert was a short, grey-haired man who seemed very well-to-do to us back then. He'd been a famous crooner himself during the fifties, with three top forty hits. Now he and his wife Daphne set about trying to restyle us. For the first time, we had costumes specially designed for us. It was all very Beverley Sisters, with us kitted out in the same clothes. None of us ever felt comfortable with that, particularly if Coleen was on stage with us. She was only nine and wearing the same thing as Anne, who was twenty-one. That was never going to work. The first outfits that we had made for us are still imprinted on my mind: red catsuits with eighteen-inch flairs and the letters 'NS' studded in diamante on them. Well, it *was* 1974!

We didn't mind the catsuits too much at the time, as they were actually quite trendy, but halfway through the show we had to change into these big, floaty lemon evening dresses. They were just hideous!

Robert Earl brought in a guy to meet us called Stewart Morris, who was head of light entertainment at the BBC and who'd produced hundreds of shows. Stewart came to watch us a few times at the London Room, then introduced us to Alan Ainsworth, who did musical arrangements for the BBC Orchestra.

Make-up artists came to teach us how to do ourselves up properly and Nigel Lythgoe, who'd been choreographing the Young Generation, was brought in to devise our dance routines. Nigel was really slim, with wavy hair down to his shoulders. He was bursting with ideas and enthusiasm and I think we all had a little bit of a crush on him.

Within a couple of months, we were a much more slick-looking group.

Robert Earl's next step was to bring in A&R men from the big record labels to see us at the London Room. But our big break came when Cliff Richard came to the show one night. He was huge at the time and was about to start filming a new six-part series for the BBC.

When we were told he was in the audience I was so nervous I thought I might collapse. We were desperate to meet him, but unfortunately he had to leave before we got a chance to say hello.

A couple of days later one of our management team ran into the dressing room with the most incredible news. 'Cliff loves you,' he said. 'You've been booked for every one of his six shows.'

We all started screaming and jumping up and down like jack-in-a-boxes! We were thrilled. This was all our dreams come true.

All six of us sisters were booked to appear on the series, which was to air towards the end of 1974, and we set about rehearsing for it almost every minute of every day. At about this time, Mum and Dad found us our own home in Granville Road, in Ilford, east London. It was a shame to be moving out of Joe Lewis's palatial mansion into something a bit more down to earth, but I think we were pleased to have our own home again and the house in Granville Road was still far larger than our terraced house in Blackpool. It was double-fronted, with steps up to the door, a downstairs cloakroom, a massive lounge and a conservatory at the back. It had previously been used as a doctor's surgery, so the room were big and airy with high ceilings. Even when Mum and Dad insisted on inviting the world and its wife round for one of their parties, that house never felt squashed.

Every morning we would get up before seven o'clock and take the train to Gants Hill, then change onto the Central Line for the twenty-two stops to North Acton, where the BBC rehearsal rooms were based. We'd get on the train before the rush hour started, then all fall asleep. By the time we woke up at Leicester Square, the tube carriage would be packed and there would be the six of us, all asleep on each other's shoulders, with the rest of the train laughing at us.

In rehearsals we'd have to learn our own song for that week's show, one that we'd perform with Cliff and finally a big medley for the end. All day long we'd work on our harmonies until we were fit to drop and then it was back on the tube to the West End for our nightly slot at the London Room.

Cliff was fantastic to work with because he was always so patient. He really was – and still is – one of the nicest people you could come across in show business. Even now, he still remembers all our names if we bump into him at an event. And because he was so lovely, it made it quite an easy introduction into the new world of television. He was very down to earth, like us, and I think that prevented the whole experience from being really scary.

It's Cliff Richard was pre-recorded, so on the night of our first performance the whole family crowded round to watch it on our big telly in the front room at Granville Road in Ilford. It was a very weird sensation seeing ourselves on screen, but the most exciting part was when the titles rolled up at the end and it said: 'With special guests, The Nolan Sisters'.

After a few weeks, people started recognizing us if we were out together in the street. We were still pretty anonymous if we were on our own, but all together there was no missing us. We thought being spotted by people was just fabulous, although one group of girls did try to chase us down the road. I'm not sure why; maybe they didn't like our harmonies! Anne stood up to them though. She might have looked like butter wouldn't melt in her mouth on the telly, but she was still rock hard! Anne wasn't frightened of anyone.

Bernie and I were enrolled at Clark's School for Girls, which was a private school around the corner from our house, but I had no interest in my lessons by then and left just months after arriving in Ilford, when I was still just fifteen. The only good thing was that it did introduce me to a few girls living in the area, with whom I'd sometimes be able to go out to the cinema or discos.

Soon I was going out and about on the nightclub scene in London with my older sisters too. One night we went to one of Joe Lewis's restaurants on Regent Street. There was a bowl of olives on the bar; we'd never seen them before. Denise and Maureen decided they must be grapes, so they tried one and nearly collapsed. You didn't get many olives in Blackpool in those days, and we were still very simple girls at heart. I could have died laughing!

We hadn't been in London long when we were signed by Warner Bros record label. We were still being managed by Robert Earl, who remained convinced that we would become the new Beverley Sisters. We went along with it, not wishing to make a fuss, but we hated it when they wanted us to dress the same every single time we left the house.

Mum and Dad paid us each a £150 in cash every week, but we weren't bothered about the money. We were still living at home and we were totally swept away with all the clothes, parties and limousines that were being thrown our way. I don't think we stopped to wonder who was paying for all those things. It was only later that we discovered it had actually been us footing the bill all along! If any of us had read the small print on our contracts properly, we'd have discovered that every penny that was spent on promoting The Nolans came out of our earnings. That's why, at the end of it all, we were left with virtually nothing.

Then, in 1974, Frank Sinatra was due to perform his 'Ol' Blue Eyes is Back' tour across Europe. Dad had always adored Sinatra, so as soon as he heard the concert dates had been released, he dashed out to try to get ten tickets for the whole family. But they'd sold out so fast that he couldn't get any and they were so expensive that he couldn't really afford them anyway. Instead, he managed to find two tickets for £100 each on the black market. He was delighted.

At the same time, our manager told us that Frank Sinatra was looking for a musical act to support him on the European leg of his tour. In America he'd had a comedian going on stage before him, but that wouldn't work in Europe because of the cultural differences. Because of his huge knowledge of light entertainment, Stewart Morris was asked to suggest five bands which might be suitable – and he included us.

When we told Dad, he was stunned. 'But calm down, girls,' he said. 'Don't get overexcited, they'll probably go for an

American band.' I think he was worried we'd all get our hopes up so much that we'd be devastated if we weren't chosen.

For weeks we waited while Sinatra and his people watched footage of the five bands. Every time the phone rang during that period, we would all hurtle into the hall, desperately hoping it was a call about the tour. Then, one afternoon, Stewart Morris asked to meet us. We were sick with nerves.

'You've got it!' was all he said. It was mayhem as all of us started screaming and crying. We'd grown up with our Dad crooning Sinatra songs and now we would be sharing a stage with the man himself! Dad was shaking when we told him.

Our first night was at the Palais des Congrès in Paris. We were on stage for about twenty minutes, during which we did an a cappella version of 'Scarlet Ribbons'. But Bernie had come down with a terrible cold and coughed all the way through it! The audience were sniggering initially, but by the time we finished they were openly laughing at us. Somehow we struggled, but we were dreading meeting Frank Sinatra backstage afterwards. We knew what a professional he was and were terrified he would just go mad at us.

When we went into his dressing room, he looked at us all and then, in that really smooth voice, he said, 'So, who's got a cough?'

We all turned and looked at Bernie.

'Don't worry, honey, it's all going to be great,' he smiled. Then he put his arms around us and said, 'Ah, you're like my daughters.'

We didn't really see Mr Sinatra, as we called him then, very often during the tour, but whenever we did, he was lovely.

Then, one night, when the show was at the Royal Albert Hall in London, we took Dad backstage to meet his idol.

'Mr Sinatra, this is our dad,' we said all together. The pair shook hands and, for the first time in his life, Dad was speechless.

Mum came with us for the rest of the tour around Europe. We flew from Paris to Vienna to Frankfurt with a sixty-piece orchestra. Until then, the biggest band we'd ever played with must have been twelve people, but all of a sudden we were working with a full orchestra which had a thirty-piece string section! It was so much bigger than anything we'd ever experienced before, and we were visiting cities we'd only ever seen on television. Looking back, it sounds incredibly glamorous, but we just got on with it. We remained incredibly normal and down to earth, and we still are today. Maybe that was because we were sisters and our day-to-day life still consisted of bickering over who'd nicked the hairdryer or giggling about blokes we fancied. That did keep us very grounded.

Things were going well for us and Dad felt confident enough to pack in his job in Blackpool to move down to London so he could concentrate full-time on being our manager. There was so much happening and I think he wanted to be on the spot so he could keep control over it and to protect his girls. Coleen stayed in Blackpool with Tommy and Brian. I think she was pretty much allowed to run wild, which seemed incredible, bearing in mind us older girls had barely been allowed out of Dad's sight when we were that age.

In London, Dad found himself in endless meetings with TV executives, music producers and sharp-suited businessmen. He only ever had our best interests at heart, but I think the job quickly became too big for him. The music industry is ruthless and there were people out there who sadly he couldn't compete with.

If we were performing at the London Room, we normally

finished at about half past ten, and then Maureen, Anne and Denise would go out on the town. I was still only sixteen, but more often than not I was joining them too. It was strange because in Blackpool Dad had been so strict with us all. But in London it was almost as though he had given up. I was a bit of a rebel too. I'd ring Dad at home after we'd finished a show and say, 'I'm just going out with the girls now, Dad.'

'No, you're not,' he'd say. But there was nothing he could do any more, and we both knew it. I was off! If I was working until the early hours in a nightclub, he could hardly stop me from staying out afterwards.

Samantha's Nightclub was our favourite haunt. It was quite small but very cool, and we loved it. Another of our regular favourites was a place called the Valbonne. We became friends with the managers and DJs of both those clubs and we'd be there night after night, dancing for hours on end without stopping.

All the boys would be falling over themselves to get to Maureen. 'I really fancy your sister with the dark hair,' they'd say to me.

'Yeah, you and a million others!' I'd reply.

Because we all looked a little different, we all attracted different men. I was always described as 'the one with the blonde hair and big boobs'. Charming!

After partying till three or four in the morning, we'd often go for breakfast at a place called Mike's Diner, next door to Samantha's in Greek Street. There was a group of guys who would usually be there at the same time, after having just finished work as croupiers in the West End casinos. It'd be dawn when us girls and the croupiers all fell out of Mike's

Diner and walked along the Embankment, singing songs from the shows, as other people set out for work.

When we finally rolled home, we'd find the key where Mum had left it, in the milk bottle next to the front door. We'd fall into bed, only to be up again three hours later for more rehearsals.

One night we were in the Valbonne when this really handsome Persian guy came up and started chatting me up. I was sixteen and he was much older than me and utterly gorgeous. I fell head over heels for him – I was a teenager; what did I know? – and he asked me out. He lived in an amazing penthouse suite at Hyde Park Gate, but I was far too naïve for him and nothing happened beyond a very innocent kiss. Then, one day, he announced he was moving to America and asked me to go with him. That suddenly sounded way too serious. I really liked him, but there was no way I could leave my family and move abroad with him. I was heartbroken when he left, but I felt I was having far too much fun to settle down with a guy.

I was a teenager living in London, doing a job I loved, partying every night and meeting glamorous people. How much better could it get? I was having a ball!

5.

Bernie

The Big Time

Anne was calling out to me from the other end of the counter in the BBC canteen, but I couldn't understand a thing she was saying. She was waving her arms about, holding the big purse that held the money for all of us girls' lunches.

'Your brother's saying, "What do you want for your lunch?"' said a voice from the middle of the queue. I looked up. It was Eric Morecambe, a TV legend.

I went bright red, but called back. 'A ham sandwich will do.'

'Your little brother says he wants a ham sandwich,' Eric Morecambe yelled back up the queue to Anne.

He really was hilarious. The Nolan Sisters appeared on *The Morecambe and Wise Show* three or four times, usually at Christmas, and we always had a great time. Whenever I saw Eric Morecambe in the corridor, it was his joke with me to say: 'And how are your brothers?'

It was incredible really that half the time my sisters and I were mixing with some of the biggest names in television, but the rest of the time we were totally normal school kids.

At that time, it seemed like we were on television almost every week. We did *The Two Ronnies*, Vince Hill's show, Cliff

Richard's show, Harry Secombe's Christmas show, *The Mike Yarwood Show*, *The Val Doonican Show*, and loads of other one-off programmes. This was at a time when the weekend TV schedules were packed with the kind of light entertainment shows that we fitted into perfectly.

I'd always loved performing. By the time I was born – the seventh child – it was no longer a case of: 'Will it be a boy or a girl?' It was purely: 'Will it be able to sing?'

Luckily I could, and I loved performing from the very earliest age. I can't really remember winning that watch at the Uncle Peter Webster Show on Blackpool's Central Pier, but I can remember always adoring being on a stage. Even when we weren't performing professionally, I'd be busy making up dance routines with Linda, and creating stories in my head and acting them out. I was always full of energy and constantly on the go. I guess I'm still a bit like that now.

I think of my childhood as really quite idyllic. As my sisters have said, it was at a time when kids could play out all day without their parents having to worry, and I was always playing in the street outside our house in Waterloo Road – riding my bike, pushing my dolls in their buggies or playing 'two balls' in the alley.

I loved all kinds of sports, particularly netball. I was chosen for the school team, and I remember Dad coming to watch one or two of my games. I was so chuffed about that. I honestly don't ever remember being pressurised to go and do shows. As I remember it, Dad was always fine if I wanted to play netball rather than perform with the family. And while I know there were dark things going on in my family, all my memories of that time are good. Maybe I was too young to realize what was going on, but all I remember is fun.

I was thirteen when we came to London, and I loved performing at the London Rooms and appearing on telly. There was only one downside – the clothes! There is a ten-year age gap between me and Anne, which now seems like nothing at all, but back then it was enormous. Yet despite this, our management still insisted we dress the same. And the clothes were bad. Grim, grim, grim! One dress still sticks in my mind. It was cream, with wine-coloured flowers on it and a big bow at the back. It was from Jaeger and, although I haven't got anything against Jaeger now, at the time I was thirteen! I wanted to be wearing drainpipe jeans and winklepickers like all my friends. I really resented it.

Even on our first day at Clark's School for Girls in Ilford, Linda, Coleen and I all had to turn up dressed the same. As if starting a new school isn't hard enough already, there we were in matching knee-length Jaeger frocks with cap sleeves and sweetheart necklines. I was delighted when Mum finally got our regulation brown uniforms and we could fit in with everyone else.

Our stage and TV clothes were even worse. Robert Earl's wife, Daphne, was trying to style us in the look of the Beverley Sisters, and I hated that. Daphne was very posh and very bossy, and she and I did not get along. I can remember crying lots of times when we were out shopping because of the things she was choosing for us. One day we were in a shop far more suited to middle-aged women than teenage girls when she picked up matching velvet jackets for each of us. They were rank.

'I'm not wearing that,' I said. Even at that age, I was very serious about my work as a singer and I had very strong opin-ions on what I liked and what I didn't like. And I most certainly did not like those jackets.

'Now, we'll have no Sarah Bernhardt's from you, dear,' Daphne said, sweeping past me. If I hadn't been a polite, well-brought-up girl, I'd have told her where to stick her velvet jackets. But I was, so we bought them. That made me really angry because I felt that none of us had any say in how we were being managed. I regret that we didn't all get together and stand up for ourselves a bit more.

To make things worse, at the end of the year, we were presented with a bill for all our clothes! We never realized that we were paying for everything along the way. No one had read the small print on our contracts; we'd been totally naïve. We were idiots really, but we'd come from the sticks and didn't realize how the music industry worked and how you had to be so careful that you weren't being cheated. When the bill arrived, we were so mad that we were being charged to wear some particularly foul jumpsuits that we got a pair of scissors and cut them into shreds. It was fantastic!

From then on, we took more control over what we wore and although we still stuck to a theme, we each had far more say in the way we looked.

I quickly settled in Ilford and made some great friends at Clark's School for Girls. Occasionally we'd get the mickey taken out of us for being on television, but I was never bullied. I wouldn't ever take that kind of crap.

I carried on playing netball and dreamt of becoming a PE teacher if my singing career didn't work out. I got nearly enough O levels, apart from maths. Mum and Dad were quite encouraging about us having interests outside singing. Maybe by the time Coleen and I came along our parents had relaxed a lot more.

Dad was always sparking with energy. Whenever our mates

came round, he would remember their names and would chat away to them for ages. And if something had happened at school, I was desperate to tell my dad.

Mum was amazing and was the one with the kisses and cuddles when we were little, but she was so busy cooking, washing, cleaning, ironing, scrubbing, shopping . . . It was never-ending for her. But Dad would sit down and listen to whatever we were saying. He probably didn't give a toss about our teenage stories most of the time, but he did a great job of pretending to be interested! He had the time to do that because he'd be sitting around getting waited on hand and foot by Mum. I never once saw him cook or clean. I look back sometimes and it pisses me off because Dad was a real chauvinist. But then I think men of that generation were, and most women of that time, like our mum, just put up with it.

When we were living in Ilford, I'd go to school and play netball most days and then perform at the London Rooms two or three nights a week. Linda and I did half a week each at the club, which was all we were legally allowed to do at our age. Some days I'd get home at three in the morning and then have to be up four hours later for school. I'd be exhausted, but it was fantastic. And on top of that were all the television appearances. I'd never let my daughter work those hours and sometimes I wonder what my parents were thinking of, letting a thirteen-year-old do that. But they weren't being cruel or horrible – they truly believed it was the best thing for us. And I guess, in many ways, it was.

It was at the London Rooms in 1973 that I met Christine Lepley, who is still my best friend now. Christine's mum, Joyce, was head waitress at the club and became like a second mum to me there. One night she said to me, 'I've got a daughter the same age as you. I'll have to bring her in to meet you.' So she brought Christine in and we got on brilliantly. Once Mum said she could come back to Granville Road for a sleepover. When we got back there, Christine and I were moving the beds around when she suddenly broke wind. We started giggling – and, thirty-seven years later, we still haven't stopped! (She'll kill me for saying that!)

By 1976, the year I turned sixteen, we had become household names and that was at the height of our television appearances. I think people like the Two Ronnies and Val Doonican liked working with us because we were not showbizzy kids. We weren't pretentious or obnoxious; we could just sing.

The following year, 1977, we toured South Africa with Rolf Harris and the comedian Stu 'Stewpot' Francis. If I'd been a bit more grown-up and in control of my own career, I would probably have refused to go because it was still at the time of apartheid. But back then I just did what I was told. And the country was beautiful. We went to Durban, Johannesburg and Port Elizabeth, and it was fascinating. Linda and I were only allowed to go if we took tutors with us, so that we wouldn't miss out on our schooling. Someone hired two young girls from New Zealand, but they were great – we all just went swimming and shopping together all the time.

One afternoon we went to the sauna at the hotel and who was sitting in there, wrapped in nothing but a towel, but Tom Jones! We couldn't believe it! We tried to act dead cool and he was absolutely lovely, saying how much he enjoyed our singing and that our harmonies were spot on. I might only have been sixteen, but I was old enough to look at a semi-naked Tom Jones and think: 'Oh yes, I like this!'

But when we got home, I didn't tell a soul about everything we'd got up to on our trip. Linda and I were desperate to keep our lives at Clark's School for Girls very separate from our lives with the group. I'm still friends now with kids that I met then.

After my O levels, I left school to sing with the band full-time. With shows and tours, there just wasn't time to think about A levels. And singing was still my first love.

'I've met this lovely lad,' Dad said. 'You'd really like him.'

We were performing on a cruise ship called *The Orsova* in 1978 when, one night, Dad came back from the bar and made this announcement. I bet my older sisters couldn't believe their ears. When they were my age, Dad wouldn't even let them look at a bloke, let alone introduce them to one. I didn't dare to imagine what kind of lad my Dad might think I found lovely. However, it turned out that he was right. His name was Mike and although he was from Derby, he had an Irish family, like me. He had thick, jet-black hair and big blue eyes and I thought he was gorgeous. We ended up going out together. He was away working on the ship a lot, but whenever he got back to Britain, he would come to meet me wherever we were touring and we sent dozens of letters to each other when we were apart. He was my first love, sexually and emotionally, but it was difficult being so far apart and, after about a year, the relationship fizzled out.

Then, when I was about nineteen, our cousin, Angie Breslan, came over from Dublin to live with us for a while. Her dad, Charlie, was Mum's brother and when he couldn't cope with Angie's nagging about wanting to live in London any longer, he sent her to stay with us.

Angie was a bit older than me, but we became bosom buddies. Almost every night that I wasn't performing we'd be at the Villa nightclub in Gants Hill. One night we were in there messing about and I saw this guy looking at me. He came over and offered to buy me a drink. He told me his name was Bob Allison and he worked nearby as a car salesman. He was about a year older than me, funny and warm, and we quickly hit it off. In fact, we were together for the next three years.

Bob and I started dating regularly and had a great time. We were part of a big crowd of couples who were out all the time. Each week we'd have a No-Solids Sunday – which meant no food, but an awful lot of drink! We had such a laugh. To them, I was just one of the gang. The fact that I was on telly and sometimes had to go off on tour didn't bother them at all.

The television success of The Nolans was great, but all of us really wanted to make records and, most importantly, to have a hit. Me, I just wanted to be on *Top of the Pops*!

Between 1974 and 1977 we recorded seven singles, but despite our massive TV success, every single one of them flopped. Being household names was fantastic in some ways, but we realized that it was actually working against us in terms of selling singles. Our reputation was so sickly sweet that it was getting in the way.

We talked it all through with Joe Lewis from the London Rooms, who was still looking after us, along with Stuart Morris, our producer, and Robert Earle, our manager. Then, in 1978, it was decided that we should record an album of cover versions called *20 Giant Hits* with Warner Bros. In the picture on the cover, we were all wearing floor-length pink dresses. Foul! But despite the hideous picture, the album was a hit and got to number three in the charts. Suddenly the record companies were all over us like a rash. Maybe we were marketable after all! But the success had one other result.

'I'm leaving. I want to go solo,' Denise announced one evening.

It wasn't entirely unexpected, but it was still a shame. We'd all been aware for ages that Denise wasn't happy in the group. She hated it when we were given choreography to learn for a show. She found it a struggle to do and wasn't that good at it – she admitted it herself. She was also self-conscious about her appearance and felt she looked bigger than the rest of us in our costumes.

She was twenty-six, was going steady with her boyfriend Tom by then and felt the time was right to go it alone. She didn't feel like she fitted in, and that's not good in a group because if one person isn't happy, you can all end up feeling like that too. We all knew that Denise was a great solo artist. When she was out on stage on her own, she had a lot more confidence than when she had all her sisters around her.

I thought: 'Yeah, this probably is the best thing for Denise. And for us too.' There wasn't any bad feeling or a big show-down; we just accepted it and moved on. Because we were sisters and knew we'd still see each other all the time, it made it far less of a big deal than it would have been otherwise.

So it was the four of us – Linda, Maureen, Anne and I – who signed with CBS to start recording singles. Coleen still hadn't joined the band full-time at that point. We were introduced to the songwriters Ben Findon and Mike Myers, who were really well-respected musicians and who had been asked by the record company to work with us. One day at the beginning of 1979, we met with them at a studio and they played us a ballad called 'Spirit, Body and Soul'. It was to be our first single with CBS.

I really liked the tune and always thought it could do well in the charts, but when it went straight into the top thirty we were all just delighted. In those days you could only go on *Top of the Pops* if your song had charted, and you didn't find that out until the Tuesday lunchtime. We were all at home in Ilford when Nicky Graham, our A&R man at CBS, called us with the news.

'You're top forty,' Nicky said. 'And . . . ' He paused. 'You're on *Top of the Pops* this Thursday.'

They must have been able to hear the screaming coming from our house the full length of Granville Road. This was a major moment in my life. Yeah, appearing on the Two Ronnies' Christmas show had been good and sharing a sauna with Tom Jones had been OK too, but this was mega!

That evening, when we turned up at the *Top of the Pops* studios, I was beside myself. This was now like being a proper pop star. We wore knee-length dresses in a range of colours and so even our outfits weren't too bad that night!

'Spirit, Body and Soul' climbed to number thirty-four in the charts, which we were pretty pleased with. A month or so later we were called back to see Ben and Mike again and they played another track. It was a jingly disco tune and I instantly hated it. I loved black soul music at that time and was a big fan of Motown, like Stevie Wonder and Chaka Khan. I hated pop songs like the one Mike and Ben were playing that day. But when they asked us to take it in turns to sing the words so they could decide who should take lead vocals, I just got on with it. I went up to the microphone and started singing the words: 'I'm in the mood for dancing. Romancing . . .'

It was the song which was to change our lives forever. Even now, you can't go to a wedding, a hen night or a seventies disco without hearing it. It fills dance floors every time it's played. It was even played before each ad break during a recent series of *The X Factor*. But that first time I heard it, I just hated it. In fact, it was years before I warmed to it. And although I'm very grateful for that tune and I appreciate that it gave us a huge amount of success, if I'm honest, it's still not one of my favourite songs.

Even so, I was chosen to take the lead vocals and the song became a massive hit. It went straight into the top ten and for the next few weeks it kept on climbing. We couldn't believe it! Everywhere we went, people were singing 'I'm in the Mood' to us. Finally, the single peaked at number three in the charts. But it still wasn't on the Radio One playlist because we weren't deemed to be cool enough for that. They *had* to play it once a week during the Top Forty countdown though, which we thought was hilarious.

With the success of 'I'm in the Mood', we were on *Top of the Pops* week after week. Back then, they had to have a certain amount of live acts on every show and, without blowing our own trumpets, we were one of the few acts who could perform live, so we kept getting called back.

In 1980 we released more singles. 'Don't Make Waves' reached number twelve and 'Gotta Pull Myself Together' made it to number nine. Then 'Who's Gonna Rock You', which was co-written for us by Billy Ocean, went to number twelve too. We released more singles over the next couple of years, but none had the success of 'I'm in the Mood'. With concerts, tours and TV commitments too, life was very hectic.

Away from show business, my life was very normal and

very happy. I carried on going out with Bob and hanging around with our big gang of friends. At twenty-one, I moved into Bob's house in Barkingside in Essex and we loved living like a proper couple.

It was a fabulous time. My only disappointment now is that we made so little money from it all. Even now, I'm still not sure what happened to all the money that we earned. It simply didn't come to us. But we were young and naïve. After Robert Earle stopped managing us, Dad felt he had to take over, but he was out of his league by then and there are some real sharks in the music industry. I'm ashamed that I was now a young woman in my early twenties, but still didn't do anything to stop it happening. But even though I can be quite bolshie at times, I also hate to hurt people and I couldn't tell my Dad he shouldn't be our manager any longer. I dread to think how much money other people have made at our expense.

Even now when people hear 'I'm In The Mood' playing they say to me, 'Oh you must be coining it in from that song,' but we didn't write it so we don't get royalties every time it's played, just relatively small performing rights. I can imagine how much money other people have made from it though.

The other shame was that we always felt that the press was very much against us and we were under attack simply for being too 'nice'. Don't get me wrong, I'm not ashamed to be a nice girl, but there was more to us. But it felt that no one in the British media wanted to see that. We were saddled with a goody-two-shoes image whether we liked it – or deserved it – or not. And I think our songs irritated some people. To be honest, I never really liked our music back then very much myself. I'm more into pop music now than I was in the late seventies and early eighties.

But whatever some people in Britain – including me – might have thought of our music, in other places around the world they were going totally mad for it.

6.

Coleen

The Baby Grows Up

Oh yes, they were mad about us abroad – and nowhere more so than in Japan. When we stepped off the aeroplane at Tokyo Airport for the first time in 1980 there was a sea of people screaming and shouting. There were literally thousands of them, all working themselves into a total frenzy.

'There must be someone dead famous on the plane,' Bernie said to me, and we looked the other passengers up and down in the hope of seeing someone from the movies. But then I saw a teenager holding a placard which read: 'We love The Nolans!' It wasn't someone else they'd come to see – it was us!

It was pretty crazy for all the girls, but it was even more amazing for me – I was still just fifteen, and a couple of months earlier I'd been an ordinary Blackpool schoolgirl who spent every spare moment mucking out at the local stables.

I was the baby of the family, and I still am today in many ways. There are seventeen years between me and my eldest brother Tommy and, oh boy, did I play on that! If any of the others picked on me, I'd start wailing and Mum would yell: 'Leave my baby alone!' while I'd be sticking out my tongue at them out of sight. Generally though, I was content to watch and listen to my older brothers and sisters without really feeling the need to say much myself. I was a very quiet kid and happy to go with the flow. It seemed to me there was already plenty of noise in our house without me joining in too! I'd just let them get on with whatever it was they were doing and mingle in quietly in the background.

Being the youngest, I was the last to properly join the band, just before our first tour to Japan. I'd sung with the rest of the family in the clubs and theatres around Blackpool before my sisters moved to London and I'd gone down to do occasional shows with them afterwards, but the rest of the time my life was pretty normal.

I enjoyed singing, but I wasn't crazy about performing in the way that Linda and Bernie were. I was two the first time I walked out on stage at the ABC Theatre in Blackpool, and I can remember it vividly. It's the Syndicate Nightclub now, and the red pull-down seats have been replaced with a dance floor and DJ booths. But back then 2,000 people had turned up for a night of music and entertainment. I think every one of them must have gone 'Ahhh' as I emerged from the wings to sing 'Santa Claus is Coming to Town'.

'Why are they doing that?' I thought to myself, totally unaware that what I was doing wasn't what every toddler did of an evening. I had never known anything different.

But as I got a bit older, I grew to hate the nightclub circuit. Everywhere we went there would be someone stinking of booze and fags wanting to cuddle me, squeeze my cheeks and ruffle my hair. 'Ugh, leave me alone,' I'd be thinking. But because we'd been brought up always to be polite, I just had to smile and accept it.

And although Bernie says she remembers being allowed

nights off from performing, I can't recall that. I remember having to do the show come hell or high water. When I was at school and all my friends were out playing in the street, I'd be getting ready to drive to Glasgow or somewhere, to be on stage at ten o'clock at night.

One evening all my friends from school were joining the Brownies and I was so desperate to go with them, but I couldn't because we were working. I was devastated.

I'm sure that whenever I said, 'But, Mum, I don't want to go to Glasgow,' or wherever it was we were headed, there was a very simple answer: 'Well, you have to.' My parents couldn't have just left me at home on my own, so I had to go. It was only when I got older that I realized my parents weren't just being strict; we had to perform, it was our livelihood. They were only doing what everyone did back then: earning a crust with which to keep their family.

I was never desperate to get out on stage. I just wasn't really that into it, probably because I'd done it from such a young age. So many times, at two o'clock in the morning, I'd be asleep on a couple of chairs pushed together in a club. Or I'd climb onto Mum's lap and she would rock me to sleep, singing to me all the while. But after that, there would still be the long journey home before school the next morning. I'd then have that awful tired feeling that totally takes you over when you're a kid.

Those experiences definitely affected the way I brought up my kids. I never made the boys or Ciara go out in the evenings when they were little. Even if we were on holiday with a group of people and everyone was going out, I still preferred to stay in and let the kids go to bed rather than drag them out and hope they fell asleep in a buggy. I knew how horrible that feeling could be. And I hate seeing kids being fussed over by adults, the way I was, ruffling their hair and tweaking their cheeks. 'Just leave them alone,' I think.

My older brothers and sisters doted on me. Tommy had a drum kit in his room and I'd run in there, sit on his lap and say, 'Let me play, Pom, let me play.' I called him Pom because I couldn't say Tom and the name sort of stuck. It must have driven him mad because he'd have been around twenty by then, but most of the time he was very patient. But, of course, there were times when he wasn't. 'Mum, can you get Coleen OUT of my room!' he'd yell down the stairs.

I don't remember sleeping in the drawer, but when I was older I'd just squash in with one of my sisters every night. I certainly didn't feel hard done by because I didn't have my own bed – I felt special. Usually I slept with Anne in her single bed. Sometimes I'd wet her bed in the middle of the night, but she never got angry with me. She just lifted me out and sat me on the bedroom floor while she changed the sheets.

Anne was fifteen years older than me and she was my second mum in many ways, bringing me up while Mum was keeping the house and caring for everyone else. It was Anne who put my hair in pigtails before we did a show and Anne who bathed me before bed.

Bernie and Linda were closest to me in age and became my playmates. Linda was a bit of a rebel. She wasn't scared of our dad in the way that the rest of us were. While I'd listen as the rest of my older sisters would sit around discussing how they were going to get out the house without Dad noticing, Linda would just say, 'Right, Dad, I'm off now,' and she would go before he had a chance to disagree. I think Dad met his match in Linda.

Bernie and I always got on great, although it must have been hard for her because she'd been the baby of the family for almost five years before I turned up. But if she was annoyed by it, she never showed it. She used to have this thing about my cheeks and would stroke and pinch them because she thought they were so cute. The only problem was, she did it so much I'd end up crying!

Like my sisters say, Dad was the one who'd listen if you were having problems at school and he was great to have a laugh with. But if I was sick or upset, Mum was the only one I wanted. Mum was always so busy, bless her, and if she didn't have time for us, it wasn't because she didn't love us – she just had so much to do. There was never a time when I didn't feel loved and Mum was always the one who was there with the cuddles and kisses, who made everything right. Sometimes she would sit me on her lap and sing lullabies to me: 'Give Her the Moon to Play With' and the old Irish lullaby 'Tora, Lora, Lora'. When I grew up and had my own kids, I'd sing the same lullabies to them.

But, like my sisters, I was disappointed when Mum and Dad were too busy working to come to parents' evenings and sports days. The morning after parents' evening would be horrible, as the other kids sat around discussing what their parents had been told – and I knew my Mum and Dad hadn't even been there.

Dad did come to a school show once, in which I was singing 'Burlington Bertie' as a solo. In all the years I'd been performing, I'd never been so excited as that night, when I saw Dad in the audience. I got a standing ovation, but the best bit for me was that Dad was there to see it. I was so proud, I could have popped.

And one time Dad came to a sports day where I came second in both the 100 metres and the relay race. Knowing Dad was watching me collect my medal was better than being at the Olympics. Because Mum and Dad rarely came along to shows and sports days, it made me determined I'd always be there when I had children. Whenever a class of kids comes out for an assembly, carol concert or school sports day, they're always looking out to see who is watching them, and I couldn't bear for my children to have no familiar faces in the audience.

School was OK, but my real passion as a little girl was horses. I was only tiny when I became obsessed with them. I nagged my parents for ages to let me go up to the local stables in Blackpool at weekends and eventually they agreed. From the age of six, I was there every spare moment I had, riding, mucking out and grooming.

My best friend was Alan Fleck, who lived next door. He was Linda's friend Suzanne's younger brother and the same age as me. We went everywhere together. We even made our First Holy Communions on the same day; he looked like a groom and I was like a bride. I was convinced it would only be a matter of time until we were playing the roles for real! Whenever I wasn't performing with the family or at the stables, I'd be playing with Alan, building dens or riding our bikes.

When my older sisters got their big break and moved down south, I went to join them for a while and enrolled at Clark's School for Girls in Ilford with Linda and Bernie. We were all stood next to each other on that dreadful first morning when the teacher asked us to sing to our new classmates. We were doing a three-part harmony, but as I sang the words all I could hear in my head was 'Noooooooooooooo, please let this not be happening!' All I wanted was to be normal, but I was being marked out as different from day one.

That time in Ilford was great for me though because I was too young to get a licence to sing at the London Rooms in the evenings with the rest of the girls, so in many ways I was able to be normal. There was no more driving for hours on end to do shows in dingy nightclubs. Instead, I could go round to mates' houses after school or just sit in front of the telly in the evenings. I was having a totally normal childhood and I loved it, absolutely loved it.

I made loads of friends at school and Mum was always brilliant about letting me invite them round to play or stay over. Sometimes the house would be overrun and Mum would rush around making breakfast, dinner and tea for dozens of people. Was the house spotlessly clean? Not really. But who cares? Mum was never one to be saying: 'Don't do that, I've just cleaned the floor,' or any of that stuff. She'd given up on all that house-proud stuff by then.

My best friend at Clark's School was Liz Nicholls. She seemed to me to be a genius academically, but she was also up with all the latest trends, and I was way behind on them. When it was trendy to have a long skirt for school, mine was up by my knickers! I'd probably be quite cool now, but back then everyone just laughed at me.

When my sisters started appearing on television I just tried to play it down as much as possible. I was still desperate to be normal and my close friends ignored the whole thing. But there was always the odd bitch who'd come up to me in the playground and say, 'Your sisters are s★★★!' I'd just go: 'Yeah, I know, they're so embarrassing.' It took the wind right out of their sails!

At weekends I'd go back up to Blackpool to stay with Auntie Theresa or my brothers, so I could spend time helping out at the local stables, and when I was about thirteen, I went back permanently. My sisters had started touring a lot and Mum went with them, so it was thought better for me to be back home with the rest of the family.

Dad was constantly travelling between Blackpool and London and my brothers were out at work, so mostly I just looked after myself. I'd get myself up for school in the morning and cook my own tea at night. By then, I was at a private school called Brewood College, but God only knows what was going on there because there were only four of us in the entire place and we wouldn't start till half past ten and be finished by two o'clock. My best friend there was called Donna Rutter and we had such a laugh – even if we didn't learn a thing!

Every evening we'd get ourselves all dressed up in our pencil skirts and high heels and walk the whole length of Blackpool Prom, down the Golden Mile. Donna would turn up wearing something like a white see-through blouse and tangerine bra and my brothers would go mental about it. 'You're not going out dressed like that,' Brian would say to me when I put on my matching (but a lot less revealing) outfit. They would even try to barricade the front door so we couldn't get out, but Donna and I always found a way. We'd hang around the arcade on the prom and let the guys who ran the waltzers flirt with us. Then, at the end of the evening, we'd walk all the way home again.

I loved living with my brothers. With Tommy being the eldest and me the youngest, I always felt we had quite a lot in common. In some ways we were the outsiders of the family. Tommy didn't conform to everything that was expected in our family and I loved him for that – I still do. Being the youngest, I think I'm a bit more independent from the rest of the family too. I turned up so long after the others that my life was very different from my older sisters'. I had my own bedroom as a teenager, which they never did, and I had loads of friends outside of the family. During the time I was back in Blackpool without Mum and Dad I had a huge amount of independence, which they were never allowed.

After a while I went to live with Auntie Theresa. She was eight years younger than Mum and had never had kids, so I became like a surrogate child. I had a great time there. When my sisters landed a regular slot on Mike Yarwood's show it was somehow assumed that I'd be part of the act, so for a while, every Friday night, I'd get the train down, spend Saturday rehearsing before the live show that evening, then return home on Sunday.

Looking back, it is incredible that I was an ordinary school-girl from Monday to Friday but was on one of telly's biggest shows on a Saturday night. But at the time I didn't think it was particularly exciting at all. I was just doing it because it was expected of me, when really I'd have been far happier hanging around the waltzers with Donna.

I still lived for horses and at weekends and holidays I would be at the stables from seven in the morning until it got dark. I was never going to be good enough to ride competitively, but I loved being out on the horses and, most of all, I enjoyed looking after them, leading them out into the fields in the morning, grooming them, sweeping out the stables, tacking them up and feeding them. I just adored being around them.

For ages I dreamt of being a vet. Then I found out how many qualifications you needed, so that idea was knocked on the head. So I thought maybe I could do some other kind of work caring for animals, or maybe be a journalist or a social worker. Or, best of all, a football manager! At that point, I really didn't have much enthusiasm at all to join my sisters singing full-time. They had toured with Frank Sinatra and were playing to massive audiences, but that just didn't really appeal to me.

If I ever discussed my future with Dad, he was very relaxed and never put me under any pressure to perform. 'Don't join the group if you don't want to,' he'd say. 'I can see you living on a farm with loads of animals and being really happy.' He knew how much I enjoyed working with horses and I think he admired me for doing something on my own.

Then, in 1979, Anne married Brian Wilson, who'd been a footballer with Blackpool, and fell pregnant. Brian had been transferred down to Torquay, which meant he and Anne were living on the south coast.

Suddenly it felt like all eyes were on me. Would I take Anne's place? I guess the question had always been lurking at the back of everyone's minds, but now I felt they were all desperate for me to make a decision. Our record company, CBS, were saying, 'If she is going to join, it has to be now.'

It was make-your-mind-up time for me. I was fourteen and a year away from sitting O levels, but bearing in mind that I was only in school for about four hours a day, it would have been a miracle if I passed a single one. So the choice was: stay at school, which I wasn't very good at, or join the group and start singing, which I was good at.

I was a bit of a lazy teenager and took the easy option to sing with my sisters, but even then I wasn't driven by any huge ambition. That sounds really ungrateful, considering how hard some people work to break into the music industry, but it's the truth.

At the end of 1979, we released 'Spirit, Body and Soul', followed soon after by 'I'm In the Mood for Dancing', and then, in 1980, came the Japan tour. Everything was moving so fast that it was hard to get my head around it all.

We were number one in Japan before our aeroplane had even touched down and we were surrounded by thousands of screaming fans. It seemed that everyone there was totally mental about us. They even had to draft in the army to escort us from place to place because we couldn't walk down the streets without being torn to pieces by overeager fans trying to kiss us or touch us. There were teenagers swarming around the reception area of our hotels day and night and special security staff had to be brought it to keep them at a safe distance. It was fabulous in some ways, but also a bit of a shame because it meant we didn't get to see much of the country. One day we decided to escape from our hotel and managed to sneak out of a back exit and walk to a nearby shopping centre. We were browsing the clothes rails in one shop when I heard some girls giggling. I looked up and about twelve girls were crowded round the shop doorway, staring and pointing at us. 'Uh, oh,' I thought.

In less than a couple of minutes the number of girls outside the shop had grown to fifty. And in ten minutes it was up to about 300. I felt like a rabbit in a trap. We had no idea how we were going to get out of there. There was no back exit, so we were going to have to force our way through them.

'Just put your head down and run,' Linda finally ordered us all. So that's what we did. We barged our way through this mass of people and sprinted all the back to the hotel. I was scared to death. It was like Beatle-mania. Looking back, I think I should just have sat back and enjoyed it, but at the time I was straight out of school and very shy, and I found the whole thing really scary.

It was a gruelling tour. We were getting up at 5 a.m. and doing about fifteen TV show appearances every day and then a gig in the evening before getting back to our hotel after midnight. I was also terribly homesick. I'm a real homebird and all I really wanted was to be sleeping in my own bed and going down the Golden Mile with Donna every evening.

My sisters were used to touring, they'd been doing it for years, but I found it hard to adjust. I was still the baby of the family and they looked after me, which made it easier, but I was pretty much expected to just do what I was told. If the other girls had arguments about something to do with the group, I just kept out of it and did what was decided at the end of the row. My sisters did like a good old row every now and again. Bernie and Linda in particular felt very strongly about the songs and harmonies that we did, and neither of them were backward in coming forward about voicing their opinions. Maureen, like me, tended to be a lot more laid-back about it all. When we really couldn't make a decision about something, it would go to a vote, so it was fairly democratic.

My education ended at the time of the Japan tour. I was supposed to have a tutor, but he never showed up and no one was very bothered, so that was that.

After that first tour to Japan, we went back another five or six times. Then, in 1981, we won the grand prize at the Tokyo Music Festival for our single 'Sexy Music'. We were the first European act ever to win the festival and it was a huge achievement, although it was barely noticed back in the UK.

Each time we returned to Japan the hysteria was just as great as before. We sold nine million records there – more than The Beatles – in two years. And one of our tours sold out entirely in two hours. Japanese people place huge emphasis on the family and I think they liked it that we were all sisters. And they loved our kind of pop music too.

We also went to America, where for two weeks we were the support act for Engelbert Humperdinck. He was nice enough, but he didn't half love himself! He thought he was God's gift to women! And then there was a tour to Australia too. Sometimes Mum and Dad would come with us on the tours, but other times they didn't. They loved travelling, although Mum wasn't so keen on foreign food. When we went to Japan she packed tea bags, McVitie's biscuits, bread and even butter. She didn't want to take any risks with all that sushi!

After our first trip to Japan we got our own band, which came with us everywhere. One of the keyboard players was a guy called Robin Smith, and he was drop-dead gorgeous. I was still only fifteen and he was twenty-three, but I didn't let the age gap bother me. Touring all over the world with my older sisters had made me grow up fast and I was quite mature for my age. At first it was very flirty but pretty innocent. I hadn't snogged a boy before I met Robin, but the first time we kissed, outside the Westbury Hotel in London, I never wanted it to stop.

Shortly after my sixteenth birthday, Mum and Dad went away and Robin stayed over at our house in Ilford. There was no doubting what was going to happen that night! Looking back, it seems like I was very young to lose my virginity, but at the time I felt like a fully grown woman. And I was so in love with Robin that sleeping with him felt totally natural, and very nice!

I couldn't keep something like that to myself though, and I soon told Linda, and then Bernie.

'Don't tell anyone,' I said to Linda, 'but I've slept with Robin.'

'Oh my God,' she replied. 'Are you alright? Was it all OK?'

'Yeah,' I replied grinning. 'It was great.'

'Oh, that's OK then,' she said. Both Linda and Bernie were cool about it – they knew their baby sister was growing up fast.

About four weeks later, though, I started feeling horribly sick. We'd had a lot of stress in the family because Anne had been seriously ill while having her daughter, Amy, and for a while we were terrified neither of them would pull through. Thankfully they did, but part of me still thought my sickness could be delayed shock at everything that had gone on.

But, to be honest, even I wasn't quite that stupid. I had a pretty good idea what the symptoms of pregnancy were, and these were spot on. As I had a wee on the tester stick in the bathroom of our house in Ilford, I already knew what the result was going to be.

'I can't have this baby,' I said to Robin, showing him the positive result a couple of hours later. 'My parents will be devastated,' I said. 'They'll kill me.'

It was a horrible, horrible time. Robin was great and didn't put any pressure on me, but I knew I couldn't go through with the pregnancy. I was sixteen and it would have destroyed my parents. I couldn't even bring myself to tell my sisters. I thought they'd be furious too, although they would probably have understood.

So Robin helped me arrange to have a termination at a private London clinic. I told Mum and Dad that Robin and I were having a day out together and wouldn't be back until late that evening. Then Robin drove me to the clinic. He wasn't allowed to stay with me, so he gave me a kiss and left me sitting in a waiting room. It was then that I started to cry. I thought I would never stop. I felt so ashamed.

A doctor came into the room and could see what a state I was in. 'Coleen, you don't have to go through with this if you don't want to,' he said.

But that wasn't an option. I just shook my head and trudged off down the corridor towards the operating room. When I came round from the general anaesthetic, I felt totally fuzzy, but after a couple of hours I signed forms to discharge myself. Even though I knew there was a danger of haemorrhaging, I had to make sure I was home that evening. Robin collected me and took me back to his house for a while, where I slept before returning home that evening.

'Are you OK?' Mum said the minute I walked in the front door.

'Yeah, I'm fine,' I said. But I was so pale and puffy-eyed that she must have known something was up. I was also wearing a new dress Robin had had to buy me when I couldn't get my skin-tight jeans back on after the operation because of the amount of padding I had to wear.

I went straight to my room, where I spent the evening crying and feeling utterly miserable. Mum kept popping into the room. She knew something had happened, but I could never have told her what I'd done.

It took me a while to recover, both physically and emotion-ally, from the abortion, but Robin was incredibly supportive and we were closer than ever. When we went on tour together, everyone treated us like an old married couple and we slept together every night, as Mum and Dad rarely travelled with us by then. But then Dad came on a tour to Japan and there was a very awkward moment. One night he pulled Linda to one side and said, 'Look, the Japanese are asking if Coleen and Robin want one room again. I don't want to embarrass her by asking, but what do you think?'

'One room,' was Linda's straightforward reply.

I was still only sixteen, but Dad was fine about it. He'd given up fighting us all by then. I know that pissed off my elder sisters though. When they were sixteen they were still wearing knee-high socks and weren't even allowed to hold hands with a boy.

My sisters must have been even madder when I moved in with Robin later the same year. Each of us sisters had earned £50,000 from the last Japan tour, and it enabled me to put down a deposit on a small house in Hillingdon in Middlesex. Robin and I set about playing happy families – I was still really young and should probably have been out clubbing, but we loved staying in, cooking meals and watching TV together. I was very happy.

Around then, Mum and Dad decided to sell the Ilford house and move back to Waterloo Road in Blackpool. I didn't like them being so far away, but Maureen was living just around the corner from me in Hillingdon and we saw each other all the time.

Then, at Christmas 1983, when I was eighteen, Robin handed me a tiny wrapped box. Inside was a diamond ring. 'It's beautiful,' I said putting the ring on the fourth finger of my left hand. But Robin never formally proposed and I think it was more a sign of commitment than a definite 'let's set the date' type situation.

By the summer of the following year things had changed between us. It was hard to pinpoint what was different, but I could feel it because of the way Robin talked to me and even the way he looked at me. It's horrible when you can just sense that someone has stopped loving you.

We carried on like that for a few weeks, until one day I suddenly said to Robin, 'Are you seeing someone else?' It turned out that she was a backing singer from the group Imagination, who he'd been working with.

'Get out!' I screamed at him. I was heartbroken. Utterly devastated. What made it worse was that we were still working together. For months I would see him every day and would have to spend all my energy concentrating on not bursting into tears every time he walked into the room.

I was single for a while after that – with the exception of a few drunken fumbles – until one day I kept feeling my eyes drawn to the tall, skinny drummer who had joined our new Nolans band. He was a bit weird – or 'alternative', I should probably say – and was really into Frank Zappa and obscure bands I'd never heard of before. But he was very, very funny, and I found that hugely attractive.

He was called Stewart and, after a few weeks of high-intensity flirting, we got together. A month or so after that, we'd moved in together. We had a good laugh, but we were very different. He'd be sitting there listening to his Zappa records and I'd say, 'I'm going up to bed to watch the telly.'

For more than a year everything was great between us and we got on really well, even though deep down I did sometimes get a nagging feeling that maybe Stewart wasn't really 'the one' for me.

Maybe I should have seen the warning signs when Bernie developed a massive interest in Frank Zappa. 'Weird. Never realized she was into all that,' I'd think when she'd turn up at our house with a bag of his records and spend hours on end talking to Stewart about his music collection. The pair of them got on really well, but it never occurred to me that anything might happen between them. She was my sister!

Their friendship seemed to be going great guns, but gradually I could feel my relationship with Stewart getting wobbly. 'Maybe he wants me to be more of a party animal, like Bernie,' I'd think. But nothing I did seemed to bring back the spark between us. It was like the situation with Robin all over again. I could just sense that he was falling out of love with me.

I was devastated that this was happening to me again, just like the last time. I became convinced there must be something wrong with me. For weeks I tried to ignore the signs, but in the end Stewart brought things to a head. 'I'm not sure what I want,' he said. When a bloke says that, you can be sure he knows damn well what he wants – and it's not you. But back then I was still young and very vulnerable. All I could do was nod and concentrate all my energy on not bawling my eyes out in front of him.

I decided I needed some time off men. Well, that was the plan anyway. The reality wasn't going to be quite so straightforward . . .

7.

Linda

The Naughty Nolan

'I know someone who really fancies you,' my sister Denise laughed one evening.

'Oh yeah?' I replied. 'Well, I'm not interested.' I'd just discovered the guy I'd been seeing for a couple of months was married. I'd been well and truly led up the garden path and was feeling a bit sorry for myself.

'He must be a man of taste though!' I joked. 'What's his name?'

'Brian Hudson,' she said. 'My new agent.'

It's funny how one conversation like that can shape the rest of your life. But it did. I hadn't even met Brian Hudson then. All I had at that point was the name of the man who was going to be the love of my life.

Denise had left the group in 1978 and gone solo, recording her own songs and performing gigs around the country. Brian was working for her management company.

Soon afterwards, we were all recording a slot for the 1979 *Nationwide Christmas Special*. In those days it felt like the nightly magazine-style show was watched by virtually everyone in the country, so it was very exciting for us. We were singing 'Have

Yourself a Merry Little Christmas' in a five-part harmony with Denise, who'd brought Brian along.

Well, what can I say? He was gorgeous. Dark hair, blue eyes, great smile, nice bum, a sense of humour. He had everything I wanted in a man. But he also had one thing that I certainly didn't want – a wife! I'd had my fingers burnt by a married man once before and I wasn't going to make the same mistake again. Or was I?

Afterwards, I said to Bernie: 'Oh my God, he's gorgeous.'

'Well, don't come crying to me!' she laughed.

That Christmas, Mum and Dad threw a massive party at our house in Ilford. The huge conservatory at the back of the house was perfect for parties, and everyone loved Mum's dos. Denise brought Brian, along with his wife, Caroline, their four-year-old son, Lloyd, and his parents. Our parties were a bit like that: the more the merrier! I was a bit down that night because a guy I had a crush on hadn't called me all Christmas. I must have been moping around about that because Brian came over and tried to cheer me up. 'You've just got to remember the good times and forget the bad,' Brian said, smiling.

At the end of the evening Brian and his family were leaving and he cornered me by the front door. He looked me straight in the eyes and said, 'You and I are going to end up together.'

And that was it; he walked down the drive and got into his car.

I was a bit taken aback. I really liked him, but he had a wife, so it was completely ridiculous. I tried to put it right out of my mind.

The next day he phoned me.

'I'm not interested in married men,' I told him firmly, even though I wasn't feeling at all firm inside.

'My wife and I have fallen out of love,' he replied. 'It's sad, but we're only together now because of Lloyd.'

I know. It's the sort of thing a million married men have said before, but Brian seemed so genuine and so sincere that my gut feeling told me it was true. But still, I stuck to my guns. On top of anything else, if Mum and Dad thought I was seeing a married man, they'd kill me!

But despite my determination to avoid Brian Hudson, he was equally determined to see me. He rang me over and over again, begging me to have dinner with him. Finally I agreed to let him take me out for dinner a couple of days before my birthday in February. I didn't tell my parents where I was going and made up some elaborate story to cover my tracks.

Brian took me to a little Italian restaurant in Hampstead, north London, and from the moment we sat down at the table, we didn't stop chatting all night. Brian told me how he had been brought up in Plaistow, east London, and had played drums and sung in bands since he was a teenager. He had been in a string of harmony bands – Tony Rivers and the Castaways, Harmony Grass, and Sparrow which had won *New Faces* many times as the people's choice and had been tipped for great things. He loved show business, just like me, but after a while he'd lost his passion for performing. He was determined to stay in the industry though, and that was when he went to work for the agency which looked after Denise.

Then Brian talked about his home life. Not only was he still married to Caroline, he had also had a first wife too, who he'd been with when he was very young. They'd had a daughter called Sarah, but after the marriage broke down he'd agreed for the little girl to be formally adopted by his ex's new partner.

At that time he was in bands, constantly touring, and thought it would be the best thing for her, but he always hoped that when she was older they would be able to have a relationship again.

Brian told me he and Caroline were now living totally separate lives, even though they were still under the same roof. 'She wouldn't mind me seeing you,' he said softly.

'Really?' I asked. It certainly sounded an unusual situation to me, and it was far from perfect, but there was no doubting that I was falling for him big time. We had so much in common: we both loved music and we were both obsessed by show business. And he was so attentive. He'd even arranged for the waiters to bring me out a birthday cake. Mind you, we had to throw it out the car window on the dual carriageway on the way home, to avoid my parents asking where it had come from.

I was nineteen by then, but they would still have been horrified to think I was out with a thirty-year-old married man. Mum was still a practising Catholic who went to mass every single Sunday without fail, and going out with a married man was just thought to be totally wrong. Dad rarely went to church, but he would hate the idea just as much. I'd always been far more of a rebel than my sisters and didn't pay too much notice to what Dad said I could or couldn't do, but even *I* thought it best to keep quiet about Brian at first.

I fell for Brian very fast. He was funny and kind, and he adored me. I'd had boyfriends in the past, but Brian was my first proper physical relationship.

We had been seeing each other for a couple of months when I dropped it into conversation that I was going out with

Brian Hudson. Of course, Mum and Dad had met Brian through Denise – and his wife!

'What the hell do you think you're doing?' Dad yelled at me one night. 'He's married.'

'But they're living separate lives,' I said. 'He told me.'

I know it's a cliché, but Brian seemed utterly genuine and I had no reason to disbelieve him. Everything he did and said convinced me that his marriage was over in all but name.

It still took a long while for Mum and Dad to come to terms with me seeing Brian. They didn't really think any man was good enough for their daughters, let alone a married man with kids! I think they must have seen how much I adored him though, and gradually they came to accept the situation. And even if they still had their concerns privately, they always made Brian feel welcome. The girls liked him too, although I think Denise got a bit fed up that he was spending more time with me than with her!

After a while Mum and Dad even allowed Brian to stay the night in our tiny spare room. When everyone was asleep, I'd sneak down and climb into bed next to him. Mum never said anything, but I'm sure she knew what was going on.

From the very beginning, Brian was mad about me. I'm not saying that to blow my own trumpet; it was just true. He would ring me ten or twenty times a day. If I was away performing with the girls, we would exchange two or three telegrams every day and love letters saying: 'I miss you, I love you, I can't wait to see you again.'

At first I found it a bit overwhelming, and at one point I talked about breaking up with him. I was still quite young and it felt as if it was getting a bit too heavy, too soon, but he wouldn't consider us splitting up.

'How can I get your sister to fall in love with me?' Brian asked Bernie one night, a few months after we'd started going out.

Bernie has always been a straight-talker and not one for a lot of fuss. 'Just stop bloody phoning her all the time,' she said. And he did.

'Why's he stopped ringing me?' I started panicking. 'Maybe he's gone off me.'

Bernie's tactic had worked. A few evenings later, I was going into town for the evening with the girls. Brian gave me a lift to the club where we were meeting and came in for a quick drink. Afterwards I walked him back to his car and watched him drive off. 'Oh my God,' I suddenly thought, standing on the pavement outside the Beetroot Nightclub. 'I love that man. That's who I want to spend the rest of my life with.'

And that was it.

Brian moved out of his family home and he and Caroline began divorce proceedings, although they kept things amicable for the sake of their little boy, Lloyd. Exactly one year after we'd first met at that Christmas party, Brian was squashed up with the rest of us in the front room in Granville Road, Ilford, opening the mound of presents under our tinsel-laden tree, surrounded by laughing and whooping. Brian handed me a box of Rive Gauche perfume. 'Go on, open it,' he said.

Everyone else in the room was staring at me, so I guess they must have known something was going on, even though I didn't realize it at the time. I opened the box and could see immediately that there was no perfume inside. I tipped it upside down and an engagement ring fell out onto my lap. It had a large diamond in the middle, surrounded by a cluster of smaller diamonds. It was beautiful.

'Oh my God,' I said, smiling over at Brian. Then I threw myself on him and we hugged and hugged. I didn't need to say yes; there was no other answer.

We married eight months later, on 28 August 1981. As Brian had been married before, we had a small civil ceremony at a register office in Blackpool first, then the following day we had a blessing at St Paul's Church just down the road. It was brilliant. All our family and friends were there. Even Brian's ex, Caroline, came along, as we had all become good friends. The girls sang the Andy Williams song 'May Each Day' and Mum sang 'Ave Maria'. She still had the most beautiful, clear singing voice.

I wore a massive meringue dress – well, it was 1981, the same year as Charles and Di got married! It was lace, with diamante, and cost £3,000 from a really posh shop in London. Ever since I was tiny, I'd dreamt of getting married in a dress with a really long train and then being whisked off on honeymoon to Paris by my handsome new husband. When I really did marry, I had a ten-foot train and veil and Brian had secretly booked for us to go to Paris on honeymoon. And, my God, my husband was handsome! It was really all that I'd ever dreamt about.

We had a magical time in Paris. We went to the Eiffel Tower, the Arc de Triomphe and the Moulin Rouge. Then, one night, we went into a club and ordered a bottle of champagne and a live sex show started! We were blushing at first, but then we couldn't stop looking!

Back home, we moved into our own little flat in Ilford, just up the road from Mum and Dad. It was great. I loved playing the role of wife and would get up in the morning to get Brian's tea and toast before he went to work. But if I wasn't working,

I'd be straight back into bed the minute he stepped out the door. Then, later, I'd get the tube into London, just to be able to come home with him when he finished work. People say the romance always goes out of a marriage after a while, but none of it ever went out of ours. For the first three years of our time together, I got a dozen red roses every week!

Brian's little boy, Lloyd, often came to stay for the weekend, and I loved looking after him. He was a gorgeous little boy, with beautiful blond hair and blue eyes. He was so polite and funny, and we could sit and chat to each other for ages. If his mum dropped him off, she'd come in for a cup of tea, and if we dropped him home, she would sometimes invite us for dinner. Brian and Caroline worked really hard to try to make sure their divorce didn't affect Lloyd, and I think that bene-fited all of them in the end.

It was then that Brian became tour manager for The Nolans. His job was to ensure that all our gear travelled from venue to venue with no problems, that our journey was straight-forward and that we had everything we needed in our dressing rooms and on stage in each club and theatre. It meant that Brian and I were together every minute of every day, but that is exactly how we liked it. It might not work for some couples, but we were only really happy when we were together.

We were all still on just £150 a week each, paid to us by Dad, who was our manager. But then our record company, CBS, rang Brian one day and said they needed an album we were working on finished by the following day. Because we were touring, this meant we'd have to work through the night. We'd been doing so many live performances that the deadline had been pushed further and further back.

'These girls are still on a pretty small weekly wage,' Brian explained. 'You'll have to give them an incentive if you want them to work through the night to finish this while they're on a tour.'

The record company bosses said that if we finished the album by the deadline, there would be a cheque in the post immediately. We were expecting maybe £5,000, but when the cheques arrived they were for £25,000 each! We were staggered. It was enough for me to be able to put down a deposit on our dream family home, a house in a village called Great Dunmow in the Essex countryside. When we weren't away touring, we loved it there. It was a four–bedroom, detached house with beautiful views over the fields. It was so peaceful and enabled us to really get away from all the craziness of London.

Brian had been fantastic getting us all that money from the record company, but at the same time relations between him and the other girls were becoming increasingly strained.

Brian was a perfectionist in his work, but that meant he would worry about things all the time. If we were ten minutes late to a venue, he would be panicking. He'd want to carry all our bags and make sure everything was just so in all our dressing rooms and that irritated the others.

By then we were having hit records and were recognized everywhere we went, so if we wanted to pop out to the shops, Brian would try to stop us, in case we were accosted.

'Brian, we're grown women,' we'd say. But that was the way he worked. He liked to make sure everything was under control at all times, so that nothing could go wrong. And he worried about us. He adored 'his girls'.

But it was leading to more and more tension within the group. I think maybe the girls thought Brian was trying to take over from Dad as our manager, but he really wasn't. He loved Dad and would never have tried to kick him out, but he was very good at what he did and sometimes people at the theatres and clubs would turn to him with questions rather than Dad. Maybe the girls thought that was undermining Dad, but that was certainly never Brian's intention.

The situation was getting awkward though. More and more, I felt caught in the middle between my husband and my sisters, and it was making me really unhappy. There weren't any big rows, but there was an atmosphere growing between us and it felt like it was Brian and me against the rest of them. One day we all sat down and the girls said to me that they didn't think Brian should be our tour manager anymore because of the clash of personalities.

I was devastated. I felt like I was being asked to choose between my husband and my sisters. It was horrible. There had always been rows between us sisters at times, but this was more than that. I couldn't understand how they didn't see that Brian was just trying to do everything he could to make us successful.

There was no question of me staying in the group without Brian. There wasn't a big row, but if they didn't want him, they didn't have me, and I said I was going. The tensions in the group had really upset me and I needed to get out. But then things became even more difficult because I needed to sort out my final settlement with the group. When Anne had left to have her daughter, she'd got a tax-free lump sum of about £10,000. Then we went on to have all the big hits and the sell-out tours in Japan before she rejoined two years later.

But when I said I wanted to leave, I just got a little bit more than Anne had – about £13,000 – even though I'd done all the big hits and the foreign tours. Dad spoke with the other girls, then sat down with the accountants, and somehow that was the figure they came up with. The money was only just enough to cover a tax bill I'd received, so in effect I walked away with nothing. It didn't seem fair that after twenty continuous years in the band, I'd got virtually nothing. I felt hurt and angry.

'I'm just not happy about this, Dad,' I said one day.

'Well, we've worked it out, and that's what you are owed,' he said.

I was too hurt to argue. Perhaps with hindsight the money just wasn't there – we never made as much as you might expect – but I felt that, after years of hard work, my sisters and Dad were now happy to let me walk away practically empty-handed. It took a long while to get over that. For almost a year, I didn't speak to my sisters, and things were pretty frosty with Mum and Dad too.

It was December 1983, and for the first time in my life I was on my own without my sisters. It felt scary. Brian was my manager and he quickly lined up work for me. But, with other sisters having joined and left the group, it was a bit confusing for the public. As Terry Wogan said one day on his radio show: 'It's like a Nolan factory.' We knew that if I was going to be successful as a solo act, I needed to create a strong image that would make me stand out.

Brian hired some great publicity people for me, and they fixed up for me to do a photo shoot with John Paul, who was a famous fashion photographer at the time. The idea was that I would do some quite sexy pictures that would really get me noticed. I'd always been complimented on my blonde hair and good boobs, so maybe now was the time to use them to my advantage.

On the day of the photo shoot, I was there from seven in the morning, and spent most of the day posing in lovely little sexy dresses. Then, at about seven in the evening, I popped out of the room and when I walked back in Brian was saying to John Paul: 'Well, you'll have to ask her – I'm not going to!'

And that was when he suggested I should pose as though I was naked, with just a sheet covering me. I was really nervous when he took the shots because I'd never done anything like that before. It was very suggestive, but when I saw the finished pictures, they did look great. And, of course, out of all the hundreds of pictures that were taken that day, it was the one of me draped in a sheet that made it into all the tabloid newspapers a few weeks later, under the headline: 'The Naughty Nolan'.

I was thrilled with the pictures, but there was a big furore about the whole thing, and I wasn't expecting that. It had certainly worked in terms of getting attention for my solo career, but I was terrified about what Mum would say. When I rang her, she couldn't stop laughing about all the fuss there had been in the papers. 'I've seen you in less on the beach,' she said.

My first time on stage without my sisters was on a tour supporting Gene Pitney in 1984. I hadn't heard a word from my sisters since I'd left the group, but I'd really hoped they would send flowers, or even a card, for my first night on stage without them. But there was nothing. That really hurt.

I waited in the wings at the Opera House in Belfast, feeling utterly terrified. Then, when I was about to walk out onto the stage, I became convinced I couldn't remember the words to a single song. 'You'll be fine,' whispered Brian. And, of course, when I went on, it was fine. But it did still feel strange to be on a stage without my sisters all around me.

Brian and I had been really struggling for money, as my entire Nolans settlement had gone on clearing my tax bill. Brian arranged for me to be paid in cash for the Gene Pitney tour, and when we took the wad of money back to our hotel room, he threw it all up into the air – it was like something out of a film!

After a couple of nights, I found my confidence again on stage and it was great. I was independent at last and I didn't have to sit down and discuss five different points of view before a decision could be made. After having felt very unhappy for the last few months I was with The Nolans, I found myself really enjoying performing again. But I did miss the girls terribly.

For the next few years, I travelled around the country doing gigs and cabaret, but it was still quite hand-to-mouth financially. After a couple of years of struggling to get by, we decided to sell our perfect home in Great Dunmow and move back to a smaller house in Blackpool.

I loved performing solo though. My only big regret was that I never recorded anything independently. When Bernie went solo, she recorded a fabulous CD of her ballads and she'll have that for the rest of her life. I wish I'd done that too. But for me, the best part of going solo was that it meant Brian and I were together all the time. It really was the two of us 24/7 and that was the way we liked it.

I didn't speak to the girls for more than a year, which was

very sad at the time, but gradually things thawed between us and we had the occasional phone call. Then we started seeing each other at family parties and things returned to normal. In fact, not working together any longer actually made it easier for us to return to being sisters – and friends!

8.

Maureen

Men, Music and Me

If Linda was the 'Naughty Nolan', then I guess I must have been the 'Virgin Nolan'.

Oh, I was always out and about in nightclubs, but I never drank much, and for years I was incredibly innocent. Back then my hair was long and dark and I was very slim, but I'd inherited my Mum's big breasts, so there was no shortage of male attention. I didn't have to buy myself a drink for years! But I'd always been a bit quiet and dreamy, and maybe I was still just expecting some handsome prince to come along and sweep me off my feet. My sisters told me I was holding out for something that didn't exist, but that didn't stop me.

In the meantime, while I was waiting for that handsome prince to turn up, I was content just to flirt with guys. I'd go on dates and have a bit of fun, but there was no way I was getting into anything serious. Maybe I was a bit of a bitch to them really, leading them on when I had no intention of going steady. I certainly couldn't even consider getting into a serious sexual relationship. It just wasn't how we had been brought up.

When we were still living in Blackpool, I went out with this lovely guy called Paul. He was really mad about me and was always buying me little gifts. Then we moved to London and he wrote me love letters all the time. Soon after we moved down, it was my twenty-first birthday and Paul bought me twenty-one presents. It was actually very romantic and sweet of him, but at the time I just thought, 'Whoa, that's a bit serious.' So, just after he'd shelled out for the twenty-first gift, I wrote him a letter dumping him. He was a lovely lad and I treated him really badly, but I just didn't want to get tied down.

In London, I loved going out with my sisters to Samantha's and the Valbonne straight after coming off stage at the London Room. We were in Samantha's one night when this really handsome blond bloke with blue eyes came up and started chatting to me. He was gorgeous. He was called Billy Jennings and he played football for West Ham. We started talking and he was a lovely guy, really easy-going, funny and charming. When he asked to see me again, I immediately invited him round to our house the following day. He turned up in Ilford the next afternoon with a Turkish player who was on loan to West Ham. For a brief spell, he went out with Linda while I began dating Billy, and we'd have a great laugh going out together as a foursome. I went to watch him play football and we'd go out to Samantha's in the evenings, but it wasn't like a singer/footballer relationship would be nowadays. We weren't snapped by photographers or splashed across the newspapers. We were just an ordinary couple.

We were together for about six months, but it still never went further than a kiss and a cuddle. I was twenty-two by then and nowadays that must sound incredibly innocent, but that was just the way I was. I was really sexually immature, more like a fourteen-year-old than a woman in her early twenties.

'Would you like to stay over at mine tonight?' Billy asked one day. But as much as I adored him, the whole idea of sex really embarrassed me, and I said I couldn't.

In the end our relationship just fizzled out. He stopped calling me and I was far too proud to ring him. Looking back, I think I really loved Billy Jennings, but I was too immature to realize it at the time. I was ever so upset when we split up, but I was soon back having a laugh and flirting with men that we met on our nights out, like some soppy teenager, rather than getting into anything serious.

A few months after splitting up with Billy, The Nolans went to work at Kings Nightclub in Eastbourne for the summer season. It was right next to the tennis courts where the Queen's Club Championship is staged. One evening John Lloyd came to see our show and afterwards he invited us to go along to watch him play the following day. We had a fantastic time watching the tennis and afterwards John and I started talking and found we got on really well. He invited me out and from then on we started dating.

John was a very sincere guy who was very family-orientated, and we had some wonderful times together. At the time he was one of the country's best tennis players. I even went to watch him play at Wimbledon and compete against Björn Borg at the Wembley indoor arena. But he was often abroad competing in championships, while I was constantly touring with the group, so in the six months we were together, we didn't see each other that often.

Then he went to play in the Australian Open and did really well. As soon as he got back to England, he came straight round to our house in Ilford with loads of presents for me.

But while he'd been away, I'd got used to being without him and was feeling worried about getting into something too serious again. And that still meant going absolutely no further than a kiss and a cuddle. He was such a lovely guy, but that day I told him it was over.

'Maybe we could stay friends,' I said hopefully.

'Maybe eventually, but not right now,' he said. I'd really hurt him.

I felt terrible about the way I had treated him because I think he was upset for quite some time, but I just wasn't ready for a serious relationship.

Soon afterwards, there was a headline in Nigel Dempster's gossip column in the *Daily Mail* which said, 'Maureen dumps tennis idol,' which was awful. I felt terrible in case he thought I'd given them the story when I hadn't at all.

Some people might think my issues with commitment and sex were to do with having such an obsessive father, but my older sisters, Anne and Denise, both had steady boyfriends. No, I think it was more that I was just a lot quieter and more emotionally immature than my sisters for a long time. And because I'd held on to my virginity for so much longer than most girls, I'd also become a bit embarrassed about going to bed with a man, in case I didn't have a clue what to do. Sex had never ever been discussed at home when I was growing up, and I was massively shy about it.

As the months went by, I became more and more desperate to lose my virginity – mainly because it was becoming such an issue in relationships that I just wanted to get it over and done with. But I didn't want my first time to be with someone I really liked. That might sound strange, but I didn't have the confidence for that, in case the guy might think badly of me for being so inexperienced. Instead, I decided my first time should be with a total stranger.

In the summer of 1977, Bernie, Linda and I went on our first holiday without the rest of the family. Anne had already met her future husband, the Blackpool footballer Brian Wilson, and Denise had met her partner, Tom, who was in the band at the London Room, so it was just us younger ones. Bernie was sixteen, Linda was eighteen and I was twenty-two, and we were up for a great time.

There's no way Dad would have let me go on holiday with just my sisters when I was Bernie's age, but by that time we'd been in London for a couple of years and he had given up trying to control our every move, so Bernie came with us.

We went to Palma Nova in Majorca and shared one cramped little room, with our beds lined up next to each other.

The first night we got there, we went out for something to eat, then just sat talking about missing the others and how homesick we were feeling. 'Come on,' said Linda eventually. 'We'll be fine in a while, let's just go and party.' So we put on our glad rags and went out. We found a nightclub and stayed up all night dancing. We were having a great time and, after a while, the DJ came over and started chatting me up. We had a good chat and got on well. It was almost light by the time we staggered home.

We went back to the club almost every night and on our last evening before flying home, the DJ asked me the question I'd always dreaded before: 'Would you like to come back to my place?'

I took a deep breath, but I'd already decided on my answer: 'Yes.'

Even though I didn't know him that well, it just felt right

to sleep with him that night. He was really lovely, and we actually had a really nice time. By then, I just wanted the whole virginity thing over and done with, so it suited me to do it that way. I bled all over the bed and the next morning, when he saw the sheets, he couldn't quite believe it. 'That was your first time?' he asked, totally amazed.

'Yes,' I said, smiling. 'It was.'

We went out for breakfast together and he wanted us to meet up again, but we were returning home that day, so that was the end of my holiday romance. Walking back into our hotel room, I was greeted by raised eyebrows from Linda and Bernie.

'So?' they both screamed at me. 'What happened? Come on, how was it?' They wanted to know all the details. I was just happy that it was all over.

I was twenty-four before I had another serious boyfriend. It was summertime and we were doing a season at the ABC Theatre in Blackpool. By then Anne was engaged to Brian Wilson and she brought him along one evening when we were going out. Brian had also invited along one of his teammates, Pete Suddaby. He was tall and blond, with a great body, and he was a lovely, lovely guy. I fell for him immediately. For the first time, I felt someone was talking to me like a person, rather than 'just' a girl.

We started going out and, because I'd already lost my virginity, I was able to let the relationship progress naturally. Within a couple of months, I'd moved into his house in Blackpool. He was thirty-one, eight years older than me, so it seemed perfectly natural that we should live together, even though we weren't married. Even Mum and Dad were OK about it.

Then he was put on the transfer list and went to play in

Brighton, so we lived there for two years. I loved being there and could still commute into London to do shows with the girls.

The following year 'I'm in the Mood for Dancing' came out and suddenly I had a bit more money, so when Peter was transferred to play for Wimbledon, I was able to buy my first house, in Hillingdon in north London, where we lived together for another five years.

Going out with a footballer in the 1970s was very different from how it is now. There were no celebrity parties and magazine shoots, and we certainly weren't ever photographed falling out of nightclubs.

In many ways, Pete and I were soul mates; we were incredibly similar. Neither of us drank. We both loved the countryside and would disappear for weekends to the Lake District for long walks and pub lunches. In the evenings we'd cook nice meals, then just sit and chat. He was intelligent, thoughtful and kind. We could talk about anything. It really was like my handsome prince had turned up at last.

As well as being an amazing footballer, Pete was also incredibly clever. Before he'd gone professional, he'd got a degree in maths, which meant that when his football career came to an end, he was able to get a job as a teacher in an American community school near where we lived.

Then, in 1986, I did a summer season with my sisters in Bournemouth. The girls and I had a ball that summer. We went out every single night, and I found myself trying to live out the teenage years which I'd never been allowed to have first time around because of Dad's rules and regulations. Sometimes you never really get over the childhood that you've had. Maybe that was my problem.

I hardly saw anything of Pete that summer because he was

teaching, and gradually I realized I wasn't missing him as much as I should have been. Towards the end of the season, I thought, 'Oh God, I'm enjoying myself too much. Maybe I'm still not ready to settle down.'

I rang Pete and told him we needed to talk. 'I'm so sorry,' I said, when we met up. 'But I don't think this is right anymore. I think we should have a break.'

Even though we hadn't spent much time together for months, I think he was still very hurt. There was no screaming and shouting, just a very sad conversation that it was all over. For a while I think he was heartbroken, and I hated hurting him like that, but I couldn't stay in a relationship if I felt it wasn't right for either of us.

Afterwards, I felt like I'd lost my right arm because not only had he been my boyfriend, for a long time he'd been my best friend too. But, deep down, I knew the spark had gone and it was the right thing to do. I did still want to settle down one day, and I desperately wanted to have children, although I had no idea when that might be.

Pete bought the house in Hillingdon from me and I moved back up to Blackpool and lived with Mum and Dad, who had returned there by then.

I'd missed out on so much fun in the past that I set out to make up for it – even though I was in my thirties! I'd been back in Blackpool a couple of months when a guy called Jimmy Higham asked me out on a date and we started going out. He was lovely and we had a great time for nine months, but then the romance fizzled out. We remained friends though, and still see each other now. But, back then, I was more interested in having fun than settling down.

I loved being back in Blackpool because Linda, Denise and

Anne were all living back up there too and I could see them all the time. And it meant there was always someone to go out with.

By 1987, our chart success was over and, rather than big world tours, we were doing summer seasons and cabaret. That's not to say I didn't still enjoy being in the band, because I did. And having made so little money from our career, we had no choice but to carry on working anyway. One morning, a couple of weeks before our summer season of '87 was due to start, we had a day of rehearsals booked at the Opera House in Blackpool. Coleen and I arrived early and had to walk across the back of the stage to our dressing rooms. We were halfway across when I couldn't help noticing this guy, who was about six foot three, with thick brown hair, blue eyes and a moustache, wearing tiny shorts and playing the theme from *Love Story* on the piano.

I thought, 'Oh, he's nice.' He was very young – he looked like he was in his early twenties at most – but watching him, I was struck by the fabulous combination of a really big, strong bloke who could play such wonderfully romantic music.

Coleen and I introduced ourselves and the guy told us his name was Ritchie Hoyle and explained he was going to be assistant stage manager during our season. For the rest of the summer, he was part of a big crowd of us who hung around together, going for drinks after the shows, then partying round my house until the early hours. There would be us girls, Cannon & Ball, who were also in the show, the crew, dancers and various other hangers-on, all crammed into my front room, dancing and singing until it got light. Coleen and Ritchie got on really well. They would spend ages talking about anything and everything, and became great mates.

At the end of the season, Coleen and Bernie went back down south and it felt very quiet in Blackpool. I stayed friends with Ritchie and his mate Mick though, and we would go out together occasionally. And, very gradually, I felt myself falling for Ritchie. I knew he fancied me too – well, he'd told me! But he was very young and pretty cool. He was certainly not long-term boyfriend material.

'Look, you're lovely,' I told him one night. 'We can go on the odd date, but I'm not looking for anything serious – I'm seeing two other guys too!'

So that was what we did – we went out on occasional dates, but it was all very casual.

Then, one night, we slept together for the first time. It was all very passionate and, in the heat of the moment, we didn't use any protection. 'I'm going to be pregnant,' I said to Ritchie immediately afterwards, as we lay next to each other in bed.

'Don't be ridiculous,' he said. 'How could you know?'

'I'm telling you now,' I replied. 'I'm pregnant. I've never had unprotected sex before and if I'm anything like as fertile as my mum, then we've got a baby on the way.'

I swear that within two days I was having the symptoms. I decided the best idea was to ignore them and hope it was all my overactive imagination at work.

One day, a couple of weeks later, Coleen rang me, really excited. She had been with her boyfriend, Shane Richie, for around two years by then, and we all knew they were mad about each other. 'I'm pregnant!' Coleen shrieked down the phone.

'That's fantastic, Col,' I said. I was delighted for her, but secretly I was wondering whether I might be pregnant too.

A couple of weeks later, I called Anne, who by then had given birth to her second daughter, Alex. We chatted for a bit about this and that before I plucked up the courage to broach the real reason for my call. 'So,' I said, 'when you're pregnant, what are the symptoms?'

'Well, there's the sickness,' said Anne. Got that, I thought.

'Sore boobs.' Got those.

'And starving hungry.' All three – it had to be true.

'Why?' asked Anne. I was a bit vague, but it didn't take a genius to work out what was going on!

I went out and bought a pregnancy test, rushed home and did it straightaway. As I sat waiting for the stated two minutes before checking the result, I prayed it would be negative. I really liked Ritchie, but I barely knew him; and this really wasn't how I'd planned on becoming a mum. But in my heart I knew the result before I even looked at the stick. I immediately phoned Ritchie. 'I'm pregnant,' I said.

'You're kidding,' was his reply.

'Nope.'

'Oh, OK.'

'Look, we don't know each other that well, so you don't have to stick around, but I'm not getting rid of it,' I said.

'I'll stay,' he said. 'We'll be OK.'

And that was it – with that conversation, we became a family.

In the weeks that followed, things didn't really seem very OK at all though. I'm ashamed to say it now, but back then I kept hoping I might miscarry the baby because although I wouldn't consider an abortion, I did think that if the pregnancy came to an end of its own accord, that might be for the best. At the same time though, I felt ecstatic that I had this new life growing inside me. It was exactly what I'd wanted one day, but not really in these circumstances.

Ritchie never once suggested getting rid of the baby. I'm a pretty laid-back person, but he is even more laid-back than me. 'We'll be OK,' he just kept saying.

My parents and Anne hardly even knew Ritchie. Anne had been pregnant the summer we'd met, so she hadn't come out in the evenings very often, and I hadn't taken Ritchie home to meet the family. It sounds awful, but when I told them all I was pregnant, they had to sort of ask: 'Who's the father?'

But Mum and Dad were so relaxed by this time that they took it all in their stride. By then, Mum was hugely involved with her local church, but what mattered to her above everything else was that her children and grandchildren were happy and healthy. Dad was the same.

Ritchie moved into my house almost straightaway and we set up home, but it was very strange at first because we still hardly knew each other. There I was discussing baby names with this guy and I barely knew how he took his tea. But we muddled through – probably more through ignorance than anything else. Neither of us had the first clue how having a baby was going to affect our lives.

Danny was born on 10 January 1989 at Blackpool Victoria Hospital. The labour was horrendous and went on and on and on. After eighteen hours of hell, during which I threw up the whole time, they gave me a caesarean. All that effort and he still didn't come out naturally! But from the moment Danny was born, I was instantly obsessed with him. He was the most gorgeous baby I'd ever seen.

Those first few months, and even years, were very tough. I was thirty-four, but Ritchie was still only twenty-five. He was determined that having a baby wasn't going to change his life at all. He still went out every night, working on shows or partying with his mates.

On top of that, we still barely knew each other because we'd only been together a few months. We shared a love of music and theatre, but in other ways we were quite different; he liked going out and getting drunk with his mates, while I hardly drank at all and was more than happy to stay home with my new baby. Ritchie would roll in drunk in the early hours of the morning, and even if he was at home and the baby woke up in the middle of the night, it was always me that had to get up for him.

Most of the time, I wasn't really bothered because I'd been prepared to bring up my baby as a single mother from the start. But, thankfully, Ritchie's parents were fantastic at helping me out with childcare. They lived nearby and did everything they could to help look after their first grandchild, particularly when I had to go back to work with my sisters when Danny was just five months old.

For quite a long while, I let Ritchie get on with whatever he wanted to do, while I put all my energy into looking after Danny. But sometimes I would think: 'What the hell am I doing? I can't believe I have finally got the gorgeous baby I longed for, but it is with this father!' If I did challenge him, there would be a big row. 'You can't carry on like this!' I'd yell.

'Well, I'm not going to change,' was his flat reply.

I didn't want to be a woman who flitted from one relationship to the next, having a succession of babies along the way, so I stayed. And I always knew Ritchie had everything going on that could make him a brilliant partner and dad. He just needed to get it together. Every now and then, I'd see flashes of how thoughtful and supportive he could be. He just needed to show it a bit more often. I was mostly devastated for Danny that his daddy was rarely around. Even Ritchie now admits that for the first few years I brought up Danny on my own. I was up to my eyes, juggling looking after a new baby and working, but I didn't care about the hard work because I loved every minute of being a mum.

My sisters were always careful not to have a go about Ritchie, but they would sometimes ask gently: 'Are you sure about all this, Maureen?'

'I know what you're thinking about him,' I'd say. 'But he's got such potential. One day he'll grow up!'

But at the end of that summer season, I decided I'd finally had enough of Ritchie's partying and drinking. He was rolling home in the early hours, while I was looking after Danny all day, putting him to bed, going out and doing a gig, coming home, giving him his night feeds, then waking up with him again at the crack of dawn. One night Ritchie stumbled into bed really drunk and I decided enough was enough.

'Look,' I said, 'I'm off. We can still be friends, but I'm not doing this anymore.'

I have never seen anyone sober up so quickly. 'Please don't leave me,' he said. 'I'll change.'

It wasn't an overnight conversion or anything, but gradually Ritchie did become more involved in mine and Danny's lives. And so, slowly, long after we'd become parents together, I fell in love with him. But we still didn't discuss marriage. It wasn't a priority for me, after everything I'd seen in my parents' marriage when I was growing up. And it was still way too early for us to consider it.

For the next few years, things rolled along pretty smoothly and I was able to juggle looking after Danny with touring. As Bernie said though, it was getting tougher and tougher to get decent venues. Then, in 1994, I was doing a panto in Hastings and loads of the family met up at Coleen's house for Christmas. We were all about to open our presents when Ritchie asked me to go upstairs with him. In our room, he handed me the most lovely card, with a beautiful message written inside about how much he loved me. Then, at the end, it said: 'And this is why I want to spend the rest of my life with you.' By the time I got to that bit, I was already crying, and I thought maybe I couldn't see it properly. 'Oh my God,' I whispered.

Then he took a ring out of his pocket and handed it to me. He is such a big, strong guy, but his hands were shaking.

We decided we'd get married two years later, but as the time got closer and closer, I started panicking. I definitely wanted to be with him, but I was scared about the commitment of marriage. Maybe I was still scarred by my parents' marriage. Ritchie was very relaxed about my concerns though and said he'd wait until I felt ready. So that's what we did.

By 1998, things were very difficult for the band. We were performing in bingo halls and pubs, and none of us was happy about that. Then Bernie said she was going to leave. Coleen had already quit, which meant just Anne and I remained. With two of us, it was going to be hard to do the harmonies and choreography, so we thought it might all be over. But then a music producer called John Conway suggested that we try the Butlins circuit for six months. We both needed the money, so gave it a go, and ended up doing it for two years. We were joined by two dancers, Julia Payne and Leigh Davis, and we had a ball. That period actually turned out to be one of the best we ever had because we were able to take our kids with us everywhere we went. We got on so well working together that at the end of a season we'd go off on holiday together too.

Danny was almost ten then and he was best friends with Anne's daughter Alex, who was only a bit older than him. Anne's eldest daughter Amy loved singing and when she was sixteen she joined our group. A friend called Julia Duckworth also joined us and we worked together like that until 2004. We did some amazing gigs in nightclubs and theatres, and we still got a fantastic reception, particularly in the gay clubs.

Sometimes we'd get a rough gig though, where we'd have to drive to the other end of the country, only to hang around until two o'clock in the morning before going on stage. There'd be no dressing room, and we would have to put our outfits on in the club's back office. By the time we went on stage, everyone in the club would be so drunk that they'd heckle us and chuck beer around. Then we'd have to drive all the way home again, through the night. Anne and I both thought that we should consider trying something different because a lot of the fun of singing had been taken away from us. Bernie, Denise and Linda had all been on stage in *Blood Brothers*, so we thought we could try acting too.

Then an agent offered Coleen a part in a show called *Mum's the Word*, which was a series of monologues about being a mum. Coleen was pregnant with her daughter, Ciara, and didn't want to do the show, but her agent asked if she'd mind her offering it to Anne and me. We both auditioned, but knew that if one of us got it, that would totally be the end of The

Nolans, so we made a pact that if one of us got it, she would give some of the wages to the other. And that's what we did when I got the part.

For the first time in thirty years The Nolan Sisters no longer existed as a group. It was sad, but we all felt it was time to try new things, and that was very exciting.

9.
Bernie

The Wild One

The Nolan Sisters' image was so squeaky clean that we made Snow White look racy. It made me sick. That wasn't me at all. I liked to party; I drank; I smoked; I stayed up all night. I had a ball!

I particularly liked it when we were touring and doing one-night shows, either in Britain or abroad. I loved doing the show, going out, getting drunk and falling into bed, then getting up the next morning, going on to a different place and doing it all again. It is harder than spending several nights in one place, but I loved the party aspect of that, probably more than my sisters. I'm totally a night-time person, but don't talk to me before one o'clock the next day!

After a gig, my sisters would probably join me and some of the crew for a couple of drinks, then go off to bed. I'd stay up with the band, or anyone else I could find to talk to, until five or six in the morning.

Because I sang the lead in 'I'm in the Mood for Dancing' and quite a few of the other singles, I did feel quite a lot of pressure when we were touring. My voice always had to be bang on. I think I coped with the pressure by partying. Of course, all the time I'd be thinking I really shouldn't be smoking and drinking because it was so bad for my voice, but it was my release. I did lose my voice a couple of times on tour, but considering how much I sang as well as drank and smoked, it wasn't very often at all. I'd been smoking since I was eleven and had my first fag literally behind the bike sheds at school. By the time we were touring as The Nolan Sisters, I was on between thirty and thirty-five a day.

And I could certainly put the booze away back then too. In the early days, I drank Bacardi and Coke, but then someone told me that was bad for my throat, so I moved on to vodka and lemonade. At my height, I was probably doing a bottle of vodka a day. I was drinking a lot, but I certainly wasn't an alcoholic or anything like that. I wasn't addicted to alcohol, I just liked it, and it became part of my lifestyle. If we weren't on the road, then I could go days without having a drink at all.

I was lucky too because I'd never get hangovers and if we were touring, I could just spend the whole day sleeping on the tour bus. However drunk I was when I got back to my hotel room, I'd always pack my bag for the following day, so next morning all I had to do was roll out of bed, pick up my case, get on the bus and go straight back to sleep. My sisters used to laugh at me, but they thought I was a good drunk. I'd never stagger or fall over or be sick, and I was certainly never aggressive. I just liked to party.

I was young, it was great fun, so why not?

When Linda left the group and went solo, she did a photo shoot for a tabloid newspaper wrapped in a sheet and nothing else! It was really revealing, and that was how she became known as the 'Naughty Nolan'. But that just made the rest of us look even more sickly sweet and innocent than ever. That was difficult for us because we knew there was so much more to us than just that, but no one wanted to see it.

I may have partied hard, but I was always loyal to my boyfriend, Bob, even when we were away touring abroad for weeks on end. I hated being away from him when we did the big Japan tours, but those trips were the only things that ever really earned the group any money. Fortunately, I used mine to put down a deposit on a little house for Bob and me in Loughton in Essex. The rest I put in the bank, so at least I had something for a rainy day.

Over the next year or so though, I felt like I wasn't missing Bob as much as maybe I should have done when I was away on tour. We both realized we were growing apart and, after three years together, we decided to split up. It was really upsetting, but it was quite amicable, and we are still friends now.

In 1986 we were booked to do a big tour of Russia. The line-up by then was Anne, Maureen, Coleen and me. At that time, Russia was still really backward; the people seemed really oppressed and there was literally no food in the shops. But when we went out to play our first gig in Baku, there were 25,000 people in the stadium. I'm sure hardly any of them had heard a Nolans song in their lives before, because they weren't really allowed to buy records, but I think they just wanted to see any kind of live concert.

There were soldiers lining the aisles and if any of the audience so much as moved, they were kicked out of the auditorium. Dancing was totally out of the question!

It was my twenty-sixth birthday while we were there, and I decided to have a party in my hotel room after one of the gigs. A big, fat, scary-looking woman soldier was stationed at the end of each landing, and we'd barely cracked open the vodka when one came banging on my door. 'You can't have a party here,' she said.

'But it's my birthday,' I said, hoping she'd understand.

'No parties here. You will go to bed now,' she repeated sinisterly before stomping off.

I wasn't going to let some old bat in a uniform get between me and my stash of Russian vodka, so we carried on drinking and laughing. Ten minutes later, there was a battering at the door. This time, when I went to answer it, the woman was accompanied by a bloke in full Soviet uniform and carrying a rifle, which was pointed at us!

'You will go to bed now,' the old bag said one more time.

'OK,' I said, feeling more than a little scared. 'We will go to bed.'

We spent ten days in Leningrad, which was beautiful but so boring. There were no shops, no cinema and no telly. There was one museum, but, really, one visit was enough.

So every night we'd take a bottle of vodka back to our room, play cards and have a good laugh. If we stayed up late enough, it meant we'd sleep through most of the next day.

The hotels were filthy and the food was rank. Some days we'd get a dinner plate with a bat on it – well, it certainly looked like a bat – flavoured with dill. Everything came with dill. I hate dill! And there was vodka with everything – breakfast, dinner and tea.

After the tour to Russia, we went back to doing summer seasons, which I never enjoyed quite as much as touring. In 1986 we did Bournemouth with Cannon & Ball, which was great because Bobby Ball and I have always been great friends and we'd be out together in the pub every night after a show. After a pub, we'd go on to a club, where we'd sit and get drunk, then have a bit of a dance. He was like another older brother to me. If I was ever getting chatted up by a guy, I'd suddenly hear Bobby yelling across the club: 'Oi, I'm watching you!' We'd also have fantastic house parties in the big place we'd rented for the season near Bournemouth.

It was around this time that I started dating Coleen's ex-boyfriend, Stewart. We'd become really good mates when he was going out with Coleen, but nothing happened then, even though I had fancied him for a long time and he flirted a lot with me. We only got together after they'd split up, but it was still very awkward for a long time. But just because you're sisters, it doesn't mean you can't fall in love with the same guy. It was just one of those things, even though it was awful at the time and I felt terrible because I knew Coleen was really hurt by it all. I'm sure I would have felt exactly the same if it had happened the other way around. Stewart and I were together for two and a half years, and he became part of the family, which must have been horrible for Coleen at first, but she was great about it.

At first things were great between Stewart and me. I really loved him, but I think he gradually fell out of love with me. That was when I rented out my house in Loughton and moved back to Blackpool. Stewart and I would still see each other occasionally if I was working down in London, but by then I think I was probably just using him for sex. I was single and still liked him, even though we weren't together, so I didn't feel I was doing anything wrong.

With work, we carried on doing summer seasons and cabaret shows in winter. Like Maureen said, we were still working just as hard, even though the singles had come to an end and we weren't on television as often. But we couldn't just stop working; none of us could afford to do that.

'Bradley says hi,' my friend told me.

It was the summer season in Blackpool, 1989, and for months I'd been getting funny messages from a Bradley Walsh, even though I'd never set eyes on him. Bradley was a regular on the comedy circuit then and it seemed that we had loads of mutual friends, even though we'd never worked together.

'Bradley Walsh sends his love,' another friend, the comedian Brian Conley, told me cheekily one night.

'Who on earth is this Bradley Walsh guy?' I thought to myself. This was long before he was regularly on TV as a game-show presenter, and even longer before his big break in *Coronation Street*.

One evening Coleen and Maureen came running into my dressing room. They were really excited and giggling like kids. 'Oh my God,' said Maureen. 'We've seen THE Bradley Walsh and he really fancies you, AND he's gorgeous.'

'Oh really?' I said. I was acting pretty cool. I couldn't really believe that someone could fancy me just from having seen me singing on the telly. But later that evening a single red rose was left for me at the stage door. With it was a card saying: 'You don't know me, but I know you, and I'd love to know you better.' It was all very romantic.

Coleen was with Shane Richie by then and, one evening, they said they were going to see Bradley, who was doing a comedy act at the Horseshoe Showbar in Blackpool. Bradley and Shane were mates who'd got to know each other when they were both touring around Britain as comedians. I said I'd go along to the show with Shane and Coleen. I wanted to see this Bradley Walsh guy for myself! If he'd been crap, I'd probably never have seen him again. It might sound a bit immature, but if someone isn't very good at what they do, I find it really puts me off them. But, of course, Bradley was great, really funny, and in my eyes that made him gorgeous.

After the show we chatted for the first time. It was a bit embarrassing because I already knew he fancied me, but it was awkward in a nice way, and from that evening we were together. Bradley was twenty-nine when we met, funny, charming and appeared to utterly adore me. He had started out as a professional footballer before he had to give it up because of injury. After that, he'd worked for Rolls-Royce before getting into comedy. That first summer we were together was just a dream; it was fantastic. We never argued, we went for picnics in the Lake District, sex was amazing – it was just wonderful. I was crazy about Brad, and I think he was crazy about me.

But at the end of the season we had to go our separate ways because of work. I stayed in Blackpool and Bradley had to move back down south to his house near Watford. We decided we still wanted to be together though and agreed we'd take it in turns to go and stay with each other between jobs.

Over the next few months, when we were together, it was still really, really good, but when we were apart, it was always difficult. I quickly realized that whatever Brad did, there would be a woman involved. If he had tennis lessons, it would be with a woman; if he was in a show, he was surrounded by dancers. He wasn't creepy or sleazy, he was just a ladies' man and got on well with women. He was a great guy, although maybe not so great to go out with at that time. But it was only later that I realized that.

Not long after he'd gone back to living down south, I was with him one day and a woman phoned up to speak to him. I could hear her talking down the phone and it was obvious she was really upset about something. It didn't take a genius to work out that something fishy was going on.

Her flat got burgled and she was a bit shaken up,' Bradley explained when he put the phone down.

'Oh, OK,' I said. I was incredibly trusting and, at that time, I had no real reason to doubt my boyfriend. It was only later that I found out from a mutual friend that there hadn't been a burglary and the other woman was upset for far more obvious reasons! But when I confronted Bradley, he was full of remorse and apologies.

'I'm so sorry,' he said over and over again. 'Please take me back, Bernie. I love you.'

What could I do? I loved him too. So we got back together.

But then I discovered Bradley had been sleeping with someone else. Maybe I'm an idiot, because Bradley and this girl were sharing a house for a while. After the first time he'd been unfaithful, I did say I wasn't particularly happy about the situation, especially as Bradley had to walk through the girl's bedroom to get to the bathroom in that house.

'There's nothing to worry about. I love you,' Bradley told me.

So I gave myself a lecture: if I was going to forgive and forget what had happened in the past, I really had to trust Bradley in the future and not question his every move.

But then I overheard another phone call which made it crystal clear what was still going on between Bradley and this girl.

'That's it,' I told Bradley. 'It's over this time.'

'Please don't leave me,' he said, starting to cry. 'I'm so, so sorry, Bernie. I don't know what's the matter with me. All I know is that I love you and want to be with you.'

It went on like that for ages and, in the end, I relented again and we carried on going out together. I'm sure a lot of people will think I was mad for taking him back again, but I really, really loved him and everything that he said made me think he loved me too. I think he did love me; it was only later I realized that he just couldn't stay faithful to me.

Bradley's happily married now though, and he is obviously a changed man, but back then I think we were both fighting for our independence in the relationship, and it caused problems.

Then, in the summer of 1991, two years after Bradley and I had first met, our whole family was rocked by the most terrible shock when our brother's wife, Linzie, died at just twenty-six. Brian had been with Linzie for years and she was one of the family in every way. She had been a really successful dancer, then turned to choreography, and had choreographed one of our routines that year for our summer show at the Sandcastle Waterpark in Blackpool.

One Monday, Brian called me and said Linzie had a cold.

'Oh, poor thing,' I said. 'Send her my love and tell her I'll see her soon.' At that point, no one realized how serious that cold was to become.

By the Wednesday, Linzie still wasn't feeling any better and was having trouble with her breathing. Brian called their GP, who prescribed Sudafed. But the following day Linzie's condition had become so bad she had to go into hospital, where she was diagnosed with pneumonia. We were all stunned when the doctors said they were going to have to put her into a coma while they drained her lungs. None of us could believe what was happening. But worse was to come.

On the Friday, doctors told Brian that Linzie urgently needed a heart transplant. They had detected a serious underlying heart disease. By then, she was on a life-support machine, and to have any chance of having a heart transplant, she would have to be taken off that and transferred to the Victoria Hospital in Blackpool. But taking her off the life-support machine was fraught with danger. Brian was left to make the most awful decision.

Linzie was taken off the machine, in the hope she could be moved to Manchester in time for a transplant, but then, on the Saturday, she died at the Victoria Hospital in Manchester.

It was just one week since she'd first come down with the cold.

It was horrific. Brian was devastated. We all were. We'd loved Linzie so much. We were all overwhelmed by shock and anger. All the family congregated round at Maureen's house. It was while I was there that Bradley phoned me. He'd known Linzie too and, like the rest of us, he was really shocked.

'How is everyone coping?' he asked.

'OK,' I said. 'But no one can believe what's happened.'

'I love you so much, Bernie,' he said. 'I really do. You know, I would really like to marry you. Will you marry me?'

It was so strange because I was too upset to be excited by what he saying. 'Yes,' I said. 'Yes, I will.'

Looking back, I wonder if we were both reacting to the shock and grief. But I did love Bradley hugely, and I really wanted to marry him.

I didn't tell anyone about the proposal for weeks. With everything Brian was going through, I didn't want to be talking

Maureen, aged about five, with
Dad at Dublin Zoo (*left*) and Bernie
and Linda with Dad (*above*).

Dad singing 'Thank Heaven for Little Girls' as we step on the stage one by one.
From left to right, Dad, Mum, Coleen, Bernie, Linda, Maureen and Denise. This is us
at Cliff's Hotel in Blackpool, where our lives were to change one Christmas.

Above The baby of the family.
Coleen as a toddler.

Right Linda (on the left),
Brian and Bernie about to perform.

Linda, aged nine, belting
out 'Hey Big Spender'. She loved
this glamorous dress.

Coleen, aged about seven, not letting
a broken arm stop her as she sings at
the Brunswick Club 1972.

The Nolan Sisters' television debut on *It's Cliff Richard*.
Singing with Cliff and Pearly Gates, in 1974.

Backstage at *The Royal Variety Show* 1978 – from left to right, Maureen, Anne,
Max Bygraves, Linda and Bernie.

By 1981 Anne had left and Coleen had joined the group permanently. Here we are, The Nolan Sisters, with Tommy and Brian (*right*). And (*middle*) so excited to finally be on *Top of the Pops*!

Bottom The Tokyo Music Festival when we won!

On tour in Japan. Left to right, Phil Cranham (bass), Linda, Robin Smith (keyboard, musical director and Coleen's boyfriend!), Coleen, Paul Donnelly (guitar), Eddie Peacock (keys). Front row Maureen, Dave Early (drums), Bernie.

On stage in the 80s, when we'd got control of our wardrobes.

Above Linda leaving our house at Waterloo
Road with Dad, on her wedding day.

Right Linda and Brian,
a very happy couple.

The Naughty Nolan! After leaving the
group, Linda dared to bare all in this photo
that was splashed over the tabloids.

Linda looking quite
naughty as Maggie May.

Above left Linda and Brian with Brian's gorgeous son Lloyd.

Above right Linda with Brian's daughter Sarah, who she loves spending time with.

Right Although she was in the middle of her chemo, Linda and Brian went to Paris for their Silver Wedding.

Above Coleen and Shane with their two gorgeous boys, Jake and Shane Jnr.

Left Ray with Ciara.

about my good news. When I did finally tell my sisters that Bradley and I were engaged, they couldn't believe it – no one had ever thought I'd settle down. I was always the one out partying and drinking. But I desperately wanted to be with Bradley and even in my wildest days, I had always hoped that one day I'd meet the right man for me and we'd have kids together. I loved having children around. And so I really thought Brad and I would marry and it would be for keeps. Mum even took me out shopping to look at wedding dresses. But, sadly, from then on, the relationship just went downhill.

We were working in different resorts again and although we tried to see each other at weekends, we were having to spend a lot of time apart. Then, one night, a friend called me and said she'd seen Bradley out with another couple and one of the dancers from the show. I rang Bradley and asked him about it.

'There's nothing going on,' he said. 'It's just I feel a right gooseberry spending all night with a couple, so we asked this girl to come along with us a few times to make up the numbers.'

I wasn't quite as trusting as I used to be, and I still wasn't sure about it. 'Everyone will think she's your girlfriend,' I said.

'But she's not,' Bradley replied. 'You are.'

I still wasn't happy, but I tried to let it lie. Even Maureen told me that I had to try to trust Bradley if I really did want to put his other affairs in the past. But I just kept hearing more stories from mutual friends about Bradley hanging around with this dancer.

'You're sure you only ever go out in a foursome, not as a couple?' I asked him again on the phone one night.

'Certain,' he replied.

'OK, then,' I said.

But a couple of weeks later I got another phone call from a friend. 'Hi, Bernie,' she said. 'I'm really sorry to have to tell you this, but I think you need to know. I saw Bradley in a restaurant last night with that girl again. And they were definitely on their own. It was a candlelit table and most definitely just for two.'

I felt sick. I'd tried to trust him again and again, but each time I'd been made to look like a fool. I was due to visit Bradley that weekend, but I called him straightaway. 'Hi, Brad,' I said. 'Did you go out last night?'

'No, I just stayed in,' he replied.

'Oh, Bradley, you are such an idiot. Don't you realize people tell me things? You were seen, in a restaurant, with that girl.'

Quick as a flash, Bradley had his answer ready. 'Oh, we were just waiting for the other two to turn up,' he said.

'It was a table for two,' I replied.

'The waiters just put us there while they were getting the bigger table ready,' he said.

It was all so obviously rubbish.

'Just stop lying, Bradley,' I said. 'Look, I'm not coming this weekend, and in fact I don't want to see you anymore at all.'

It was that easy to do in the end. It was over. But I put the phone down and cried my eyes out. I'd adored Bradley and I felt utterly heartbroken, but even then, while I was sat there crying my eyes out, I still felt I'd done the right thing. Bradley was never going to change in our relationship.

As I've said, he has got a lovely wife now and they have a gorgeous son. He seems to be really happy, and I'm sure he wouldn't do anything like that now he is married, but I think if we had stayed together, it would just have happened again and again.

For a while, Bradley would ring me up and do his crying routine, begging for forgiveness and another chance to prove himself. But there was no doubt in my mind that I'd done the right thing. One day I received a letter for him asking if we could still be friends. I wrote back to him: 'I don't want to be your friend, I've got loads of friends, I wanted to be your wife.'

I didn't hate him, and was quite happy to be civil to him if we bumped into each other, but that was it. He couldn't have me in his life as a friend if he couldn't be faithful to me as a partner. When I think about it now, I feel I had a lucky escape. If we had gone through with the marriage it would have been a disaster.

I was thirty-two when I split with Bradley and for a while I was convinced that I would never settle down. I loved children and had always wanted to have my own, but I suddenly felt very old and seriously doubted whether that was ever going to happen for me now.

After a couple of months, I started dating a guy called David Ian. We'd first met a couple of years earlier, when we were in panto together in Hull. David was lovely, a great singer and very good-looking, but we were both in relationships at the time, so nothing happened between us. But when we met up again we were both single, and that's when we got together. By then David was moving out of acting and into producing. He had bought the rights to *Jesus Christ Superstar*, which became a massive success. After that, he was behind the stage productions of *Grease*, *Saturday Night Fever*, *Evita* and *The Sound of Music* and became one of the biggest theatre producers in the country.

He was a lovely guy and we are still friends now, but the relationship had fizzled out by the following summer. I think David was worried that I was still hung up on Bradley. Maybe deep down I was.

A year after splitting with Bradley, I was booked to do a summer season in Weymouth. And guess who else was on the bill? Bradley Walsh! I told myself I just had to get on with it and not make a fuss, but it was still a bit strange at first. The first time I walked into rehearsals and saw him there, I said, 'All that time we were together and we never got a job in the same place. And now, here we are.'

We had a good laugh about it and from then on things were fine between us.

By then, someone else had caught my eye. Every evening after the show, a group of us would go to a bar across the road from the theatre called the Roundhouse. People used to say that if the comedian Johnnie Casson, Bradley, the new drummer in our band, Steve, and I were there, then it was going to be a funny night.

Steve had first played with us earlier in 1991, when our regular drummer had to pull out of a gig in Ayr at the last moment. A friend suggested we try a guy called Steve Doneathy from Stockton-on-Tees. He was the closest person we could find, but it still took him hours to get there, and he didn't make it in time for the sound check. But he played the gig perfectly; he was brilliant. So, after that, Steve became our drummer.

By then we were only doing one-off gigs, so we didn't spend much time with the band and until we got to Weymouth, I hadn't really got to know Steve. It was only that summer, when we all went out every night till four or five in the morning and everyone was falling about laughing at his jokes, that I thought: 'Oh, I really like him'.

He was dark, tall (6ft 2ins next to my 5ft 1ins) and seemed very manly, the sort of guy who could protect me. But for me the most attractive thing was that he was very well-read, intelligent and witty and he had opinions on all sorts of things. I thought that was brilliant.

Over the next few weeks it was clear we were both falling in lust. I was single, but Steve had a girlfriend, which made the whole thing very difficult. One evening Steve offered to walk me back to the flat where I was staying. We were walking over a bridge and stopped to talk and then he leant down and kissed me. It was very romantic. From then on, we were together.

At the end of the season in Weymouth, Steve said he was going to drive straight to London to tell his girlfriend that he'd met someone else. I'd done enough summer seasons to know that very few romances lasted long after they'd finished, and I didn't know whether Steve would really end things with his girlfriend or not. As I drove home to Blackpool that day, I felt pretty low. But that evening Steve called me. 'I can't wait to see you,' he said. And then I knew it was all going to be OK.

Except that it wasn't totally OK immediately. One day, when Steve came up to visit me, we found ourselves chatting about children. 'Nah, I don't want kids,' Steve said quite casually.

'What, never?' I asked, feeling a bit sick.

'No. Never,' he said.

So that was it. It was 'See ya' because I did want kids, and I wasn't going to let myself fall in love with someone who didn't. When Steve left, I was utterly heartbroken. I'd really, really liked him.

A couple of days later the phone rang. It was Steve. 'Look, about kids.' he said. 'Maybe we can talk about it . . .'

At first we commuted between his house in Stockton-on-Tees and mine in Blackpool. Then, in 1994, I bought a new place in Blackpool and Steve moved in with me. But work was becoming more and more difficult. Coleen had left the group the previous year, and good work was becoming harder to find. The cabaret clubs were closing down and increasingly we were having to perform in nightclubs or bingo halls. Then, because of costs, we had to get rid of our own lights, and then the band, so we had to perform to tapes instead. It felt like a bit of a comedown, and I'd had enough.

We were hardly making any money and Anne and I were clashing. We love each other, but we have very different outlooks on life. I'm sure she thinks I'm a bit loud and crude, but I'm also a perfectionist, and there were things we just couldn't agree on. I should probably have left the group years earlier, but I'd stayed because I felt loyal to the others. For years we'd had it drummed into us that 'We're the Nolans, we stick together,' and that's how I felt.

Maybe I was also a bit scared about leaving, but certainly by the end of 1993, I realized I had to give it a go. At the start of our summer season in 1994, I told Maureen and Anne that I'd be leaving at the end of it. I knew it was putting them in a difficult position because it'd be a struggle to make the group work with just two members, but I couldn't hang on any longer. I think they understood though.

The first year and a half after I left was desperate. I didn't get a single gig. Nobody was interested. People kept telling me, 'You'll be fine, you're a Nolan.' But it was all crap. I was only doing some session work for a local act. At that time, being a Nolan sister was a disadvantage not an advantage.

Steve kept me going and paid my mortgage with his drumming work, while I just hoped something better was around the corner. Then my agent got me a job on a cruise ship and Steve came along as my musical director. It was a nightmare because you could never get away from the punters, day or night, but Steve and I had a laugh.

Work remained thin on the ground until I was offered a summer season at the Layton Institute Working Men's Club in Blackpool. I'd filled in when someone was sick the previous summer, but this time they wanted it to be all my own show. It was a good offer – they were going to pay me £1,300 a week – but I'd left the group because I didn't want to be doing working men's clubs and venues like that anymore. I'd done them when I was a kid and it felt like a step backwards.

'I just feel it's accepting my lot if I take it,' I said to Steve. 'But you're paying the mortgage, so it is up to you.'

'Don't do it,' he replied. So I turned down the job and carried on hoping for a break.

Finally it came, when I was asked to audition for a big part in a touring production of *Billy Liar*. It was my first professional acting job and I was so nervous, but it was what I wanted to do. On the evening of my final audition, I was flying off to Venice to meet Steve, who was working on a cruise ship out there. I'd just arrived at the airport when I got a call to say I'd landed the part. It was amazing – that was huge for me.

When I got off the plane, I was so excited about seeing Steve and telling him about the job. I was wearing a gorgeous new blue suit that I'd bought, with a long jacket and pencil skirt. It was just brilliant to see him again, and when we got to his cabin on the ship, there was a huge bouquet of flowers waiting for me and my favourite wine. That evening, as we headed out into Venice, all Steve's mates on the ship were shouting, 'Have a good night!' I thought it was a bit strange that they were all being quite so friendly, but I didn't think any more of it.

At the restaurant, the waiter had only just served our dinner when Steve said, 'Come on. Hurry up and eat this because I want to take you somewhere afterwards and we've got to be back on the ship before it sails at eleven o'clock.'

So we bolted our dinner down and then walked and walked and walked around Venice, looking for this mystery place which Steve couldn't seem to find. Finally he turned, all hot and stressed, and said to me, 'I'm looking for a particular bridge, and I just can't find it.'

'Don't worry, it's fine,' I said. I really couldn't understand why he was stressing so much over a bloody bridge.

'But you do love me, don't you?' he went on.

'Is this still about the bridge?' I thought. It was all getting weirder and weirder.

'So do you think you want to spend the rest of your life with me?' Steve then asked.

'What are you saying?' I said, the pieces finally falling into place.

'Will you marry me?'

It was amazing. I couldn't believe it! 'Yes,' I said. 'Yes, yes, yes.'

We were so late going back to the ship that it was getting ready to pull out of the port when we got there and we had to rush up the gangplank to get back on. All Steve's mates were sitting on the deck drinking champagne.

'She said yes!' Steve shouted to them.

'Yes!' everyone cheered.

We were together for the rest of the cruise, and it was wonderfully romantic, but my run of luck ran out when, two weeks before *Billy Liar* was due to open, the show was cancelled and we all got paid off. I was absolutely gutted.

Steve and I married in 1996. It was a fantastic day. In the morning I walked round to our house in Waterloo Road, where we'd grown up and where Mum and Dad were still living. We drank Buck's Fizz and Dad and I had some time alone. 'So are you happy?' he said.

'Oh yes, Dad.' I replied.

His breathing wasn't very good that day. It had been getting gradually worse over the last few years, which we put down to years of smoking and performing in smoky clubs. He looked a bit poorly too, but he was so delighted and proud to be giving me away.

We had a church wedding in Blackpool because even though neither Steve nor I are particularly religious, I felt I needed that to feel properly married. It was a big white wedding, with two of my sisters, Anne's daughters, Coleen's kids and Steve's neice as bridesmaids and page boys. During the service my brothers and sisters sang 'One Hand, One Heart' from *West Side Story*. I cried my eyes out. Then Mum sang 'The Prayer Perfect', which was wonderful. She still had a brilliant voice.

I looked out from my seat at the top table at the wedding breakfast at the Grand Hotel in St Anne's, and there was a sea of faces that I loved. Then, in the evening, we had the most brilliant party, which ended with me in the hotel foyer at four in the morning, still in my wedding dress and with my feet up on the piano. What a night!

Work started picking up for me in the year after we married. I landed work on the world premiere of *Oh What a Night* in Blackpool, which was great. As well as appearing on stage, I was also singing backstage a lot. That was very technical, but I've always loved that side of performing just as much as being on stage. As soon as that show finished, I'd be stripping off at the side of the stage and putting on my outfit for my second performance of the night – at the Stakis Hotel in Blackpool. I was booked there for an entire season of cabaret with my own band and dancers.

Sometimes I'd arrive during the opening overture, but Steve was my musical director, so between us we always ensured I made it just in time! It was incredibly hard work, but the money we earned that year meant we were able to buy our second home in St Anne's. As Steve would say to me when I sprinted, out of breath, into the Stakis Hotel every night: 'Just suck the cheque!'

10.

Coleen

Men and Boys

What with Robin cheating on me and then Stewart dumping me, I didn't feel like I was having a lot of luck with men. Maybe I was attracted to the wrong kind of man. Certainly I liked a fella with a twinkle in his eye. And no one had a twinkle quite like the fella who bounded up to the table where my sisters and I were having a coffee one morning.

'Alright, gels?' he blustered. 'Anyone seen Dave?'

We were in the canteen of the Bournemouth International Centre, where we were about to start a summer season. Dave, we guessed, was Dave Wolfe, who was a comic in our show. But who was this guy with the shoulder-length wavy hair and the cor-blimey accent? I didn't know, but I was sure as hell going to find out!

I tracked down Dave and his mystery mate, who it turned out was also a comedian, in the bar, drinking bottles of beer. We chatted for a bit, and I knew then that I fancied him. 'We're having a party tonight at the house where we're staying,' I said casually. 'You should drop in.'

Then I rushed back to the canteen and found Maureen. 'Right, we've got to have a party tonight,' I told her. 'We'll have to run out to the shops and get some food and booze.'

'What's his name then?' said Maureen, smiling. She knew me too well!

'Shane,' I replied. 'Shane Richie.'

In actual fact, his surname was Roche, but he used Richie for work. That night Shane and I sat up chatting until four in the morning. It was brilliant. That was a bit of a weird night all round really because it was the same evening Maureen took me to one side for a quiet chat.

'Look, I think you ought to know,' she said. 'Bernie is going out with Stewart.'

I felt like I'd just been kicked in the stomach. I knew Bernie had always got on well with Stewart when we were living together, but actually going out together? How could she? Bernie knew exactly how cut up I'd been when Stewart dumped me. And, of course, I couldn't help but wonder if something had been going on between them while Stewart and I were still together. Would she? I never asked. The next day, when I saw Bernie in the dressing room, she looked terrified, as though I was about to swing for her, but I walked over as though nothing had happened and said, 'Can I borrow your blusher?'

It was much more our family's style to make sure anything a bit awkward, like sleeping with your sister's ex, was swept right under the carpet!

Thank goodness I'd just met Shane though, because otherwise the news would have hit me far harder. Thankfully, I had my own love life to think about, rather than my sister's. That night Shane came back to our house again after the show and we talked until the early hours about anything and everything. He was a year older than me, very outgoing and made everyone laugh. He was just great to be with. When we kissed for the first time that evening, I really did think, 'This is it!'

We arranged to meet again the following day, and Shane picked me up in his Ford Escort convertible. Don't be too hard on him, it was 1986! When I got back home after our date and walked into the kitchen, I immediately knew something was up. Everyone was really quiet and staring at the floor, and I knew those lino tiles weren't that fascinating.

'What is it?' I said.

'Brian's got something to tell you,' Maureen replied.

Our brother Brian had been down visiting us for a few days.

'Erm, I'm sorry, Coleen,' said Brian, 'but Shane is engaged. I bumped into him a few days before you met and we got chatting. He told me about his fiancée.'

I was gutted. I'd even asked him if he was seeing someone and he'd said he wasn't. Even though we'd only known each other a couple of days, I was utterly devastated. I'd really thought he could be 'the one'.

I was supposed to be meeting him later that evening in the bar at the International Centre where we were performing. 'So, are you engaged?' I asked flatly when I finally got him away from his mates that night.

He didn't even take a breath. 'Yes, but it's over,' he said. 'Sorry, I should have told you sooner.'

That was probably the clearest warning sign I could ever have been given about what lay ahead if I started seeing Shane. It was the way he didn't even need to pause while he spun me a line. But all I could see back then were his sparkly eyes and cheeky grin.

'Maybe we should just be friends for the time being,' I said, desperately trying to be tough. But he wasn't having that. We walked down Bournemouth High Street, with him making a total show of me. 'Please don't leave me!' he was screaming, just to embarrass me and try to make me laugh. 'Pleeeease! I really want to go out with you!'

He explained that he wanted to finish with his fiancée face to face at the end of the season rather than do it over the phone, and I thought that sounded reasonable.

What could I do? Truth be told, I was already in way too deep. This was love.

That summer was like something out of a film. We had such a great time together and within weeks we'd told each other that we were in love. Then, just before the season was to end, Shane's fiancée found out about us and turned up in Bournemouth. It was our last day there, but he spent all of it with her. By then I'd fallen for him hook, line and sinker, and I was utterly terrified that he might stick with her and dump me. In the evening I went off to the theatre feeling really down. But I'd only been there twenty minutes when Anne's little girl Amy, who was then about seven, ran into my dressing room.

'Auntie Coleen,' she was shouting. 'Shane's got a message for you. He says he's all yours.' I felt like screaming, I was so happy.

After the end of the season, Shane moved into my house in Hillingdon. This really was 'It'. And it was 'It' for fourteen years.

I was still doing gigs and tours with The Nolans and he was picking up more and more work as a comedian. It was hard because it meant we were often apart, particularly in the summer. And in show business there are always rumours going round. One summer I heard stories that Shane was seeing a dancer in his show, but I knew how nasty gossips could be and I put it out of my mind. We knew we wanted to be together forever; we told each other that a million times a day, although sometimes I did worry whether I'd really be able to hang on to Shane for that long.

One afternoon we were sat eating a McDonald's in Uxbridge when Shane turned to me and said, 'So, d'you wanna get engaged or what?'

'Yeah, alright,' I replied.

And that was it. We finished our chips, then went into a jeweller's, where Shane bought me a gold ring with a tiny diamond in it. It cost £160, but to me it was the most precious thing in the world.

We hadn't got round to setting a date or anything like that when I missed a period. I was pregnant. We hadn't been trying for a baby, but we hadn't been not trying either, if you get what I mean. This time, I was ecstatic – and so was Shane.

The first person we told was Bobby Ball from Cannon & Ball because Shane was on tour with them. Bobby Ball was like a second dad to me. 'I'm warning you,' he told Shane. 'If you hurt this girl, I'll break your legs.'

Then I had to tell Mum and Dad. Since moving back to Blackpool, Mum had rediscovered her faith and went to mass almost every day. While she could just about cope with her daughter living in sin, she would be really upset about me having a baby when I wasn't married. I rang Dad and told him the news, then asked him to pass it on to Mum. Apparently, when he told her, she cried. Thankfully, I didn't find that out until years later. Gradually though, Mum came to terms with it. And when, a few weeks later, Maureen made her announcement that she was pregnant by a fella they hadn't even met, it certainly took the heat off me!

The baby was born four months before my twenty-fourth birthday and we called him Shane Jnr. It was a tradition in our family to name kids after their parents. When he was born, I could sit and look at him for hours. I couldn't quite believe that I'd created him. It made me think of Mum in a whole new light – she'd done that eight times!

Shane, the baby and I were a family, and we were happy. But it wasn't easy financially, as I stayed at home for seven months after the birth, so Shane was the only breadwinner. Sometimes he'd travel for six hours to do a gig, or he'd be compering hen nights, which might just earn him £40. Gradually work picked up for Shane, and the summer after Shane Jnr was born, The Nolans did a summer season in Blackpool. Maureen had her baby, Danny, with her too, so we shared a house and a friend babysat for us when we were working at night.

Shane Jnr was such a good baby. I'd have to wake him to feed him, while poor Maureen was up and down all night with Danny. We all really felt for Maureen at that time because she wasn't getting any support from her boyfriend, Ritchie. The fact that he'd become a father and couldn't stay out until all hours was totally lost on him. There were times when we were all desperate for Maureen to leave Ritchie, for her own good, but Maureen is so laid-back that she just got on with it. 'He'll grow into it,' she'd say about Ritchie. We thought she was being a bit over-optimistic, but in the end she was proved absolutely right – even if it did take a good few years!

Shane was doing a season in Weymouth that year and, again, I started hearing rumours that he was seeing someone down there. Obviously it worried me, but Shane was always so attentive that I just didn't think it could be true. He'd travel seven hours every week from Weymouth to Blackpool to visit us. And he'd phone me 25,000 times a day!

After that season, Shane and I had been due to marry, in a proper church service back in Blackpool, with me in a big meringue, all my sisters lined up as bridesmaids and a sea of aunties and uncles filling the congregation. But the deeper we sank into the palaver of wedding preparations, the more I could tell Shane was hating the whole idea.

'You don't want to do this, do you?' I said to him one day.

He just looked at the floor. That wasn't really the response I'd been hoping for! Something like: 'Of course we'll do it,' was more what I'd expected. So the wedding was off. I cried for a couple of days, but Shane kept reassuring me that it wasn't me that was the problem; it was the big traditional wedding, where he felt he'd simply have a walk-on role.

'Let's elope to Florida,' he suggested a couple of months later.

I was still a little disappointed at missing my big day, but it sounded so exciting. And, more than anything, I wanted us to be married. 'OK,' I agreed.

We told our families we were just going on holiday, and Shane's mum agreed to look after Shane Jnr. The only person I confided in about it was Maureen. Then, as a surprise for me, Shane fixed up for her to fly over with Ritchie, so she could be my bridesmaid. It was all a little surreal, and in some ways it didn't feel to me like a proper wedding, exchanging vows at the edge of a lake, thousands of miles from home, but it was a lovely day.

My family were all great about it and thrilled for us, apart from Denise, who I think was angry that they hadn't all been invited. She always felt that family should be put above everything. She got over it in the end though.

When Shane Jnr was two and a half, I decided it would be

nice to give him a brother or sister, so Shane and I set to work! Jake was born on 16 September 1992, just at the end of a summer season. He was chubby and gorgeous, and his elder brother adored him. By then we had just moved into a big, five-bedroom, mock-Tudor house in Hillingdon. Shane had been presenting a show called *Caught in the Act* for the BBC and was suddenly earning big money. Our financial problems were in the past. Or so we thought! Within months, the show was dropped and we were left with a huge mortgage on a massive house which we couldn't even afford to furnish. We were really scrabbling around for cash to pay the bills and even had the bailiffs round. They left with Shane's old banger of a car that, quite frankly, I would have paid them to take off our hands!

I had to start working again as soon as possible, to help pay the bills, but it was tough doing that as well as looking after a newborn and a demanding toddler. Shane didn't do much to pitch in. He'd play with the kids if he was around, but everything else was down to me. That made my sisters mad. 'We'll look after your kids while your wife's having a nervous breakdown,' they'd snipe at him sarcastically when they came to visit and saw me crumbling under the strain.

Shane was at home less and less as the months rolled by, and when he was there, it felt like he rarely noticed me at all. Then he landed a part in the musical *Grease* in the West End. He was surrounded by adoring girls and just lapped up the attention! Meanwhile, I was feeling fat and frumpy, my shoulders rounded and a baby almost permanently connected to my hip. I felt virtually invisible to my husband, but a lot of the time I'd think: 'To be honest, I don't blame him. I'm overweight. I look crap. I feel crap. I'm knackered. Why would he still fancy me?' My self-esteem was sinking like a stone.

And, of course, there were the rumours that Shane was seeing other women again. Always the same old rumours. By then, I didn't dare confront him about them. I couldn't risk giving him the chance to turn around and say, 'Yeah, I am shagging around because I don't fancy you anymore.' I couldn't bear the thought of bringing things to a head and possibly losing my husband and the father of my children.

Instead, I stuck with the 'sweeping it under the carpet' approach. I became locked in a vicious circle of feeling utterly worthless, but because I felt like that, I couldn't do anything to improve the situation.

Looking back, I can see that it was all a disaster waiting to happen. And it did happen. We were doing a summer season in Weymouth and there was a guy in our band who was just lovely to me. I never once thought, 'Right, that's it. My husband's being a bastard to me, so I'm going to have an affair.' It wasn't like that at all. I was just vulnerable and this guy came along, paid me a little bit of attention and I fell for it.

He was quiet and gentle, the total opposite of Shane. When he told me I looked gorgeous, it meant so much because I'd not had a guy say that to me in years. I'd think, 'Oh, right, maybe I am still a little bit attractive after all.' Now, I know that as soon as I began to enjoy that attention, I should have said to Shane, 'I'm not happy. I'm feeling neglected and vulnerable and now someone else is paying me attention and I like it.' But, of course, I didn't say any of that and, instead, over that summer season, the musician and I started an affair.

My sisters hated the way Shane had been treating me and how I'd lost every ounce of self-esteem. They could see why I was attracted to the musician, and they were pleased he was boosting my confidence, but they were cautious too.

'Be careful,' Maureen and Bernie both told me. 'We under-stand why you're doing it, but you are vulnerable. Be careful.'

The musician and I went out for romantic dinners and drinks together and, yes, we slept together and it was lovely. But although part of me enjoyed it, another part of me absolutely hated it because I was carrying the most terrible guilt with me all the time. I might have had a lovely evening with him, but I'd wake up the next morning feeling so awful about what I'd done that I'd want to be sick. All summer long I was hearing stories from people in the industry that Shane was messing around with other women in London, but even that didn't stop this crippling sense of guilt that I had. It was dead in the water with Shane by then, but I still felt terrible about what I was doing.

As for the musician, I seriously thought we might have a future together, but then one night he told me that he didn't think he could ever take on another man's children. So where did that leave me? I really didn't know. If he'd said he would have been happy to help bring up Shane Jnr and Jake, maybe I would have gone with him, I still don't know. Knowing he wouldn't, though, meant that it was only ever going to be a fling. So, at the end of the season, I packed my car up and drove home alone with Shane Jnr and Jake.

I was heartbroken and confused. The thought of never seeing the musician again was devastating, but at the same time I still loved Shane, even if he had become so distant. On top of that, the guilt I was feeling was horrific, and I was going to have to live with it for ever. I knew I would never have an affair again. It was just too awful and upsetting for everyone involved. The only good thing about the affair was that it had given me back some of my self-confidence.

I spoke to my musician once or twice after I returned home, but I was determined we would never see each other again. I had to concentrate on rebuilding things with Shane.

But one evening Shane came home from *Grease* and I could tell something was up.

'Anyone ring tonight?' he said.

'Only Maureen,' I replied.

'Really? You sure?' he asked.

'Yeah,' I said, feeling distinctly uncomfortable.

The game was up. Shane had bought a bugging device and had been taping my calls. He must have been incredibly suspicious, although I'm not sure what had sparked that. Maybe he knew the signs of a guilty conscience! The phone call to the musician hadn't been romantic or lovey-dovey, and I certainly hadn't said, 'I'm missing you' or 'I want to see you,' but there must have been enough to it for Shane's suspicions to be confirmed.

He went totally mad. 'Did you kiss him?' he yelled at me.

'Yeah,' I said quietly. I couldn't lie. It was too late for that.

That was the worst moment of my life. He looked utterly devastated. Then he started asking question after question about what had gone on and when and where and why. But he never asked me if I'd slept with him. I think he didn't want to ask me because he knew I couldn't lie. I think he knew.

Afterwards, Shane went and sat in the car outside the kitchen window for about three hours and just sobbed. He cried and cried and cried, he was so hurt. I felt like the biggest s*** on the planet.

I said I was sorry almost continuously for the next two months. I tried to explain why it had happened and that it would never happen again, and I meant every word of what

I said. I just never wanted to see anybody that hurt ever again. I couldn't bear it.

After that, Shane wouldn't trust me to go anywhere without him. For the next eight weeks, I had to go to London every night with him while he was in *Grease*. Denise babysat the boys, while I spent the night watching the show or sitting on my own in Shane's dressing room. I didn't care though. I'd have done anything to make it up to Shane and win back his trust. I'd have gone to *Grease* every night for the next two years if that's what he'd wanted!

Incredibly, after all that came out, Shane and I went on to have the best two years of our marriage. It woke us both up to how things had gone wrong between us and it made us deal with things we'd previously just ignored. Shane changed beyond recognition. He acknowledged everything I did, listened to everything I said and told me all the time that I looked lovely. He was so attentive. Of course, my confidence was boosted, and I looked and felt better and so was more attentive towards him. We talked about everything, we laughed together again, and it was like when we'd first met.

Life at home was better than it had been for years. The boys were great fun to be around too, and I found myself resenting the times when I had to be away from them with The Nolans. We often had to travel really long distances to do one-off shows and, with Shane now playing the lead in *Grease*, we weren't so desperate for money.

One night in 1994, we were doing a gig way up in Scotland somewhere and weren't even going on stage until two in the morning. We had to change in the basement of a club and there were rats running around. It was foul. We went on stage and were just starting a four-part a cappella number when some tosser in the crowd shouted, 'Show us your tits!' That was it. I thought, 'I'm not leaving my kids for this anymore. It's over.'

The next day I told my sisters I wanted to leave the group. I just wanted to be at home with my boys. They all said they understood and there was no big drama about me leaving.

I was delighted not to have to work for a while, and I loved my new role as a full-time mum and doting wife. The rumours about Shane and other women still continued to bounce around though. Sometimes my sisters and friends would ask whether it worried me that he seemed to get so much female attention, but it really didn't. He was so attentive to me then, so loving and romantic, that I trusted him totally. It was to be a while longer before I realized how totally fooled I had been.

11.

Bernie

Loss

At any family party I'd be the one racing up and downstairs with the kids, playing rowdy games in the front room and organising footie matches in the garden. I loved kids. Maybe I was still a big kid at heart myself. I'd always longed to have a family of my own and soon after Steve and I married, we decided the time was right to start trying. And for us Nolan women, getting pregnant isn't usually a problem – I think we take after our mum in that!

At the end of 1997, I fell pregnant. When I did the test and saw it was positive, I was totally thrilled. Even Steve, who hadn't wanted kids when we first met, was delighted too. It was Christmas time and the whole family had gone round to see Mum and Dad. All my brothers and sisters were there – it was a real houseful!

'We've got something to tell you all,' I said, grinning like a loony. 'I'm pregnant!'

Everyone started screaming, and Dad was so shocked that he nearly fell over. By Nolan family standards, I'd left it quite late to have children, and maybe they'd thought it was never going to happen. But it was great, just wonderful, and pregnancy really suited me. I felt fabulous. I had no sickness, no scares, no illness at all. Everything seemed to be going according to the textbooks.

It was May when I went along to the hospital in Blackpool for my twenty-week scan. I lay on the couch, all excited, knowing that in a few minutes I'd see a picture of my baby. Except when the sonographer rubbed her scanning device over my belly, she kept frowning at the screen. Steve was standing next to me, and we looked at each other. Something didn't feel quite right.

'Can you just go for a walk about outside,' the sonographer said to me. 'I can't get a scan because it's lying on its back and it needs to move around a bit.'

I went outside and walked around. At that point I just accepted that the problem was purely that they couldn't get the baby in position for a good scan. Five minutes later, I was back on the couch. But as the woman stared at the screen in total silence, I knew instinctively that something was very wrong. I'd seen enough medical dramas to know that normally she would saying, 'There's the head' and 'There are the legs,' but she wasn't saying any of those things.

'OK, if you could just pull your trousers back up, one of my colleagues will be in to see you in a moment,' she said gently. This wasn't right at all. I felt sick.

I sat up on the bed just as one of the doctors came in and sat down opposite me. 'I'm afraid we're really not happy with the scan,' she said.

I still find it almost impossible to explain how it felt to hear those words. For me, it wasn't an emotional feeling at that point, it was purely physical. I needed to throw up.

'What do you mean?' I said.

'Well, there are a few things we need to check,' the doctor

said. She explained that they were going to send me to St Mary's Hospital in Manchester, where they'd be able to do a more detailed scan.

At that moment, I knew I wanted this baby more than anything in the world, but suddenly everything felt very out of my control.

Outside the hospital, I rang my sisters from my mobile phone. 'I've just had the scan, but there's something wrong,' I told each of them.

'Don't worry, it'll be fine,' they said. What else could they say? I wanted to believe them, but I really wasn't sure. Oh God, it was awful.

At St Mary's, they did another scan. Steve and I sat in a waiting room for the results. Finally a doctor emerged, holding a wad of papers. 'We think your child may have Down's syndrome,' the doctor said. 'We need to do an amniocentesis to be sure, but it does look that way to me. We'll have the results in about a week.'

The whole thing was like a bad dream. We had been so excited about becoming parents and now everything was changing. Steve was so pale that I thought he was going to faint. We went home and sat in silence for ages. I don't think either of us had any idea what it all meant. We were both in shock. My brothers and sisters all rallied round, but it was hard for them too. There was nothing any of us could do but wait.

'Look, I can't sit here staring at the walls for a week,' I finally said to Steve. 'I'm going back to work. Why don't you come with me?' I had landed a fantastic role as Mrs Johnstone in *Blood Brothers*, touring all round Britain. At least being back on the road kept me occupied while I waited for the results, but it didn't stop me thinking about it. I couldn't think about anything else.

A week later, Steve and I sat in front of a nurse at St Mary's Hospital. 'I'm terribly sorry,' she said. 'It's not Down's syndrome, it is actually worse. Your child has a condition called Edwards syndrome.'

'What's that?' I said, choking back the tears.

'Well, the baby's neck hasn't developed properly, and she has spina bifida too.'

I later discovered that Edwards syndrome is a chromosome disorder, like Down's, and that few children born with the condition live for more than a year. At the time, a friend of ours, Frank Wilcox, was senior consultant obstetrician at Victoria Hospital in Blackpool. I'd known his wife for years and we were all good friends. Frank is an amazing man and offered to do anything he could to help us. I showed him my notes and scans. 'What should I do?' I said.

'I'm so sorry, Bernie, but this is the worst strain of Edwards syndrome I've ever seen,' he told me. 'I'm afraid your baby hasn't got a chance of surviving. She'll die as soon as she is born.'

I was too shocked to cry. I felt utterly numb.

'I can book you in now to induce the birth,' he said. 'You could carry on with the pregnancy and go to nine months, and you'll feel her kicking inside you, but once she is born she won't live, I'm afraid. I'm so sorry.'

The baby hadn't started kicking by then, but I didn't think I could bear the thought of her moving around inside me if she had no chance of life. I went with the doctors' advice and decided to be induced.

The night before the operation Steve and I sat up almost

all night at the kitchen table, talking and crying. Neither of us could sleep. The thought of what would happen the next day was just too awful for either of us. We had decided to call our daughter Kate. I loved Katherine Hepburn and we both agreed it was a really pretty name.

Next morning we drove in almost total silence to the hospital. I was going to have to give birth to her as a natural labour. My friend, the obstetrician, had said that, if I insisted, I could have a caesarean, but he advised against it. 'A c-section is a major operation,' he explained. 'You might be out of action for six weeks afterwards, whereas with a natural labour you could be back to normal as soon as next week.'

Again, I took his advice. I try to remain positive in all situations and I kept thinking that maybe getting back to work as soon as possible would be the best way of coping.

I was taken into a special 'SANDS' room for the labour, which is just for people who know their children are going to be stillborn. It is fantastic that such a place exists, but it was positioned right next to the maternity ward. All day long, I could hear newborn babies crying just down the corridor, when I knew I'd never hear my baby make a single sound. It was horrific. And, walking down the corridor, I'd see hugely pregnant women who were about to give birth to healthy babies. It all seemed so horribly unfair.

It took ages to get the labour started. At one point, as a nurse examined me, I heard her say to her colleague, 'Ah, there she is, just sitting there.' I knew what she meant: 'She's dead.' My baby was just sitting there inside me, unable to help the labour along or do anything to help herself.

In the end, the labour didn't last too long. When she came out, there was only Steve, the nurse and me in the room. She was born, and there was total silence. Usually when a baby is born, there are the sounds of a baby crying or parents shouting with delight. But there was nothing. Just total silence.

Steve sobbed quietly on my shoulder, but none of us said a word. After a while, the nurse said to me, 'Would you like to see her?'

'Yes, I'd like to,' I said. 'But tell me first how bad she looks.'

I know that sounds awful, but I was scared; I had no idea what to expect. The nurse said that she was very red, because she was so premature, and that one of her eyes was shut. Then she wrapped her in a blanket, put a tiny little hat on her head and brought her to me.

I looked at my daughter and couldn't quite believe it. She was gorgeous. Absolutely beautiful.

She was very red and she was tiny, but she was lovely. She was so small that they didn't even weigh her, but I don't think she can have been more than 4oz. She had long fingers and long legs and looked as though she was just sleeping.

I didn't touch her because the nurse told me not to. I'm still not sure why; maybe her skin was too delicate.

One of the nurses brought in a camera and took some photographs of Kate, which were lovely. I keep them in a special box with her scan pictures and all the letters and cards I received afterwards.

'Would you like her baptized?' one of the nurses asked me.

'Yes,' I replied immediately. I wasn't particularly religious, but it felt totally the right thing to do. But when the nurses contacted the Catholic priest, he wouldn't come to do it. In the Catholic Church it is considered abortion if a baby is induced when it has no chance of life. I was so upset that any-one could act like that, and I've never forgotten or forgiven it.

But then a lovely female reverend came from the Church of England and she performed the most beautiful baptism. She held a Bible and said such lovely words over our little Kate. Steve just sobbed, but I didn't cry. I couldn't, not then. Maybe I was still in shock. I felt sorrier for Kate than for myself because she'd never had a chance to live.

A few hours later, Steve and I were allowed home. We walked in the front door of our house, still just the two of us. There was no baby to bring home.

The following week, we held a funeral for our little girl. It was Steve, me and a little white coffin. The funeral director asked Steve if he wanted to carry his daughter and, of course, he did, so he took her to the place where she was buried.

It was a lovely sunny day and afterwards all my family came round to the house and we sat in the garden. I'd told them I didn't want them wearing black suits or anything, I just wanted them to be around me that day. My poor dad knocked on the door and, when I answered it, he said all nervously, 'Is this OK?' pointing to the blazer that he was wearing.

'It's great, Dad,' I said.

Dad needed an oxygen tank to help him breathe by then, but he didn't have it with him that day. He was quite shy and very proud, and he hated taking it out in public.

My nephews and nieces played football in the garden and it was a lovely day. I never felt bitter when I looked at my brothers and sisters' kids. I don't really 'do' jealousy. I was just happy they were there.

While the men were all chatting downstairs, I took my sisters upstairs and laid out all the pictures we'd had taken of Kate on our bed and showed them all the beautiful cards that people had sent me. I was so grateful to have those photographs. A friend of mine had had a stillbirth years earlier and she never even saw her baby. She never got over that.

It was a lovely day, with us all together. Maybe that sounds strange, but I felt it was something special for Kate and it helped me grieve and bring the whole process to an end. Maybe another reason that day sticks in my mind as being so wonderful was that it was one of the very last times that our family were all together.

We had a little gravestone put up in the cemetery where Kate was buried. It is very simple, with just the date of her birth and the words: 'The light that burns the brightest, burns the briefest.' It is beautiful where Kate is buried. Brian's wife, Linzie, and now my Mum and Dad are there too, and it is so peaceful. I can go there whenever I want, and I like having that.

After the funeral, I went straight back to work. Working has always been my way of coping with everything. I am seriously, genuinely and to my very core optimistic about life. I think, 'There are no problems, only solutions.' That is honestly how I am. And so, after Kate's funeral, I thought, 'Well, I can either sit here and cry all night and day for the rest of my life or I can get off my fat arse and get back to work.'

Kate had died. She wasn't coming back, and that wasn't her fault and it wasn't mine. Nothing could be done about it, and I needed to get on with life. And that's what I did. I know many people just can't do that after losing a baby, but for me it was the only way to survive.

I went straight back into *Blood Brothers* and at the same time Steve and I immediately started trying for another baby. Losing Kate had brought us closer together than ever, both physically and mentally. We'd always been close, but losing Kate made us feel we'd been through something so, so bad, but together we could fight anything. Some couples can pull apart when they go through that kind of trauma, but fortunately it wasn't like that for us.

By July, I was pregnant again.

I wanted to be delighted about it, but this time I was too scared of getting my hopes up. Every day I'd be worried that something was about to go wrong. And when I went for my first scan, at just six weeks, I thought my worst fears were coming true. They looked at the scan and, again, they weren't quite happy, although they weren't sure what the problem was. I was beside myself with worry, but there was nothing I could do except wait to see how the foetus developed.

I was scanned again at eight weeks and twelve weeks, and still the doctors weren't happy with the baby's development. The doctors said I would need an amniocentesis test to get clearer results, but when the results of that came back, it still wasn't clear what was going on. The doctors thought it might be floppy baby syndrome, which is a developmental delay problem. Then they thought she might have learning disabilities.

I felt constantly sick with worry. I carried on in *Blood Brothers*, travelling backwards and forwards to Blackpool for my hospital appointments. We were told to wait a while longer while they looked again at the amniocentesis test.

'I don't know if I can cope with this much longer,' I said to Steve. We were both at our wits' end. Every day seemed to last a lifetime.

When *Blood Brothers* moved to Nottingham, Steve came with me. One morning we went shopping together in the city centre, to take our minds off what was going on. We were browsing around The Pier homeware shop when my mobile rang. It was the hospital. 'Erm, Mrs Doneathy?' the voice at the other end said.

'Yes?' I replied, my heart pounding with fear.

'Well, we've worked out that the reason the first amniocentesis results weren't clear was a fault with the petri dish,' said the nurse.

'OK,' I said. 'But is there anything wrong with my baby?'

'No, she's absolutely fine,' the nurse said.

I turned and hugged Steve, then burst into tears in the middle of the shop. I couldn't hold it all in any longer. Weeks and weeks of emotion had been building up inside me and suddenly it all burst out. Then I rang Mum and Dad and all my brothers and sisters. I was crying so much, I could barely speak, but when I managed to tell them it was good news everyone was delighted.

From then on, I had a great pregnancy. Sometimes I'd panic that something still might go wrong, but physically I felt fabulous.

But in the September of that year, when I was still just a couple of months pregnant, there was more bad news. Dad was seriously ill. For the past eighteen months, his condition had been deteriorating. He should probably have gone to the doctor's and got himself treated years before he actually did, but for ages he refused to admit he had any kind of problem. When he did go to the hospital for tests, they found he had a form of lung disease caused by years of heavy smoking.

At first he was put on loads of different tablets to regulate his breathing, but as he became sicker, he was also given the oxygen tank to help him. He was still a very proud man though and he hated having to use that tank. He loathed any kind of fuss being made about him. Towards the very end of his life, Dad was also diagnosed with liver cancer, but there was nothing that could be done to help him by that point.

Because I was away touring a lot, I might not see him for weeks on end, but each time I went home I'd be shocked by how much further downhill he'd gone. One night, in September 1998, Dad's breathing was so bad that Mum phoned for an ambulance. They took him straight into hospital and he never came home again. He was seventy-three.

I was appearing in *Blood Brothers* in Glasgow one Wednesday when Maureen called me in the morning. 'I'm so sorry, Bernie,' she said. 'Dad's died.'

I felt sick and totally lost. My dad, who'd always been there for me when I was struggling over my homework, who'd cheered me on at netball matches and who'd been so buzzing with energy all the time, was gone.

All I wanted was to get home and be with my family, but the show had only just opened and my understudy hadn't done a single rehearsal. There was a matinee performance that afternoon and if I'd pulled out they'd have had to cancel it. I could have said, 'Screw you, my dad's just died, I'm off.' But I knew Dad wouldn't have been happy about that. He would have wanted me to go on stage. That was the professional thing to do, which he'd drilled into me from the age of two.

I did two more performances, then drove home to Blackpool. It seemed so strange to be going back to my parents' house and Dad not being there anymore. Us kids sat around and talked about the good times we'd had with him and prepared for his funeral.

The service was held at St Kentigern's Church, next to where we had gone to school as kids. I wrote the eulogy and read it too, which was terrifying, but I'd loved my dad very much and I wanted to do it. I think I'm like Dad in a lot of ways. Although he was quite shy, he could also be very extroverted, and I'm a bit like that too. I love people and socialising. Dad had a mean streak, and I'll never forget the way he treated Mum sometimes, but he was my dad and I loved him.

I started the eulogy by saying, 'Well, this is the only time in Dad's life that he has been on time,' and that got a huge laugh.

Afterwards, Maureen spoke the words from the Celine Dion song 'Because You Loved Me', and despite everything that had happened in our family, those words were so fitting for our dad. Then all the grandchildren did readings. Dad had loved his grandchildren and they were all crazy about him. It was a wonderful service, but terribly sad too.

In the weeks and months afterwards, Mum was totally lost. She and Dad had spent their whole lives rowing and were total opposites; Mum didn't drink or smoke and was very religious, while Dad smoked, drank and loved going out. But they'd loved each other, in their own strange, ridiculous way.

Dad wasn't at all romantic and I don't ever remember them kissing, but towards the end of his life, I think he really realized what a wonderful woman Mum was. I think, in his last few days, he finally said to her, 'I really love you.' And I'm sure he did.

There had been all those times when he'd been a right git to Mum and us girls had said to her, 'Just leave him,' but she couldn't, she loved him too. In the last few years, Mum and Dad had done everything together. They'd do the shopping together, go out for a drive together, then watch telly together in the evenings. They still argued, but they belonged together. And, without him, Mum was lost.

'Oh God, I miss your dad,' Mum would say to me when I popped round to see her.

'I know, Mum,' I'd reply. 'Me too.'

It must have been so lonely for her in that house without him. I'm convinced the shock and sadness of losing Dad brought on Mum's Alzheimer's, which was to be the next tragedy to strike our family.

I was devastated that Dad had gone. I still feel his loss now. Whenever something great or terrible happened in my life, I was always straight on the phone to my dad because he'd have words of wisdom or advice. He was always interested in what was going on in our lives, and it is hard not having him around for that.

Obviously, with everything that Dad did to Anne when she was growing up, he must have been sick in the head in some way. I don't know how to explain that. It is so hard because, of course, that was totally wrong. All I know is that I loved my dad. I did.

After Dad's funeral, I again threw myself back into work. But, by then, I was looking more and more pregnant by the week. That Christmas, I finished playing Mrs Johnston in *Blood Brothers*, ready for the birth in April 1999. But in March, just weeks before my due date, I had a frantic phone call from my brilliant agent Tony Clayman. He'd been asked if I could rejoin *Blood Brothers* immediately in the West End.

'They do realize I'm the size of a house?' I said.

'Don't worry, you'll be fine,' Tony laughed.

Somehow the costume department managed to fix my

outfits and everything was fine. I worked up until about a week before the birth.

The day my contractions began, I was more excited than worried. This was the day I'd been waiting for for years and years. It was a long, hard labour though. I struggled through for ten hours with gas and air, but then the baby's heartbeat started dropping. My friend Frank Wilcox was there for the delivery, and he was determined not to take any chances. We decided to go for a caesarean.

Steve was standing next to me, holding my hand, when Frank shouted out: 'It's a girl!' and lifted her up. As he handed her to me, I could see she was the absolute image of her dad. 'Oh my God,' I said, staring at her tiny features. 'She's just like you, Steve.' And she still is. Frank was the first person to see our daughter, and I'll never forget that – he was so good to us through everything that had happened.

We called the baby Erin Kate. I'd seen the name Erin in a book of names and instantly fell in love with it, and we wanted the name Kate in memory of the sister she never met.

Erin was a fantastic baby and I loved motherhood. I breastfed her for seven months, even though I was back at work in *Blood Brothers* after three months. Steve and Erin came with me on tour and it worked. The three of us were together virtually all the time and we became a really tight little band.

Family had always been so important to me, and now I had my own family too. It was everything I had ever wanted.

12.

Linda

Harder Times

We were known as 'Mr and Mrs Show Business'. Brian and I loved everything about the industry. We lived and breathed it. To me, going out and performing was never just a job; it was my life.

Admittedly, it could be tough driving up and down the country to do enough jobs to pay the bills, but then I landed the most perfect opportunity – the chance to play the eponymous character in a show called *Maggie May*.

It was 1986, and the theatre at the end of Central Pier in Blackpool had been completely gutted and refurbished, with the idea of putting on shows every night where the audience would actually feel they were stepping back in time into the old Liverpool docklands. There were flagstones on the floor, old-fashioned lampposts around the building and the bar was behind a traditional pub shopfront. Maggie May was a 'lady of the night' in Victorian times and her job – i.e. mine – was to host the show for the entire evening.

As Maggie, I would be dressed in fishnet tights and a little basque top. I'd start off by doing a song and welcoming the audience, then I'd introduce each of the acts, do another slot later in the evening and then lead a big sing-along at the end.

It was a completely new idea in entertainment, and the audiences absolutely loved it.

For the first year, I did the show seven nights a week for six months. It was exhausting, but great fun. One evening, near the start of the season, Brian and I walked onto the pier more than an hour before the show was due to start and there were loads of people crowded around. 'I wonder what's going on here?' I said to Brian.

'Hope it's not trouble,' he said.

It was only as we walked up the pier that we realized that people were already queuing from one end to the other to get into *Maggie May*. It was like that every night for the rest of the season. It was fantastic.

Brian took his job as my manager very seriously. He looked after everything for me and I didn't have to do a thing. He was in charge of our finances; I didn't even know how to pay a cheque into the bank because I'd never had to do it. And he even did the shopping and kept the house tidy because if I'd been working until late at night, I wouldn't get up until mid-morning, by which time the house was spick and span and there was fresh food in the fridge.

During the day, we'd potter around. I'd do the *Daily Mirror* crossword and he'd do the *Sun* one and maybe we'd go for a walk in the park. Then, in the evening, we'd go back out to the theatre again. Brian made sure everything was perfect in my dressing room and I had everything I needed before going on stage. He'd wait for me until I finished the show and afterwards we might go for dinner or for a drink, and we were rarely in bed before 3 a.m.

Spending twenty-four hours a day together might not suit

a lot of couples, but it worked for us. It was how we wanted it.

Of course, there were times when we got on each other's nerves, and we might have a bit of a row about something once every couple of months, but we soon made it up. I don't think anyone could ever have been as loved as I was by Brian. I couldn't imagine being without him.

The second year of *Maggie May*, Brian said I had to have one night off a week, so I did six nights instead of seven. I couldn't imagine then how I'd coped the previous year.

Maggie May was just as popular the second year, and the year after that, and after that. In fact, every year people just kept coming back. In the end, I did Maggie May for eight years, until 1994, at which point the show moved to South Pier and was renamed *Rosie O'Grady's*, and then I did it for another two years there.

The money wasn't bad, but my wages had to support two of us for the whole year, even though the summer season only lasted six months. One winter I did a touring production of *Prisoner Cell Block H: The Musical* with Paul O'Grady. We became great friends and had a fabulous time. But during a lot of winters, I didn't work at all. Brian never worried me with what was going on with our finances, but I think towards the end of each winter season, before the show reopened, money would be quite tight. I never checked our account or read a bank statement though, so I had no idea how difficult things really were. 'You just do what you love doing and I'll look after you,' was what Brian always told me.

Then, one day, I came back from town with a shirt I'd bought him as a present. 'How much was that?' he asked quite grumpily.

'Only a tenner,' I said.

'A tenner?' he said. 'Linda, we can't afford it.'

So obviously then I realized things were pretty bad, but Brian still shielded me from the full truth. Maybe I should have sat down and demanded to see our bank statements, so I could share the worry of what was going on with Brian, but I didn't. Brian never wanted to worry me with that kind of thing.

Then, in 1995, we missed a payment on the car. Even though Brian told the hire purchase company that I was going to be paid for some work within a few days and they'd be getting their money, they just refused to wait for it. A couple of days later, we were getting into the car when these two guys walked up, took the keys off Brian and repossessed it.

Even then, Brian tried to protect me. I knew he was trying to stave off a bankruptcy hearing because I'd heard him talking about it on the telephone, but I didn't know any of the details. I had a rude awakening one night shortly afterwards, when Brian and I stayed over with Shane and Coleen down south because I was due to perform in a nightclub in London. It was really early the next morning when I woke to hear Shane banging on our bedroom door. The next minute, he was in our room saying, 'You'd better get up – you're bankrupt, darling!'

There it was, all over the newspapers. Because we hadn't been able to keep up our repayments on the car, I'd been made bankrupt. Bankrupt – for seven and a half grand!

That evening I was due to do my show, and I was dreading it because everyone in the audience would know what had happened. Even though it was only a relatively small amount that we'd owed, I felt so ashamed.

The court had immediately frozen our joint back account, so we couldn't even pay to put petrol in our hire car to get to the gig. Coleen lent us the cash. 'Don't worry, Linda,' she said. 'It'll all be fine.'

I wasn't so sure, but I knew that, whatever I was feeling, I still had to go through with the show. Our dad had taught us since we were tiny that you got on and did your job, however you were feeling inside.

I walked on stage that night feeling terrible, as if everyone in the audience was whispering about me. I had to break the ice. 'Hi, everyone,' I said to the crowd. 'I'm Linda Nolan – the blonde one with big boobs, and I have no money!'

The audience clapped and cheered and were absolutely lovely – it made the night a lot more bearable.

The ridiculous thing was that I was made bankrupt on a Tuesday, but on the Wednesday I got £17,000 from a newspaper for an exclusive interview about what had happened. That seemed pretty ironic. We were able to pay off the money we owed immediately and my bankruptcy was annulled, but the feeling of shame and embarrassment took a lot longer to shake off.

For the first ten days after I got back to Blackpool after the story leaked out, I didn't leave our flat. I was mortified. I only did the exclusive newspaper interview because I needed the money they were offering me for it. Trust me, talking publicly about what had happened was the last thing I wanted to do. But when I did venture into town again after the bankruptcy judgement, I was overwhelmed by the kindness of people in the street. 'I'm so sorry,' people would say, 'but keep your chin up. You'll bounce back.'

We managed to keep our heads above water, but then, at the end of 1996, *Rosie O'Grady's* came to an end. I still had pantomime and cabaret work lined up, but it was less secure than a summer season and also meant a lot of travelling to gigs up and down the country.

Sometimes people ask whether I ever thought at that point of giving up show business and getting a 'proper' job, but, no, it really didn't ever occur to me. I'd been performing since I was three years old. I couldn't imagine a life without it.

In 1999, I was booked to do a twenty-week summer season at the famous Layton Institute Working Men's Club in Blackpool. I'd sung there when I six years old with Mum, Dad and my sisters, and here I was again, thirty-four years later. When I walked in, everything looked exactly the same as it had done all those years before. It was like nothing had ever changed. I put together a good show, singing big Hollywood numbers and with my own backing dancers, but I couldn't help but think I was going backwards in life, to the kind of gigs we'd done as kids. And it was always difficult performing in working men's clubs because the club committee would try to decide every detail of the show. They wanted me to sing the ballads and didn't want me to do a sing-along at the end, which I loved. Everything seemed a problem. As the nights went by, I felt more and more miserable.

'Just leave if you're not happy,' said Brian. He always put me first.

'I can't though, if we need the money,' I said.

I rang Bernie, who is always fantastic at dishing out sensible advice. 'Just suck the cheque,' she said. Bernie was right. We needed the money, so I carried on.

But it was putting me in a foul mood and Brian and I were bickering all the time. One night we were driving to the gig when Brian stopped the car. 'If we carry on like this, it is going to tear us apart,' he said.

He was right, and nothing in the world was worth that, so I got my head down and tried to have a laugh and make the best of a bad situation.

Living in Blackpool, we still saw my brothers and sisters almost every day. I lived within a couple of minutes' walk of my sisters, and we were constantly popping in and out of each other's houses. Sometimes, if they were working, I'd help out by babysitting, and I'd loved having the opportunity to watch my nephews and nieces grow up.

For years, Brian and I had been happy on our own. Then, in 1998, Coleen gave us our gorgeous dog, Hudson, after I fell down a flight of stairs and was feeling a bit sorry for myself. 'Here,' she said, handing me the cutest little white ball of fur. 'I thought he might make you feel better.' He was a Bichon Frise, and unbelievably cute. Brian and I took him for walks every day, and he just loved being cuddled.

But apart from Hudson, Brian and I had always been happy just being the two of us. We were so self-contained that we didn't feel the need for a baby to complete our happiness – it was already complete. We did sometimes talk about trying for a family, but it never seemed quite the right time. Brian already had his son, Lloyd, who we still saw regularly, and we also loved spending time with his daughter, Sarah. Brian had agreed to her being adopted by his first wife's new husband when Sarah was tiny, hoping that one day she'd want to know her real dad too, and that is exactly what happened. When she got older, she and Brian started seeing each other again, and they got on fabulously well. Both Brian's kids had his sense of humour, and we loved having them to stay.

For years, I kept putting off having children, waiting for 'when the time was right.' But then, gradually, as I was approaching forty, I decided that, yes, now was the time. I'd maybe left it a little late, but it wasn't impossible that I could still have a baby.

Brian and I spoke about it and although he was happy to go along with it if it was what I wanted, he worried about his age. He was thirteen years older than me and thought he'd never be able to play football in the park with another child.

'But you've got so much more to offer than just kicking a ball,' I told him. 'You've got so much love and knowledge that you could give to a child.'

We decided to go for it. I spoke to my doctor, who suggested I should start coming off the pill gradually and take folic acid tablets to help with a healthy pregnancy.

'Oh my God,' screeched Maureen, when I told her. 'This is going to be amazing. If anyone should have children, it should be you two!'

It really was exciting. It was going to be the beginning of a new adventure for Brian and me. But I didn't know then that all our dreams for the future were about to be shattered into a million pieces.

13.

Coleen

It's Over

I knew the signs immediately. After Shane moved up to Manchester to star in *Grease* at the start of 1996, he stopped phoning me as much, encouraged me to go out with my friends and rarely came home. When he was there, he just wasn't really engaged with what was going on.

I'd been with Shane long enough to work out that he was having an affair. For years my sisters and friends had asked if I was suspicious of the way he flirted around other women or about the rumours that were constantly going around that he was up to no good. I hadn't been worried at all because although I knew Shane could be a flirt, I never thought he'd go any further. He appeared so devoted to me that I didn't think he could be. But, as the years went by, yes, there were times that I wondered. I couldn't prove anything, however. I was left in a position where I believed what I wanted to believe, which was that he was faithful to me because he loved me.

But after Shane went up to Manchester, leaving me and the boys at home in our big house in Denham in Buckinghamshire, it became a lot harder to keep believing that. One night, on the phone, I told him I was going out for a drink with the girls.

'OK, princess,' he said. 'Have a great time.'

I thought to myself: 'Not once in ten years have you told me to have a great time if I'm going out without you. What's going on?' Usually he hated the thought of me being out without him.

On the night of his opening show in *Grease*, I invited myself up to watch and go with him to the after-party. There was no point in waiting for him to ask me to go along! I was standing chatting to Shane's best mate, Chris Gosling, when I spotted a gorgeous-looking girl with long legs who was wearing a tight, white dress.

'Who's she?' I asked Chris.

'Just one of the dancers,' he replied.

'Hmmm,' I thought. 'She is just Shane's type.' It must have been a sixth sense, but I knew that girl spelt trouble for my marriage.

One half-term holiday soon afterwards, I suggested the boys and I should all travel up to Manchester and stay with Shane. 'There's no point,' Shane said. 'We're rehearsing all week.'

More doubts crept into my mind.

The summer holidays came around and I was all prepared for us to go up and spend the whole six weeks with Shane. 'Why don't you go to see your family in Blackpool first, then come over to me,' he said.

But we ended up spending the entire time in Blackpool because Shane never had quite enough time for us to go and stay with him. Something was clearly wrong, so when Shane said he had been asked to extend his contract for another year, I asked him to turn it down. 'Come home,' I said.

And he did. After a year in Manchester, he came home in January 1997 and went back into the West End production of *Grease*. Then, later that year, he landed a role in *Boogie Nights* in London. He was still very attentive to me, told me 20,000 times a day that he loved me and was involved with the boys, but my intuition told me something still wasn't right. The boys were at school and I wasn't working, so I was at home alone most of the time, churning it over and over in my mind.

'I'm not going mad,' I told my best friend, Carol. 'He's up to something.'

Then, one day, Shane Jnr had been playing in the basement of our house when he appeared upstairs holding a photograph. 'Who's this lady with Daddy?' he asked.

There was a whole roll of pictures of Shane and this girl at a house party. They had their arms around each other and in one he looked like he was going in for a kiss. I looked at the pictures and felt like I was going to die. 'Oh, it's just a friend of Daddy's,' I told Shane Jnr, desperately trying to smile.

I never cried in front of the kids, but I was desperate to get them into bed that night. I phoned Carol, who came straight round, and we spent hours looking at the pictures. 'There might be a perfectly reasonable explanation,' she said.

'Yeah, right,' I replied.

When Shane got home, the photos were spread across the dining room table and I was sat having a fag and staring at them.

'What are these?' he said in his usual jokey way.

'Your son found them in the basement,' I snapped.

'What? And this is what you're pissed off about?' he said, looking down at them. Then he launched into this explanation about how the girl in the pictures was the friend of one of the show's dancers and had been pestering him all that night for a photo.

'What about this one where you're kissing her?' I said.

'I'm not kissing her,' he replied. 'It might look like that in the photo, but I was winding her up. It was a joke. Look, if I had been kissing some girl, why would I have left pictures of it in the basement of our house?'

He was right. Why would he have done that? I immediately thought I'd overreacted. He ripped up every single snap and threw them in the bin. 'I can't believe you've sat here all night thinking I would do that to you,' he said, holding my hands.

'I'm sorry, Shane,' I replied. Deep down, I still knew he had done something, but he was telling me what I wanted to hear so, again, I accepted it.

One morning an anonymous letter arrived containing a newscutting with a picture of a woman called Louise Tyler, who was a dancer in *Snow White*. It claimed that Shane was having an affair with her. She was wearing a wig so I couldn't be sure she was the same girl as in the other photos. 'What the hell is this?' I screamed at Shane. But he denied everything. He was insistent that it was a fan trying to split us up. He was so persuasive and although I didn't totally believe him, I kind of accepted what he said anyway. I couldn't just break up my family and storm out when I had no real evidence anything was going on.

For months it went on like that. I went looking for a programme from *Grease* but instead found a publicity shot of a girl who looked like the girl in the photos. But again I couldn't be sure. It was signed with the name Claire. Everything pointed to the fact that he must be having an affair with this dancer called Claire, but I had no concrete evidence.

But from then on I became like a woman possessed. For

month after month I checked his pockets, briefcase, bank statements, cupboards and filing cabinets whenever I could for anything which might explain what had been going on. Because as much as I wanted to believe he was innocent, I was also desperate to find out what he'd been doing.

Then, even when Shane wasn't working, he started going out in the evenings, saying he was seeing his friend because they were writing an album together. Often he'd go out about half past ten at night and not return home until four in the morning. I hated him going out because, deep down, I knew he was going to see another woman, but of course I couldn't prove it. Some nights I would be sobbing on the kitchen floor, begging him not to leave. He would simply step over me and walk out the door.

One day I found a receipt from a jeweller's shop in his pocket. I drove straight round to the shop and concocted a story to find out what the receipt was for. It turned out he'd bought an ornament of a ballerina. It certainly wasn't for me. But when I confronted Shane, he had a perfect explanation. He always did.

One morning I discovered a receipt for a ring and, after a bit of searching, I found the ring in one of his pockets. 'Brilliant,' he said, chucking the ring at me. 'Now you've ruined the surprise.'

Then there were two bills from Interflora on his bank statement for Valentine's Day, but I'd only received one bouquet. 'So I'm not allowed to send my mum a bunch of flowers now?' he said.

The list of suspicions was endless, but every time I confronted Shane, he would look me in the eyes and, without flinching, come up with the most plausible story. The never knowing but always suspecting was like a form of mental torture. Often I'd be crying and would say to Shane, 'Just tell me if you are seeing someone because I think I'm going mad.'

'I think you are,' he would reply flatly.

There was even a story in one of the Sunday papers about a girl who claimed she'd had a one-night stand with Shane while he was on the nationwide tour of *Boogie Nights*. But again he denied everything, saying the girl must have made it all up to earn a few quid.

My sisters were worried that I was making myself ill with my constant suspicions. They had their own concerns about Shane, but had no more proof than I did. 'Can you believe it?' Shane would say to them. 'Your sister thinks I'm having an affair.'

Linda and Brian were staying with us for a while and, one night, Brian took Shane to one side. 'It's none of my business,' said Brian, 'but if you are up to something, it really is not worth it.' Shane went mad at the mere suggestion that he was cheating and said he wanted them both out of the house straightaway. They had to leave, and it was just awful. I was stuck in the middle.

It was hard for my sisters. They could see I was in a mess, but what could they say? Shane and I had been together a long time and we had two kids. They couldn't just tell me to walk out when I still had no concrete evidence that anything was going on.

It went on for months: the suspicions, the denials and the rows. Here was a man who sat me down, held both my hands and said, 'I swear on both my children's lives that I am not having an affair.' When he said that, I felt sure it must all be in my mind. He wouldn't ever say that if it wasn't true. Would he? I really must be going mad.

One night, my friend Carol and I went to see Shane in *Boogie Nights* in Southend. We were walking down a corridor back-stage when a young woman walked past us. 'That's Claire,' I said to Carol.

'How do you know that?' said Carol.

'I just know,' I replied. And I did. Although I'd seen photographs in the past, I could not have sworn to this being the same woman on that alone. But some extra intuition told me that the woman who'd just wandered past me was the one who'd been sleeping with my husband. And I was right. Months later, I discovered that the reason Claire (whose stage name was Louise Tyler) had been at the theatre that evening was to confront Shane about seeing another girl! Minutes before I turned up, she'd slapped him round the face.

'Hiya, Col. Y'alright?' Shane said as I walked into his dressing room. He must have been thinking, 'Oh my God, they're all turning up tonight!' But he never showed a flicker of concern. He always was a brilliant actor like that.

'No, I'm not alright,' I said. 'I've just seen Claire.'

'What are you talking about?' he said, looking totally baffled.

'Claire. The girl you've been shagging. I've just seen her,' I said flatly.

'Oh, you're at it again,' he snapped. 'Will you just give it a rest? I am not having an affair.'

And so it went on. At the time, he was touring with the actress Lisa Maxwell and we all became good friends. She'd ring me quite often and if I ever mentioned anything about Shane cheating, she would always reassure me. 'If he is cheating, I have never seen him doing it,' she said. 'I've never seen him with anyone.'

I heard a rumour afterwards that Shane and Claire had been going out for dinners with Lisa and her partner, but I don't know if it was true. If it was, then I suppose my asking her about Shane put her in a very difficult situation because she was his friend too, but I still felt awkward after that rumour. Lisa is a panellist on *Loose Women* now too, but we don't go on the same shows.

I really was driving myself mad thinking about what Shane was up to during that tour of *Boogie Nights*. I decided I needed something to keep my mind occupied. One day I was walking past a health-food shop when I saw a sign in the window advertising for staff. I walked in and said to the lady that I would like to apply. I was called back a couple of days later for an interview.

'OK,' said the woman who owned the shop, smiling. 'So tell me, are you really interested in health foods?'

'Not really,' I replied, deciding honesty was probably the best policy.

'Oh,' she said, looking a bit miffed. 'Then why are you here?'

'Well, my kids are at school, I'm rattling around in a big house on my own all day, I think my husband's having an affair and I'm going insane.'

'Right,' she replied, starting to giggle. Then we both burst out laughing and didn't stop for half an hour.

She looked at my application form. 'You seem to have forgotten to fill in the bit about O levels and A levels,' she said.

'I haven't forgotten,' I said. 'I just haven't got any. None.'

But despite all that, she offered me the job. I accepted straightaway, and absolutely loved it, but Shane hated me working there. 'What are people going to think about Shane Richie's wife working in a shop?' he'd say.

'I don't care what they think,' I replied. 'I love it.'

My boss was such good fun, but after I'd told her everything that was happening at home, she had a fairly low opinion of Shane. Around the same time, I also decided to enrol for a computer course because I could barely turn one on in those days and thought it might enable me to help the kids with their homework. I loved the course, and that Christmas Shane bought me my own computer.

I'm not sure how I did it, but somehow I plugged the internet into the phone socket and, unbeknown to me, the computer was recording all our calls, thinking they were answerphone messages. One afternoon I turned on my new computer and a sign flashed up saying: 'You have thirty-three missed calls.' I went through them, but they weren't missed calls; they were all the calls we had been making from the house. Two of them were Shane. I could hear his voice, but not who he was talking to on the other end. I didn't need to. Finally I knew I wasn't going mad after all.

'What time are you finishing work tonight?' I heard him say. 'It's just I really need to see you,' he went on. 'I miss you.'

My first feeling was one of absolute elation. That might sound strange, but I'd spent two years thinking I was going insane and for the first time I had proof that I wasn't. I had been perfectly sane all along. 'You total bastard,' I thought. Denise was staying with me at the time and I called her into the room and played her the recordings. We both stood there listening to them in silence. A few minutes later, Shane's friend Chris called with a message from Shane and Denise answered the phone. 'Coleen knows,' was all Denise said.

Ten minutes later, Shane was on the phone. 'I'm so sorry,' he said. He just repeated that over and over again. I barely said a word.

Even then, I didn't think my marriage was over. Whatever Shane had done, I never doubted that he loved me; after all, he told me a million times a day! And now I knew the truth, I felt I could forgive him. I had been unfaithful myself in the past and I thought that with marriage guidance or something, maybe we could rebuild things. Shane came straight home and sobbed in my arms like a baby. He said she was called Claire and had been a dancer in *Grease*. He seemed utterly devastated by what he'd done.

'But I've got to be careful,' he said. 'I can't piss her off because she's threatening to go to the newspapers.'

I thought that if she wanted to sell her story, she should just get on and do it, but Shane said that would be terrible for both of us and he had to let her down gently. Again, I accepted what he said. For weeks Shane wouldn't let me out of his sight and treated me like a princess. On my first day back at work in the health-food shop I told my boss all about Claire. A couple of hours later, a massive bouquet of red roses turned up from Shane.

'I'll just file these under "bin",' said my boss, chucking the whole lot away. She was such a laugh.

But Shane wouldn't give up. He even took me to New York on Concorde and we stayed in the Waldorf Suite at the Waldorf Astoria. He was doing everything he could to win me back, and he seemed so desperate to save our marriage that I really thought I should give him another chance. After all, he'd forgiven me when I'd cheated.

Then, after a few weeks, he became very depressed and I got really worried about him.

'Maybe I just need to get away, to sort my head out,' he said. His friends were going to Monaco for a Grand Prix, so I suggested he go with them, then have a couple of days on his own too.

He'd only been gone two days when my phone rang. 'Hello,' said the woman at the other end. 'You don't know me, but I'm Claire's mother.'

'OK,' I said, slowly.

'Where's Shane?' she said.

'He's gone away for a few days to be on his own,' I replied.

'He hasn't,' she said. 'He is in Tunisia with Claire. I hate to be the one to tell you, but I can't bear the fact that he's destroying my daughter, and he's destroying you. My daughter believes everything he says, but I don't. He has told her you're not sleeping together anymore and are only together for the kids. He says you're just friends. I thought you ought to know that.'

This poor woman was clearly livid and so upset for her daughter. I couldn't help but feel sorry for her. We started talking, and the two totally different stories which Shane had been telling us came spilling out.

'Look, I know you must hate my daughter, but I don't want you to hate her,' Claire's mum said. 'She just believes everything Shane tells her.'

At that moment it was like someone flipped a switch in my head and I suddenly thought: 'I don't want to be with him anymore'. Oh, I still loved him, but I didn't want to be with him after all those years during which he'd allowed me to think I was going mad when I'd been right all along. How could he have done that to me? And all the time he was telling another load of lies to Claire too.

I rang Shane's friend Chris and said, 'Do me a favour. When you pick Shane up from his holiday in Tunisia, don't bring him back here.'

'I don't know what to say,' Chris said quietly.

'You don't have to say anything,' I replied. 'I don't blame you for any of it.'

I told Chris that if Shane came anywhere near the house I'd punch his lights out, in front of the children if necessary. But Shane being Shane, he did whatever he wanted, and a couple of days later he turned up at the house. Of course, I didn't punch him – I wouldn't really do anything that would upset the kids – but I couldn't bear to be near him. I wanted to be at home, with my family, so I took the first train to Blackpool with Jake. Shane Jnr had a football match that he didn't want to miss, so he stayed over at a friend's house.

As the train pulled out of Euston, I could feel the tears starting to fall down my face. It was the first time Jake had seen me cry, and he just held my hand. In Blackpool, I stayed with Linda, and it felt better having my family around me. I didn't want to cry in front of Jake again, and all my brothers and sisters were under strict instructions not to slag Shane off in front of his sons, but once Jake was in bed, they were free to slag him off as much as they liked!

It had taken two years for me to reach the point where I realized that my marriage was over. But now I knew for certain. Mum and Dad were still saying, 'Oh, Coleen, but think of the kids.' But I'd been thinking of the kids for the past two years, when I'd kept accepting his excuses, even though, deep down, I knew they were a pile of crap.

And it wasn't just Claire. I suspected there might have been other girls too, certainly one-night stands, if not proper affairs. And how much longer was I prepared to put up with that for? When I got home, Shane was still in the house and begged me to give him another chance, but I couldn't do it anymore. When he realized I was serious, he agreed to move out and rented a bedsit nearby.

For a while, I was very low. I would get the boys to bed in the evening, then sit on my own in the kitchen with a bottle of wine and cry all night. When you're that low, night-time is the worst because you think the whole world is asleep except you. It is so lonely. I'd go over everything in my mind, time and time again. I knew I didn't want to be with him anymore, but I still loved him, and that was why it all hurt so much.

I couldn't sleep at night, but I'd manage to get myself together in the morning to take the boys to school, then come home and go back to bed until ten past three, when I had to go out and pick them up. Then, of course, I'd stay up the next night again. One week I drank a bottle of wine every single evening, which for me was a huge amount because I don't normally drink. But at the end of that week, I thought: 'Right, I'm on a downward spiral here. I can either sit around getting worse and worse, or I can try to rebuild my life.'

It was very hard though. I felt broken.

I made an appointment with my GP. 'I need some help,' I said as I sat in his surgery sobbing. I told him I didn't want pills if they'd turn me into a zombie or if I'd become hooked on them, but I needed something to ease the pain.

'They'll just take the edge off things,' he said, writing out a prescription. He also suggested that I should try counselling.

'I don't think so,' I said. 'I wouldn't know what to say.'

But after a lot of persuasion, I agreed. Now I think my counsellor saved my life. She made me see things that I had never realized before. The first time I went into her little office, she simply said, 'And what can I do for you, Coleen?' I started crying and didn't stop for twenty-five minutes, even though until then the only other person who'd seen me cry was Jake, on the train.

Finally, I managed to speak and began telling the counsellor everything that had happened. I went back every week for six months, and gradually she made me see things in a more rational way.

'But he does love me,' I kept saying to the counsellor.

'Do you think, Coleen,' she said gently, 'that someone who sees you sobbing on the floor, begging them not to go out, but then steps over you to walk out the door really loves you?' She had a way of making everything seem clearer.

I also felt a tremendous sense of guilt that I was splitting up the family. My parents had stuck together through thick and thin. Dad had hit Mum and, as we'd got older, we'd heard rumours that he'd had affairs too. But Mum had put up with that to keep her family together. Maybe I should be doing the same thing.

'So do you think you should bring your boys up to believe that it is alright for their father to treat you the way he has?' my counsellor asked. 'So that when they do it to their wife, they'll think, "My mum put up with it. Why can't you?"'

'She's right,' I thought. I can't just put up with anything because that's not good for my boys either.

But telling Shane Jnr and Jake that we were splitting up was heartbreaking. Shane and I had made sure that they didn't see us rowing or upset, and we had spent weeks making a show of playing happy families. Shane couldn't handle telling them, so I did it on my own. I told them all that stuff about how Mummy and Daddy still loved them, but sometimes adults couldn't live together anymore. But it was totally horrific. Shane Jnr curled up into the foetal position and screamed for twenty minutes. That killed me. I decided then that, whatever happened from that point on, I couldn't allow anything else to hurt my boys.

They just couldn't understand why we wouldn't all be living together anymore. Later, Shane told them: 'I still love your mum, but she wants to leave.' Of course, I couldn't tell them why I wanted to leave, so they would get cross with me. 'Dad still loves you,' they'd say. 'Why are you splitting up?' They were too young then to hear the whole story, so I just kept telling them how much their dad and I loved them both.

Shane carried on seeing Claire and I was determined that, whatever I might think of her and Shane, I couldn't let the boys see it. But one day I got Claire's number off his mobile and called her. As we talked, for the first time we realized quite how much Shane had lied to both of us. Claire told me Shane had told her that I'd known about their relationship all along.

'No,' I said. 'I never knew anything.'

Then Shane decided he wanted to take the boys on holiday to Florida with Claire. 'OK,' I said. 'But they can't go before they've met Claire. And I want them to see me with Claire, so they don't feel awkward or disloyal.' I knew that if we didn't handle this really well, we could risk screwing the boys up for life. The best thing was if it was all out in the open, and we tried to be friends for their sakes.

So, one day, I invited Shane and Claire round to the house for a cup of tea. Linda was furious with Shane for even considering taking the boys on holiday with his new girlfriend, and none of my sisters could understand how I felt able to invite Shane's other woman into my house. 'How on earth will you manage?' they all said.

'It'll be OK,' I replied. 'I'm doing it for the boys.'

Of course, it was all very weird when Claire and Shane first walked in. We were all stood in the kitchen for a couple of minutes and Shane said, 'I can't handle this,' and walked out, leaving Claire and me alone. 'Do you want a cuppa then?' I asked. I couldn't think of much else to say at first, but maybe being left on my own with Claire was a good thing for us both. I almost felt sorry for Claire that day – she was only just beginning to see what she was letting herself in for.

By then I was certain that I didn't want Shane back. All I wanted was for my boys to be as happy as they could be in a horrible situation. Obviously it was upsetting for the boys, but they adjusted very well. They saw their dad every day and Shane and I made a big effort to always be friendly in front of them. After a while, they probably realized their lives weren't really any different to how they'd been before, and they were fine.

Shane wanted to keep the house in Denham, so I agreed to move out to a new family home nearby in Ickenham. That way, the boys could still go to visit their dad in their old home whenever they wanted.

Soon after I moved out of the house, Claire moved in. We all saw each other quite frequently and, bizarrely, we all managed to get along fairly well. Claire could be insensitive at times, but maybe that was just because she was still very young and it was a pretty unusual situation. 'Shane would never cheat on me,' she'd tell me.

'Oh really,' I thought. If only she knew that he was

constantly trying to get back with me. One day I couldn't cope with any more of her jibes about how much Shane loved her and how he was faithful to her. As if I hadn't heard all that old baloney myself from him over the years! That evening Shane popped round, and I couldn't help it, I started flirting with him. 'I can still have you any time I want,' I giggled.

Well, that was enough for him. That night we slept together.

The next day Claire started up with her 'Shane would never cheat on me' line again. I shouldn't have done it, but I just snapped. 'Well, I know he would,' I said. 'Because he did last night with me.'

I know, I know. It was mean and I shouldn't have done it. But after years of being made to feel so crap about myself during their affair, it was my little bit of revenge. As soon as I realized how hurt Claire was, I felt awful. She walked out on Shane and he went mental. Gradually it calmed down a bit though, and things went back to normal.

But I did feel for Claire. She changed so much in the time she was with Shane. She went from being a vivacious, bright young thing who was always busy, had a great job and loads of friends to someone who looked permanently worried and exhausted, who had no friends and rarely left the house. Maybe a small part of me did think, 'Well, that's what you get for stealing my husband'. But, more than that, I felt sorry for her. She was actually a nice girl from a good family and it wasn't fair that she was being ground down in the same way that I had been. She was like a zombie from it all. It must have hurt her too that Shane dragged his heels for years over divorcing me. For ages, I was desperate for him to get on with it, but he still wouldn't sign the paperwork. It took about five years in the end, and all that time he'd ring me and text me saying: 'Come on. You know you still love me. Let's give it another go.'

Maybe he did still love me in his own way, but I think what he really wanted was for me to admit that I couldn't live without him. It killed him that I could. If I had gone back, things might have been OK for a couple of months, but inevitably there would have been more affairs and he'd have gone straight back to doing whatever he wanted, with whoever he wanted to do it with.

But by then I was long past caring what Shane Richie got up to – because by then I had found the man who really was my soul mate.

14.

Bernie

A New Career

'*Brookside*?' I asked my Tony, my agent. 'Me? Are you sure?'

'Totally sure,' replied Tony. 'Paul Marquess wants to see you.'

Paul Marquess was then producer of *Brookside* and he'd been told about me by one of the show's casting directors, who had gone along to *Blood Brothers* with some of the soap's other crew members when it had been on stage in Liverpool the previous Christmas.

It was a really big deal to play Mrs Johnstone at Christmas in Liverpool, the show's home city. Its producer, Bill Kenwright, normally only lets the West End Mrs Johnstone take on the role, not the actress who has played the part on tour, as I had done. But for Christmas 1999, Bill Kenwright asked if I would take the part. I was dead chuffed. The show's creator, Willy Russell, even came along and said how much he'd enjoyed it.

I didn't know at the time that some of the crew from *Brookside* were in the audience, but I guess they must have thought I was pretty good because it was only weeks later that Tony got their call. It turned out there was a new family headed for Brookside Close, and they wanted me to audition for the role of the mum, Diane Murray.

I'd never really done acting for television before, so it was all very scary. I'd done comedy sketches on a kids' TV show I'd appeared on for a couple of years called *On the Waterfront,* but that was about it. I'd first got into *On the Waterfront* after having been a guest on *Cheggers Plays Pop* a couple of times and thrown myself into the children's games with such enthusiasm that the director thought I'd be ideal for the Saturday morning children's programme.

But *Brookside* was entirely different. There was no joking and fooling around there – it was gritty reality at every turn. It was a great opportunity just to get an audition for a soap opera, however, so I decided to go along and give it my best shot.

When I got to the studios, I was taken into a tiny office, where I sat on a stool and was told to read from a script. It was all to be done in a strong Liverpool accent. Fortunately for me, after years of playing Mrs Johnstone in *Blood Brothers,* a Scouse accent was second nature. I had to read the scene with four different guys and it all seemed to go OK, although I still wasn't convinced they would want to hire an ex Nolan Sister for a part in a Channel 4 soap.

I left the audition and drove back to the theatre, where I was due on stage for a matinee performance of *Blood Brothers.* I'd just pulled up in the car park by the stage door when my mobile rang. It was my agent, Tony.

'Hi, Bernie,' said Tony. 'Good news – *Brookside* wants you.'

'Oh my God,' I said. 'That's amazing!' And I really was amazed. So amazed that I couldn't move out of the driver's seat for ten minutes. I just sat there, thinking about what the job was going to mean. Obviously there would be financial security, which would be incredible, but this was going to be a massive challenge – on telly! And there would be no singing either. I couldn't imagine doing a job which didn't involve singing; it was what I'd been doing since I was two. But it was too good an opportunity to turn down.

Thankfully, Bill Kenwright allowed me to break my contract with *Blood Brothers* and I was able to take the job. I'll always be grateful to him for enabling me to take up that amazing opportunity. And he wrote me a lovely letter too, saying how much he'd loved me playing Mrs Johnstone. He was so kind.

Erin was just eleven months old when I arrived for my first day on set. Steve and I had decided we wanted to be around to look after Erin as she was growing up, and didn't want to be handing her over to a nanny every morning, but the reality was that I was earning more money than Steve, so it was agreed that I would go out to work and he'd stay at home to look after Erin.

While I'd been touring in *Blood Brothers*, I'd been able to be with Erin most of the time, but *Brookside* was going to mean spending long days on set. It was a massive wrench leaving her every day, but to be honest we didn't have much choice; we needed some money coming in. And I knew I was far more fortunate than a lot of working women. I could commute to Liverpool from home, which meant I still saw Erin every morning and evening, and some days I wasn't needed on set at all.

My first few months in *Brookside* were manic. I was on set virtually all the time. My character, Diane Murray, and her family were major new arrivals for *Brookside*. We were even given our own half-hour special to launch our appearance in the show, where we were seen packing up our old house and preparing to move to Brookside Close. My on-screen husband,

Marty, was played by an actor called Neil Caple, and we had three kids played by Steven Fletcher, Katie Lamont and Ray Quinn, who was then only nine years old. I keep in touch with all of them and, of course, Ray went on to be a runner-up on *The X Factor* and won *Dancing on Ice* in the same year Coleen took part in it.

The *Brookside* cast and crew were fabulous. The camera guys, sound technicians, wardrobe assistants and floor managers – they were all brilliant. It really was like one big family, and I was used to big families! I loved it.

In my first episode I had to kiss Neil Caple, which was terrifying. I hadn't kissed anyone other than Steve for years. Before I went on set, I sat in my changing room, telling myself over and over again: 'You are not Bernie Nolan. You are Diane Murray. You are not Bernie Nolan. You are Diane Murray.'

It was only ages after our first kiss that Neil admitted to me that, at the same time, he'd been in his dressing room telling himself: 'She is not a Nolan sister. She is Diane Murray. She is not a Nolan sister. She is Diane Murray.' I thought that was hilarious!

In the end, our screen kiss wasn't too bad, but I was so embarrassed watching it. On the night that my first episode was screened, I invited all my brothers and sisters round to our house to watch it. We all wore those black, curly Scouser wigs and sat in rows in front of the television as if we were at the cinema. They were all so pleased for me, although Steve had to put his hands over his face when I kissed Neil. I think it is very hard for an actor's partner to watch them doing that.

That year was brilliant for me at *Brookside*. I loved the technical side of television, making sure I was in the right place and thinking about how a scene would be shot. And I had memorized so many song lyrics over the years that I never found learning my lines difficult either.

I didn't even miss singing, which I'd thought I might. Occasionally, Steve and I, along with our friends Rick Coates and Martin Kyle, who is an amazing singer, booked ourselves a gig at the West Coast nightclub in Blackpool, and then I got the thrill of performing again. But most of the time I was happy with life in *Brookside*. The Murrays were at the centre of loads of brilliant storylines, including Diane and Marty's attempts to have a baby through IVF. Diane finally got pregnant, but then miscarried the baby. The scenes where Diane and Neil had to flush the tiny foetus away down the toilet were gruelling.

It was only a couple of months after filming the miscarriage that I found myself going through the ordeal in real life.

Steve and I had decided we wanted more children and, again, I fell pregnant quite quickly. We were both dead chuffed. I was still only a few weeks pregnant when I told a couple of people at work, so they knew what was going on and why I was behaving a bit differently.

Then, one morning, when I was about ten weeks pregnant, we were filming a scene and I suddenly felt something wasn't quite right. 'I've got to go to the loo,' I told Neil before running off down the corridor. I'd started bleeding. I knew it was bad news.

When I came out of the toilets, the floor manager was waiting for me. 'Are you OK?' she asked.

'I'm bleeding,' I said quietly.

'Right, we've got to get you to hospital.'

But Neil wasn't having any of that. '*I'm* taking her to

hospital,' he insisted. The floor manager tried to explain that a crew member had to be with me for insurance purposes. 'Well, you can come,' Neil said, 'but I'm taking her.' By then we'd become the best of friends.

We arrived at the hospital and sat side by side in the waiting room. I'd called Steve, but he had to stay at home with Erin. He couldn't leave her, and I certainly didn't want her coming to the hospital but the problem was that, with me and Neil at the hospital together, we were getting loads of people coming up and saying things like 'So, you are husband and wife in real life then?' and 'What are the Murrays doing here?'

I knew I was in the process of losing my baby, but I still felt I had to be polite to them, even though all I wanted was to be left alone. Finally I was called into a little room, where a nurse gave me an ultrasound scan. I lay there, desperately hoping the baby would be OK, even though I knew deep down that it was looking unlikely. After waving the scanner device over my stomach for a while, the woman simply said, 'Yeah, this isn't a viable pregnancy.'

And that was it. That was how I discovered that all our hopes for another baby had been destroyed. I know she was just doing her job but at that moment it seemed so cold, so impersonal. I lay on the couch, uncertain what to say.

'You'll probably lose the baby totally tomorrow,' the nurse said briskly.

It seemed like there was nothing more to discuss. I got up off the couch and went outside, where Neil was still waiting.

'I've just got to pop to the loo and then we can go,' I said, desperately trying to summon up a grin. I felt so sorry for him, finding himself in the middle of my miscarriage. I went into the ladies' loos and totally lost it. I sobbed and sobbed and sobbed. I gave myself a couple of minutes, then pulled myself together and went outside to meet Neil. It didn't seem fair to let him see me like that.

Neil drove me all the way home to Blackpool and the following day he came back again, with his lovely wife Deborah, to return my car.

The timing couldn't have been worse because the next morning we were due to be moving to a new home we'd bought a couple of miles away, slightly closer to Lytham in Lancashire. Steve was distraught that night, but there was nothing either of us could do. We just had to wait for me to miscarry.

The following morning it happened. Steve and I were upstairs surrounded by boxes and suitcases, while the removal men packed up our furniture downstairs. I had gone to the toilet and when I looked down I saw it, a tiny little thing, just like pictures you see of a foetus, but so small. When I came out of the bathroom, I told Steve.

'Oh, OK,' he said. 'I'll go and flush it away then.'

'No,' I said. 'Not yet. I'm not ready for that. I'll flush it when I'm ready.'

Steve went downstairs to tell the removal men that there had been some bad news in the family and we'd be delayed for a short while. Then he came back into our bedroom and I started crying. It was all beginning to feel real at last. I could feel myself go limp and I sort of collapsed on the floor. Steve caught me and we were both on our knees, crying and holding each other, when Erin walked in. She wasn't even three years old, but she put her arm around me and said, 'It's OK, Mummy. She will be in heaven with Kate. And you've still got me.'

It was amazing. We hadn't even told Erin I was pregnant, but I suppose she must have heard us talking. Erin saying that had an incredible effect on me. I thought: 'Yes, she's right. I do have her, and I am so lucky for that. Thousands of couples don't ever get to have any children.'

I still felt raw and empty, but at that moment I was reminded just how much I had to be grateful for. So Steve and I got up and finished packing up the last of our belongings. Before we left the house, I went into the bathroom, said goodbye to the tiny foetus, then flushed it away.

When we got to our new house, Anne and Auntie Theresa came round and took Erin out for the day. Steve and I unpacked a few boxes, but it was a very strange day. I felt numb.

A miscarriage is such a strange experience because one minute you are enjoying this incredible sense of excitement and then suddenly there is a horrible anticlimax. It's like the flat feeling you get after you've had all your family round for Christmas or a party, and then they all go and you think, 'Oh, that's that then.' Except, of course, it is a million times worse.

By then, I'd had a baby that was stillborn, a baby that had survived and a miscarriage, and each experience was entirely different, with totally different emotions.

After Kate died, Steve and I became incredibly close, but after the miscarriage, it felt like we were grieving separately. We did talk about it, because I'm a real one for talking about emotions, but we just weren't together in the same way that we were after Kate. Losing Kate had brought us together physically, whereas this time it wasn't like that at all. Maybe Steve thought I wouldn't want that kind of intimacy after having had a miscarriage. Certainly, for a while, there was a distance between us.

I had a couple of days of feeling very low, but again I looked at the positives in my life, picked myself up and got back to work.

For a long time I really wanted another baby. At first we talked about trying again at some time in the future, but then Steve became worried about it. 'I really don't want you to go through any more upset,' he said one day. 'What if another baby died, or you had another miscarriage?'

I was just as scared of that happening myself. And we were so happy already and were so incredibly lucky to have such a gorgeous little girl that it felt like too great a risk to take. What if we did lose another baby? It would have been horrific, and who's to say whether it might have split us up if it had happened again? Dealing with that kind of loss can put huge pressures on a couple. So I thought: 'OK, let's be happy with this,' and we decided not to try for more children.

In some ways, I do regret not having had more kids, but it wasn't to be. And I am just so grateful that I have Erin and that Steve and I are so happy together.

'I'd really like Bernie to join *The Bill*,' Paul Marquess said to my agent, Tony. 'I think she would be brilliant. I just need to get the character sorted in my head.'

I'd been at *Brookside* a couple of years by now, and Paul Marquess had recently left to become producer of *The Bill*. When Tony told me what Paul had said, I felt really torn. I thought Paul was great, and *The Bill* was a primetime ITV show, which was fantastic. But I felt incredibly loyal to *Brookside*. Everyone there had been so lovely to me that I didn't feel I could just walk out on them.

But rumours had been rife for months that *Brookside* was

going to fold, and Steve and Tony both thought I might be making a big mistake turning down *The Bill* if I was going to be out of a job in the next few months. So, after weeks of heartache, I decided I had to take the plunge. *The Bill* was an amazing opportunity, and if I didn't take it I could regret it for years. But, still, leaving *Brookside* was a terrible wrench.

Phil Redmond was back in charge at *Brookside* by then, and he seemed to take it badly that I was leaving. He didn't speak to me for months in the run-up to my final scenes, and I was written out in a way that meant there would never be any chance of returning.

Diane Murray was killed when a police helicopter crashed into the shops where her hair salon was. But just before the crash Diane had walked out on Neil and their kids. We filmed the scenes of me walking out on my last day on set. We had all been dreading them. Ray Quinn had to cry and was saying to me, 'Why are you leaving? I love you.' And Neil was in the background sobbing. It was so emotional, and then I looked up and saw all the crew crying too. I had to stop then.

'Are you lot having a laugh?' I joked. 'How do you expect me to get through this when you're all crying. Now piss off!'

Thank goodness we all managed to have a laugh then, but it was still incredibly sad. When we'd finished filming, Neil walked me to my car for the last time and stood crying and waving as I drove away. I sobbed all the way home. I really thought I would never get over it. *Brookside* really had been like a family to me, and leaving was awful.

At first I'd thought I could commute up and down to work on *The Bill*, which is filmed at Merton in Surrey. But Steve was adamant that we should stay together. 'If you're going, we're all going,' he said. And he was right. It would have been miserable for all of us to be at different ends of the country.

I started on *The Bill* in October 2002. I was cast as Sgt Sheelagh Murphy, and again quickly found myself in the middle of some major storylines, which meant long hours on set.

After a while, we managed to rent a small house in Hersham, Surrey, from a friend of Linda's. It was a lovely house, but much smaller than what we were used to, and it was particularly hard on Steve, who was cooped up there all day with Erin, who was still only three. She wasn't at school, which meant it was down to Steve to keep her occupied all day long, as well as looking after the house, doing the washing and cooking all the meals. And I was often leaving the house before 6 o'clock in the morning and not getting home until eight in the evening.

When I did get home, it was quite stressful because the house was cramped and we were all living on top of each other. The only good thing was that, because we were living so close to the set, if I wasn't needed for a few scenes, I could sometimes nip home for a few hours during the day.

But Steve was struggling. Being a stay-at-home mum is a very, very tough job, but I think it is even harder for blokes. He was stuck in that tiny house on his own with a toddler, day after day after day. He adored Erin, but it was still very lonely. We had no family in the area and no friends. He even went to mother and toddler groups with Erin, but because he was a stay-at-home dad he found it very hard to make friends with the mums. And for more than a year we never went out together once. There was a lovely little pub at the end of our road, but we couldn't even pop in there for a drink in the evenings because we had no one to babysit.

At *The Bill* I became really good friends with one of the make-up girls, Bridget, and one night she offered to babysit for us. Typically, I ended up feeling really ill on the day we were due to have our night out, but I was still determined to go. I was sick just before we left the house to walk up the road to a little Italian restaurant, then got home two hours later just in time for me to be sick again!

It sounds funny now, but at the time it was really, really miserable. We were stuck in this terrible rut where I'd get in from work feeling exhausted and Steve would be there feeling incredibly low after another long day stuck in the house with a toddler. Some days he wouldn't have spoken to a single adult, so he would want to talk to me, but I would be feeling shattered and worrying about all the lines I still had to learn for the following day.

It must have been very hard for Steve too, because my career was going so well, while he'd given up work to look after Erin and me. I think that situation would be difficult for any man to deal with.

'Cooking, cleaning, washing – this is all I do,' Steve would say to me sometimes. We'd always agreed that we didn't want a nanny, but it reached a point where I thought we'd have to employ someone, to give Steve a break. But he wouldn't hear of it, and that made me angry because I didn't feel he could complain about the situation if he wasn't prepared to do anything to make it better.

But he was just incredibly down. Sometimes I'd dread going home because I was so worried about what kind of mood he would be in. I kept trying to be upbeat all the time, to lift his spirits, but it was dragging me down too. We were both exhausted and, of course, that is when you row even more. I was worried that if something didn't change soon, it was going to split us up.

For months we looked at dozens and dozens of houses on sale in the area around Merton, before finally finding the house where we live now, in Weybridge. Moving into our new home was a turning point and things gradually started to get better at home. There was more space, which meant Steve could have a music room again, and when everything became too much for him, he could go and write songs and play his keyboards and drums. Erin was getting older too, which made looking after her easier. When she started school, Steve had a bit more time to himself. Slowly but surely, things got easier.

But I was still incredibly busy. I was at *The Bill* for three years, and was heavily involved in storylines virtually the entire time. First of all, Sheelagh had an affair with PC Des Taviner, played by Paul Usher, who'd been Barry Grant in *Brookside* before I joined the soap.

Paul could be great, but if he was in a bad mood, it was difficult for everyone. And if there was a Liverpool game on that night, he didn't care about anything other than doing the scene and getting off to the match. *The Bill* was filmed with a single camera, which meant you might have to do the same scene a few times, so they could get close-ups of the different characters. One day Paul and I were doing a scene in the canteen, but when it came to shooting my close-ups over his shoulder, he'd gone and a floor manager was standing in for him.

'Where's Paul?' I asked.

'Oh, Liverpool are playing,' someone said. I couldn't believe it!

One of my storylines was that Sheelagh Murphy's baby that

she'd had with Des suffered a cot death. Paul Marquess asked me if I thought I'd be able to handle doing another plot about a baby dying after what had happened to me.

'Yes, of course I can do it,' I told him. 'What happened to me was real. This isn't real.'

And so I did the storyline, but it did actually take a lot out of me. It was far harder to film than I'd thought it would be. I had a prosthetic baby to hold, and it looked so real. Every night, when I got home from the set, I'd feel quite down and totally exhausted. But I'd pick myself up again – that was what I'd always done – and the scenes were really powerful when they were screened.

The public really warmed to Sheelagh Murphy and people in the street still shout out, 'Hi, Sheelagh,' just as much as they use my real name. I think *The Bill* was the thing that made people think of me as an actress rather than a singer. I felt really chuffed about that.

I made some great friends in the cast and I'm still in touch with Kim Tiddy, who played PC Honey Harman and is now in Hollyoaks, and John Bowler, who played PC Roger Valentine.

On *The Bill* you got paid a regular wage, regardless of how many episodes you featured in – at *Brookside* you only got paid when you appeared. So, for the first time in my life, I was like a normal person, with a fixed amount going into my bank account every month. That gave us a far greater feeling of security. The set was only twenty minutes up the road from our new house, and Steve was back to his old self again. I felt very lucky.

But all good things have to come to an end! Sheelagh Murphy got into an affair with PC Gabriel Kent, played by

Todd Carty. Todd wanted to leave and, in his final months on set, his character was becoming more and more deranged. One day I was called into a meeting with the deputy producer. She was really kind, but it was the usual spiel that a million actors have heard in the past: 'We love you, you're absolutely great, but I'm afraid we're not going to be renewing your contract.'

'Oh, OK,' I said. There wasn't much more to say.

Sometimes, after those meetings, actors reappear and announce to other members of the cast: 'Yes, I've decided to leave. I feel like I've had enough.' But we always know that the truth is that they've been given the boot, so I saw no point in lying. I went straight into the canteen and said, 'I've been given the boot, everyone.'

They were all so lovely to me. I was upset, but I didn't cry. In acting, it is just one of those things.

I had a joint leaving do with Todd Carty, at a hotel next to the studios, and it was a fantastic night. Todd is quite shy and took a lot of persuading to have a 'do', but me, I'd do anything for a party! More than 400 people turned up, and there were screens up all around the room showing our best scenes. Then I sang the Sam Brown hit 'Stop!', which is one of my favourite songs.

It was a brilliant send-off. One of the best nights of my life.

15.

Coleen

Life Begins

I was standing with Maureen in a packed-out bar called West Coast in Blackpool. She smiled at a guy with short blond hair who was standing next to us, and he smiled back. To be polite, I smiled too. But he just turned his back on me, and all his mates sniggered. 'What a pillock!' I thought. It had been hard enough for Maureen to persuade me to come out for the night in the first place. This was all I needed.

It was only later that I discovered that the blond guy had turned away because he'd been telling his mates for years that he fancied me and, now that we'd finally come face to face, he was mortified. And his mates, of course, thought that was hilarious.

Later on in the evening, the blond guy came over to talk to Maureen and me. He introduced himself as Ray Fensome, and we started chatting. I was still a bit suspicious of him, but he was great to talk to and told me he played guitar in bands, touring the world doing shows for big corporate events. Pretty quickly, I could feel he was flirting with me. And I definitely fancied him.

'So, have you got a girlfriend?' I asked casually.

'Er, yeah,' he said, explaining that she lived in London.

'That's fine,' I said. 'We'll just be friends.'

Except he had very different ideas. Later that night, as a group of us walked down the road to a greasy-spoon café for an early-hours breakfast, I found myself being yanked into a bus shelter. It was Ray, and he gave me the most incredible kiss. 'Now that's nice,' I thought. But he was drunk, I was sober and he had a girlfriend – nothing was going to come of it.

Over the next few nights we saw each other a lot in the bars and clubs around Blackpool. Linda babysat the boys for me and, after all the heartache I'd been through with Shane, it felt good to be acting like a teenager again. After my marriage had broken down, I'd had a brief relationship with a guy called Dave, but that had only lasted ten months – we weren't that well-suited and he couldn't cope with me being friends with Shane and still seeing and speaking to him regularly.

That relationship might only have been quite short, but when it went wrong, it really hit me hard. I think I was still reeling from the split with Shane, and I started to panic that I'd never meet anyone again. One weekend the boys had gone to stay with their dad and I was on my own for a couple of nights. It was my lowest point. Everything seemed so bleak. I thought to myself: 'The boys would be OK without me. If I wasn't around anymore, they'd cope.' I'm not saying I was about to neck a pot of pills, but my mind did go to a pretty dark place. Fortunately though, when the boys came home, I realized I could never leave them and of course they needed me. That gave me the shove I needed to pick myself up again, but it was a really tough time.

After that, meeting Ray was fabulous. He made me feel

young and attractive and happy again. We could talk about anything and everything, and laughed together all the time.

Then, one evening, Ray said to me, 'I'm going to finish with my girlfriend. I don't want her coming all the way up here to visit, with me thinking I'd rather be with you.' And he did it. After all the lies and cheating there had been in my marriage, I so respected Ray for being so honest. I think that's when I fell in love with him.

After he finished with his girlfriend, Ray was too cut up to even speak to me for three days. Then, one night, we met in West Coast again and he invited me back to his flat for a mug of tea. 'Would you like to watch a film?' he asked a bit awkwardly, suddenly not quite as confident as he liked to pretend he was.

'No,' I giggled. 'I'd like to see your bedroom though.'

What would my mother have said! We leapt on each other and had the most incredible night. But it wasn't just great sex; it was the fact that we could lie there afterwards and talk for hours about the most important and the most stupid things in the world.

From then on, every night we'd lie awake in his bed until five in the morning, then I'd jump up and dash back to Linda's, where I was staying with the boys. I always made sure I was there when they woke up, even though I'd be feeling like death warmed up!

'You're going to die if you carry on like this,' Linda warned me.

'I know,' I giggled. 'But what a way to go!'

My sisters were slightly less enthusiastic about the speed with which things were moving. Ray had a bit of a reputation around Blackpool as a womaniser, and he'd admitted to me that he'd messed around in the past.

'Just be careful,' said Linda. 'There's no rush, you know.'

But I wasn't rushing. I was falling in love. I knew for absolute certain that this time it was for real.

'How come you've never had children?' I asked him one evening, as we were lying in bed together.

'I never met the woman I wanted to be the mother of my children,' he replied. 'Until I met you.'

Crikey! 'Now there's a line,' I laughed.

'I'm serious,' he said. 'Really serious.'

I knew without any doubt that Ray and I were going to be together for ever. Within a fortnight, we'd said we loved each other. And so the thought of having a baby with him felt absolutely right. Thinking back, that sounds totally crazy, considering we'd only been together a few weeks, but at the time it felt entirely rational. I was 35 and knew it could take a couple of years to get pregnant, so why not start trying straightaway? Yeah, I suppose I could have ended up a single mum with three kids to look after, but Ray was forty-three, desperate to be a dad and I knew he was 'The One'.

We threw caution to the wind. 'What will be, will be,' I thought. But I don't think either of us really thought that it would 'be' quite as quickly as it was. I was in the bathroom of my new home in Blackpool when I did the pregnancy test. It was September – just over two months after I'd met Ray. But there was no doubting the clear blue line on the tester. Ray had gone over to Leeds to visit his mum. 'I'm pregnant,' I told him over the phone. He was so stunned, he missed his turn-off on the motorway on the way home.

Next, I had to tell the boys. Shane Jnr was eleven and was

delighted about it. I knew Jake, who was still my baby, despite being eight, was going to find it harder to cope with. 'What would you think if we had another baby?' I asked him casually one evening.

'I'd run away and never come back and never see you again,' he replied.

'OK.' Well that was clear then!

I waited another couple of days before bringing up the subject of pregnancy again. 'So are you?' he asked, looking a bit puzzled.

I took a deep breath and answered: 'Yes.'

Jake threw his arms round me, then ran out into the street yelling, 'My mum's having a baby!'

From then on, both boys were delighted about the whole idea. My sisters couldn't believe it when I told them, but once they'd stopped laughing, they were all incredibly supportive.

Even Mum was delighted at the idea of a new grandchild. I just had to tell Shane before the story got into the newspapers – incredibly, I'd already had calls from reporters about it. I'd told Shane that I'd met someone a couple of weeks after Ray and I got together, and the two of them had met the previous year, during the summer season in Blackpool, and had got on really well. That didn't mean Shane was delighted by my news though.

'I can't believe you're going out with him,' he'd say in one text message. Then, a couple of hours later, he'd be texting to say he was a great guy. He was just as weird about it when I called to say I was pregnant. After I broke the news, the phone line went totally silent. 'Are you alright about it?' I asked.

'Yeah, yeah, we're really happy for you,' he said quietly. 'Are you happy?'

'Yes, I really am,' I said.

'OK,' he said. 'I'll speak to you later.'

But then, the following morning, he rang and started calling me all the names under the sun. 'You're a f***ing idiot!' he kept shouting. 'You're going to end up bringing up that kid on your own. It would be better if you lost it.' It was such an awful, awful thing to say, but that is the way Shane is – one minute he is all sweetness and light, and the next he can be screaming and swearing like a madman.

I put the phone down and tried to put it out of my mind. But, of course, half an hour after his ranting and raging phone call, he was back on the line again. 'Sorry about that, darling,' he said. 'It was just a bit of a shock.'

I think that, until then, he'd still thought that me and him had a chance to get back together. He'd already been dragging his heels over signing the divorce papers, and that went on for years. He came up to Blackpool to see the boys every weekend and, apart from the occasional row, we had been getting on really well. But even if he had hopes that we might one day get back together, nothing could have been further from my mind.

The pregnancy went well, and Ray was involved every step of the way. He came to the scans and helped choose everything we needed for the baby. He was also brilliant at helping out around the house, as I was being offered more and more TV work. I was a *Loose Women* panellist, and then landed a similar role on a show called *Live Talk* and a Sky health show called *Girl Talk*, so life was certainly hectic.

Ciara arrived ten days late, at Blackpool Victoria Hospital. The contractions were vicious, and I was groaning while sucking like crazy on the gas and air mouthpiece.

'Do something, she's dying!' Ray shouted at one of the nurses. He'd never witnessed labour before and was finding it all a bit shocking.

I pulled the mask off my face. 'I'm not dying,' I snapped. 'It just bloody hurts!'

In the end, I was given an epidural and was even able to sleep for an hour before it was time to push. Ciara popped out at 11.15 a.m. on 19 June 2001. She was 9lb 4oz. with little chubby legs and a beautiful round face. She was gorgeous and Ray couldn't put her down. As for her brothers, they adored their little sister from the start.

It wasn't easy for any of us though. Ray had been catapulted into our home in the position of stepfather, and was having to work out his relationship with the boys. He spent hours with them, helping with homework or playing football, but he could also be strict. Looking back, having that discipline was brilliant for them, but at the time I would sometimes feel caught in the middle of every battle in the house.

All that and a brand new baby to look after too.

And that wasn't all. Ciara was just ten days old when I was invited down to London and, out of the blue, offered a job presenting *This Morning*. Richard and Judy had just left and it was, without doubt, one of the biggest jobs on TV. It was all very scary. Not least because I was going to have to move the boys out of school and back down south again. And I'd be getting up at the crack of dawn every morning, with a new baby. But it was the opportunity of a lifetime and would solve all our money worries, so I had to take it. We had two weeks to find somewhere to live, which was virtually impossible. We couldn't all live in a hotel room, so I was getting desperate.

Then, one day, Shane, who was still living in our big house in Denham, rang up. 'Why don't you all come and stay with Claire and me?' he suggested. I'm sure most people could have thought of a million reasons why they wouldn't want to do that, but it actually did us a real favour – we had nowhere else to go, and it was great for the boys to be under the same roof as everyone that they loved.

Claire was great and even bought the boys new school uniforms before we arrived. But there were some weird moments. On the day we arrived, Claire said, 'Hi, you're sleeping in the guest room; it's to your left at the top of the stairs.'

'Er, yes, I know,' I said.

But Claire was great at helping out with Ciara and the boys and we all got on really well. I was at work at *This Morning* a lot of the time, so it was probably harder for Ray than it was for me because he was left at home during the day. But then Shane did a musical tour and Ray went as his guitarist. I know that would be just way too weird for a lot of people, but at first it really worked for us.

This Morning was a very steep learning curve. I was presenting with Twiggy and, to be honest, the chemistry between us wasn't great from the start. We're quite different people, we'd never worked together before and it was unusual to have two women hosting a show like that together. We were also taking over after thirteen years of Richard and Judy, which was never going to be easy. The response from viewers was lukewarm at first, but we battled on and gradually things improved.

It was exhausting though, getting broken sleep with a new baby and then the alarm going off at half past four every morning. And Ray was knackered too because he was having to do the night feeds and then look after Ciara when I was at work. And although it had been fine staying with Shane and Claire at first, they were starting to have problems and it was getting weirder. They would be arguing in the kitchen, and I'd be sitting in the lounge, and Shane would stomp in moaning, 'This is a nightmare, she is doing my head in!'

Then I'd walk into the kitchen and Claire would be there crying and saying, 'What should I do?' So I was becoming a counsellor for my ex-husband and the girl he'd left me for!

Claire wasn't working, had lost all her friends and was stuck in that big house in the middle of nowhere all day, while Shane was out goodness knows where, with goodness knows who. It was like history repeating itself. I felt really sorry for Claire, but I would be a liar if I said that, deep down, there wasn't a tiny part of me which thought, 'I could have told you so!'

One day Ray said to me, 'We've got to leave now. This is driving me mad.'

It wasn't that they were horrible to us; it just became a bit too weird.

There had been changes at *This Morning* too. Twiggy had been replaced with John Leslie, whom I really enjoyed working with, and the on-screen chemistry between us was much better. Then, after three months, Fern Britton returned from her maternity leave and I was moved onto presenting the Friday slot with John and filming special reports. It was less high–profile, but the reduced hours actually suited me because of the new baby.

We were desperate to move into our own home, so I checked with my boss that my job was safe. When she said it was, Ray and I went ahead and bought a beautiful house in

Ickenham from Maureen's ex-boyfriend, Pete Suddaby. I loved that house; it was gorgeous.

We'd only been there a couple of weeks when Claire turned up one day. 'I'm leaving Shane,' she said. 'I can't put up with it anymore.' The poor girl had waited all that time for the man that she loved, and then the whole thing had turned out to be a total nightmare. Despite everything that had happened, I felt terribly sorry for her. Sure enough, Shane was soon on the phone, in floods of tears about it all. But within a couple of weeks, he met someone new – a dancer called Christie Goddard.

A crisis of my own was just around the corner. One day I got a call from my agent saying that the new editor of *This Morning* wanted to have a meeting with me. I had a bad vibe about the whole thing. Sure enough, when I sat down at the meeting, my editor said, 'Look, I'm sorry, Coleen, but we're not going to be renewing your contract.'

Even though I'd had a feeling there was trouble coming, I was still totally stunned.

'I love you,' she said, 'but the viewing figures for Fridays aren't that good.'

I could feel myself shaking with shock. 'So shall I stay until the end of my contract in April?' I asked.

'No,' she said. 'We think it is better if you go today.'

And that was it. I was gutted. We'd just bought this lovely house and got the kids settled in new schools and now we'd have no choice but to move back up north again. There was no way we could afford to pay the mortgage on our new house with no money coming in. Within days, we were packing up and driving back to Blackpool, where we'd kept our old home. I felt so embarrassed and humiliated, and I was worried too. How on earth were we going to manage?

Just at the time I'd been sacked, I'd landed a place in *Celebrity Fit Club*, where a group of us were put through our paces by that manic American marine Harvey Walden. I went in weighing 12st 13lbs and got down to 11st, but it didn't earn me any money. I did earn £11,000 for charity though, which I was very proud about.

After that, my phone hardly rang with work for more than a year. I got the odd slot on local television, for maybe £100, but that was it. Ray did occasional gigs too, but everything was very hand-to-mouth. For a long time, it was really, really tough. The boys had to settle back into school in Blackpool and Ciara was still just tiny. And we were all still learning to adjust as a family too, which wasn't easy. Ray was very keen that the boys should study hard at school and although now they both accept that if it weren't for him they wouldn't have got any GCSEs, at the time it led to a lot of rows.

Things also became tense between Ray and me about how involved Shane was in our lives. He had got into the habit of ringing me every morning for a chat, but we could be on the phone for up to an hour. As Ray normally stays up very late, he gets up late too, so the calls were usually when he was still in bed. One day he heard me on the phone to Shane again and he just went mad about it, absolutely mad. 'This has got to stop,' he yelled. 'I've got no problem with him calling before nine or after four, when the boys are home from school, but you've got to tell him to stop ringing during the day. Because if you won't, then I will.'

'But he only rings for a chat and to tell me what he has been doing,' I said.

'He's got a girlfriend to tell what he's been doing!' Ray

yelled. 'How would you like it if my ex-girlfriend was ringing up every day? I am not having three of us in this relationship.'

When I thought about it, it was obvious that Ray had a point. I told Shane he could call anytime to speak to the boys, but not just for a chat with me. He, of course, refused to understand Ray's view at all. 'I just don't get it,' he kept saying.

'Yes, Shane,' I said. 'You do get why it's a problem; you just don't want to get it.'

I was still Shane's security blanket and, even then, I think he still wanted us to get back together. One day he said to me: 'If you came back to me, I'd take Ciara on as my own, you know.' But that was never going to happen. I suppose I allowed the daily phone calls to continue for too long because knowing how much he still needed and missed me built up my self–esteem, which he'd totally destroyed when we were together.

The phone calls came to an end, but things were still tricky between Ray and me for that first couple of years. I'm convinced that Ciara was the glue that kept us together at that time and that if she hadn't been here, then we would both have thought at times: 'Sod it. This is just too much hard work.'

Another big issue for Ray was adjusting to living with not just me but my entire family! Ray has got one brother, and they get on great, but they have quite independent lives and aren't totally in each other's pockets. But my family are much more 'in your face' and, living in Blackpool, we would see my sisters and brothers all the time. And that did take some getting used to for Ray, particularly as he felt some of the men in the family had never really warmed to him. He's not really a 'beer and football' kind of bloke, and sometimes he'd prefer to sit with the women at family dos, rather than be up at the bar with the blokes.

But we battled on and gradually things became easier. I liked being back home, near my family, and I was also glad to be there as Mum was becoming a bit forgetful and frail. After years of looking after all of us, she now needed us to look after her.

Then, in 2002, I got a call inviting me back onto *Loose Women*. It was just once a week at first, but there was a smaller pool of panellists, just eight or ten of us, so we got to know each other really well. Kaye Adams was hosting it, and the regulars included Carol McGiffin and Jenni Trent-Hughes. We had a great laugh, spilling our most intimate secrets on air, even if we didn't really mean to do so!

'Do you have to keep telling the world that you're desperate for me to propose?' Ray laughed one day, after having watched me yakking on about my dreams of marriage on *Loose Women*.

'Sorry,' I smiled.

'It just takes the romance out of things a bit,' he said.

I could see his point, but I was desperate to be Mrs Fensome. My divorce had come through and I was free to marry again. I was beginning to wonder if it would ever happen though.

It was my fortieth birthday in March 2005. I woke that morning thinking, 'When I open my eyes, it's going to be there, on the pillow next to me – a little sparkling ring.'

I opened my eyes and looked at the pillow. No ring. 'Ah well,' I thought, 'maybe later.'

Ray and the kids had bought me loads of presents and, as I opened the boxes, I thought, 'It could be that old trick of a tiny ring-box inside a bigger box, inside an even bigger box.' But although all the presents I opened were wonderful, none of them contained an engagement ring. Maybe it was never going to happen.

For my birthday, Ray had organized the most amazing party. All he'd told me was that it was a black tie do and I had to buy an evening dress, so I'd got a beautiful floor-length blue frock. I knew there would be no proposal that night though – Ray was far too shy to do something like that in front of people.

When I walked into the party, it felt like everyone I'd ever met in my life was there. It was fabulous. Then, half-way through the party, a big screen came down. Ray had put together a film which was a montage of my career, then messages from the kids and all my family. Then, right at the end, on this big screen, Ray went down on one knee and said, 'Will you marry me?'

The most amazing roar went up all around the room. I was stunned. I couldn't believe it. I put my hands over my face and started crying. When I took my hands away, there was Ray in the flesh, on his knees in front of me, holding the ring. It was the most perfect moment.

Apparently, he'd already asked the boys for their permission to marry their mum, which I thought was wonderful. Then, at the party, Shane Jnr, Jake and Ray got up and sang McFly's 'It's All About You' with the orchestra.

It was just perfect. After all the heartache I'd been through over the years, I had a gorgeous man who adored and respected me. I had three beautiful children and a good career. Life was truly beginning for me at forty.

16.

Linda

The Incredibly Brave Linda Nolan

Life was good. At the end of 1999 I took over the lead role in *Blood Brothers* from Bernie. It was a major, long-running tour and our money worries were in the past. Brian and I could spend every day together and we were still hoping we might have a baby. In fact, life wasn't just good, it was great.

Then, at the beginning of 2001, Brian complained of feeling a bit run-down. At first we just put it down to the flu epidemic which was sweeping the country – so many people had been struck down by it that it was even being discussed on the news. Then, in the early hours one morning, I woke up to find Brian wasn't in bed. We were staying with Denise and her husband Tom at their house in West Drayton, Middlesex, while I was in *Blood Brothers*. I went downstairs and found Brian sitting at the kitchen table.

'I think I need to go to hospital,' he said. 'I've been coughing up blood.' He was clearly in a lot of pain, and I could tell this was serious. I woke Denise and Tom and we gently helped Brian into Tom's car. But as I went to get into the seat next to him, Brian tried to stop me. 'I don't want you to come with me,' he said. 'It's my job to look after you, and if you come to the hospital, I'll just be worrying about you. Stay here, where I know you're OK.'

'Typical Brian,' I thought. He was always acting as my manager, caring for me and thinking about me, even when he was really suffering.

We were all desperate with worry about Brian, so Tom drove like a madman to get him to the nearest hospital in Hillingdon as quickly as possible. He jumped red lights and broke the speed limit all the way, but it probably saved Brian's life. When he arrived, the triage nurse took one look at him and rushed him straight into the casualty ward, where a doctor diagnosed a perforated ulcer and internal bleeding.

'Thank God you got him here so quickly,' the doctor told Tom. 'Another forty minutes and he would have been dead.'

I sat at Denise's house, worried sick. I rang the hospital and a nurse told me: 'He is very sick and they are going to operate. You should come immediately.'

No matter what Brian had said, I was determined to be with him. When I got there, one of the nurses told me Brian was in 'resus'. I'd watched enough *ER* to know 'resus' meant resuscitation – were they saying Brian was dying? I could feel myself shaking. For the first time in my life, I felt utterly terrified. Just the previous day we'd thought all Brian had was a touch of flu.

When I saw Brian, he was actually breathing OK, but he looked terrible and was clearly very poorly. He was groggy but conscious, and we were able to talk before he went into the operating theatre. 'I'm worried about you now you're here, Lin,' he said. Even as they wheeled him off for surgery, he was still more concerned that I was OK.

We hadn't even known Brian had an ulcer, so the whole

episode was a terrible shock. In all honesty, Brian hadn't really looked after himself for years. He was never a sports fanatic and, over the years, he had become more unfit. When I'd first known him, he would drink occasionally, but in the last few years he had started drinking a lot. I hate saying it, but I think he had developed a drink problem. He wasn't a drunk or anything like that, but he probably did drink more than was good for his health.

When I landed my role in *Blood Brothers* I didn't need a tour manager at my side all the time as much as I had in the past, and that hit Brian hard. I knew I couldn't have done that job without having him there to support me, but he didn't feel as needed. He felt as if he was redundant in some way and, to while away the hours, he drank more.

In many ways, Brian had given up his career for me. He had been a great showbiz agent, and everyone who'd worked with him said so, but he had put all his energy into looking after me. Maybe it sounds a bit corny and a bit silly, but it was what we had wanted. And when Brian felt I wasn't relying on him as much, he found that difficult to deal with.

The perforated ulcer was a wake-up call for us both, and we realized that maybe we'd been taking our health for granted. As Brian gradually recovered in hospital after the operation, we both decided we would have to start taking more care of ourselves.

Brian gave up drinking whiskey because he was worried about the damage it had done to him. He switched to drinking beer, but sadly he carried on drinking more than was good for him. He was still very low in himself, and the silly sense of humour that I'd adored appeared less and less. I kept hoping he was just going through a bad patch and that things would turn out OK in time.

About six months after the terror of the burst ulcer, we were lying in bed one night at Tom and Denise's house when Brian said, 'Hey, Lin, feel this – I've got a lump on my chest.'

I leaned across and could feel it – a tiny, hard lump by his breastbone. It was so small, I thought it was just a spot. But Brian had a bad feeling about it and he made an appointment with the doctor. Again, he refused to let me go with him. 'No, if you come I'll be worrying about you all the time,' he said.

Maybe I should have insisted, but I was so used to Brian protecting me that I let him go alone. The doctor was brilliant and, even though the lump was tiny, he immediately sent him to the hospital for tests and a biopsy. I was worried, but the lump was so incredibly small, just like a pimple, that I didn't really think it could be cancer.

A few days later Brian left the house early to go back for his results. I'd been on stage in *Blood Brothers* the night before, so I got up late and went and sat in the garden in my dressing gown. It was a beautiful sunny day and I was still sitting outside, drinking a cup of tea, when Brian returned home. He walked out into the garden and started weirdly skipping round and round in a circle. It was totally surreal, but I started laughing because it was so out of character and he looked so funny.

He carried on skipping, but then said, 'I've got cancer, I've got cancer' in the way that children shout to each other in a playground. He said it a few times before it really sunk in what he meant. And there he was, still skipping around like a little boy.

'What are you talking about?' I said, feeling myself getting annoyed with him.

Above Coleen's wedding day to Ray. Linda is maid of honour, with Anne's daughters Amy and Alex, and Tommy's daughter Laura as bridesmaids. Erin (*left*) and Ciara are flower girls.

Left The wedding was one of Coleen's happiest days.

Left Coleen's two boys are taller than she is now! From left to right: Shane Jnr holding Ciara, Coleen and Jake in 2009.

Below Loose Women is a great laugh, and Coleen can't help spilling her secrets on air. Here she is on the show with, from left to right: Kate Thornton, comedian Sarah Millican, Denise Welch and Lynda Bellingham.

Above Maureen's boyfriend, footballer Pete
Suddaby (on the right), with our brother Brian.

Right Ritchie, looking like a stud, around
the time he started dating Maureen.

Below Maureen and Ritchie shortly after
the birth of Danny. It's fair to say Maureen
looks happy but shattered.

Top Maureen and Ritchie in Spain, the night before they finally tied the knot.

Left Maureen with Ritchie and Danny, on her wedding day, 13 August 2010.

Above Maureen's two lovely grandchildren Ava (*left*) and Sienna.

Above left Mum and Dad, much happier together later in their marriage than they were when we were growing up.

Above right Bernie with Bradley Walsh in Blackpool 1991.

Left Bernie and Steve on their wedding day, in 1996.

Above Bernie and Steve with little Erin, then six weeks old.

Right Bernie's other family on *Brookside* where she played matriarch Diane Murray.

BROOKSIDE CLOSE

Above Bernie as Sgt Sheelagh Murphy in *The Bill*.

Right Erin, aged six.

Below Bernie in the midst of her chemo and determined to fight. We are all so thankful she won that battle.

The Nolans reunited! It was such an amazing experience to be
back together and performing live again.

'I've got skin cancer,' he said, finally stopping his insane skipping and looking me right in the eye. 'The lump is a malignant melanoma.'

I felt sick. It really did feel as though my world was shattering into tiny little pieces. It was almost as though I was having an out-of-body experience and could see it happening in front of me. 'Sorry about the skipping,' he said. 'I just didn't know how to tell you.'

We stared at each other and I felt tears welling up in my eyes. I could see them brimming in his too.

'I'm scared, Linda,' he said quietly. Then he started crying and I started crying. We sat holding on to each other and sobbing for an age.

Suddenly the future seemed so frightening. The lump was so small that I never doubted Brian would pull through, but we both knew there was a long and painful journey ahead. Neither of us had ever thought about the dangers of skin cancer; people didn't back in the seventies and eighties. We would go on holiday to Turkey or Spain and sunbathe for hours. Brian would go a wonderful brown colour, and we thought having a tan made us look healthy. He had always had a mole on his back, which I kept a close eye on, but we'd had no warning at all about the lump on his chest.

Over the next few days, we both spent a lot of time talking – and crying. Denise and Tom were fabulous to us, and they rang the rest of the family and told them what was happening. Everyone rallied round.

One day Brian and I were sat there doing the crosswords together – me the *Mirror*, him the *Sun*, just as usual – when he suddenly said, 'I don't want to die, Lin.'

'You're not going to die,' I said. And I really believed it. He was such a strong man that I thought there was absolutely no way this would finish him off. He was sent to the Royal Marsden, which specializes in cancer, and the doctors said that rather than cut out the lump, they were going to blast it with chemotherapy. With hindsight, maybe he should have had it cut out, but we just followed the experts' advice.

By then I had moved on to a touring production of *Blood Brothers* and we were constantly moving around the country, but Brian wouldn't let me do that on my own, so, despite being seriously ill, he travelled with me to every venue. He even arranged to have his chemotherapy at different hospitals as we travelled around. I'm not sure how he got the doctors to agree to it, because it meant there was no continuity in his care, but that didn't bother Brian. What bothered him was making sure I arrived at each theatre on time and that my dressing room looked lovely before a show. He really did always put me first.

One night we arrived in Glasgow and he spent the evening preparing my dressing room, then was up again at the crack of dawn, looking for the city hospital where he was booked in for chemo. A few weeks later it was Manchester, then Nottingham, then Sunderland – all over the place.

The chemotherapy really got Brian down. He would be irritable and withdrawn, and sometimes he'd snap at me over the smallest thing. And he'd never been like that before. For years, no matter what was going on, he would always be bright and cheery, and he made me laugh every single day. Even when he started to feel a bit more down, he still made an effort to lift his spirits for me. But the chemotherapy brought him crashing down. I could tell he was getting more and more depressed. At times I could feel him dragging me down too, but I had to keep us both going.

'You're going to be OK,' I'd tell him time and time again. 'You have to be positive.'

But he was finding that more and more difficult. He would spend entire days sitting in his armchair, barely talking to me. That was hard for both of us. 'Why don't you come with me to take Hudson for a walk in the park?' I'd say.

'No, I don't want to,' he'd reply.

Sometimes that would really get to me. 'I love you, Brian,' I'd say, 'but I can't sit around here and let you drag me down too.' And I'd pull on my coat and stomp out the front door. I'd feel terribly guilty afterwards. Brian had supported me every moment we'd been together, but now, when he needed help, he didn't seem to want it.

His doctors suggested antidepressants, but, like a lot of men, he didn't want to admit there was a problem. And so it went on. Every now and again, I saw glimmers of the old Brian, and he would still make me laugh, but most of the time he was desperately low.

Then Brian's body started to reject the chemotherapy. It is such an horrific treatment and it was battering Brian each time he had it. On the second and third day after a session, he wouldn't be able to get out of bed. He was shattered. He had three courses of chemo and each one involved six sessions, one every fortnight. That went on for about a year, and it was gruelling. The doctors finally said that Brian just couldn't phys-ically take any more chemo, but they were hopeful that what he'd already had would be enough to stabilize his condition.

I'd hoped that, with the chemo over, Brian's spirits might lift. But he seemed to have aged quite suddenly and remained tired and depressed. His legs became very swollen and sore, and he found it difficult to walk.

We carried on like that for the next few years. I was so busy working and worrying about Brian that when I first felt a hardening lump in my left breast I put it out of my mind.

That probably sounds total madness, but I was dashing around from town to town in *Blood Brothers* and there never seemed time to even make a doctor's appointment. I'm not stupid, I knew exactly what it could be, but I chose not to think about it.

I'd first found a lump in the same breast when I was nineteen and had been terrified. But then my doctor had said it was simply a blocked milk duct and nothing to worry about. The lump had always remained, but during 2005 I could feel it was getting bigger and harder.

'I really must get this checked out,' I'd think when I ran my hand over it while putting on my bra in the mornings. But then something would happen and I'd never quite get round to it. I was busy, I honestly was. And with Brian so poorly, I felt I couldn't be sick too. Maybe, if I'm brutally honest, I was just scared of what the doctors might tell me.

I'm certainly not proud of putting off getting myself checked out for such a long time. Now I just think I was a total idiot, and I'd tell anyone else to get themselves down the doctor's the moment they find a lump. I told Coleen I'd found a lump, and she nagged and nagged me to go and get it examined. 'Have you made that appointment yet?' she'd say every time she rang up.

'I'll do it tomorrow,' I'd reply.

The next day: 'Have you made that bloody appointment yet?'

'Yeah, I'm just about to,' I'd say.

Then, one morning, she rang up fuming. 'If you don't fix up to see the doctor today, then I'm going to make the appointment myself and come round and drag you there.'

I finally went to the doctor in Blackpool in September 2005. As he ran his hands over the lump, I could see the frown forming on his face. 'Yes, you definitely need to get this investigated further,' he said. 'I'll refer you for a mammogram.'

But I was about to go away again with *Blood Brothers*, and after that I was going over to Belfast to do panto. I'd landed the role of the Wicked Queen in *Snow White*, which would be full-on for the whole Christmas period. Brian and my sisters were all nagging me to get myself properly tested, but all I could think about was staying well to help support Brian. So I put off the mammogram for another four months. Looking back, I can't believe I was so silly.

Finally, one Wednesday morning in January 2006, while I was still in panto, I went to the Belfast City Hospital for a mammogram and a three-needle biopsy. 'I think you probably do have breast cancer,' the doctor told me, before even sending off the sample for testing.

'But it might not be,' I thought to myself. 'It could be just another blocked milk duct.' I was desperately trying to remain positive. And, to be honest, I didn't have time for worrying or feeling sorry for myself. That day I still had to do another two panto performances.

In the evening Brian rang his cancer-care specialist at the Royal Marsden Hospital in London to talk about my symptoms. 'Don't worry yet,' she said. 'The doctor was probably just guessing. They don't give you the news that you've got cancer unless there is a specialist Macmillan nurse there.'

On the Friday, we returned for my results. I only just managed to squeeze in the appointment between a matinee and evening show of the panto. Brian and I introduced ourselves at the reception desk of the ward. A couple of minutes later, a lady walked up to me and said, 'Hi, Linda, pleased to meet you. I'm your Macmillan nurse.' Brian and I turned to look at each other and smiled. So, this was really it then.

The nurse took us into an office, where my consultant, Mr Whitaker, gave us my diagnosis. It was bad.

I had very aggressive, stage-three breast cancer (it only goes up to stage four), and the lump was about four inches long. When I got back to Blackpool, my cancer nurse told me the lump was the size of a small courgette. Needless to say, we've never eaten courgettes in our house since! I was going to need a full mastectomy of my left breast and chemotherapy.

As the consultant spoke, I could feel Brian's hand gripping mine tighter and tighter. I looked across at him and he was deathly pale. Mr Whitaker's words seemed to be bouncing around the room, without me actually being able to hang on to any of them.

'So,' he said, after a while, 'do you have any questions?'

'Will I have to have chemo?' I asked, almost automatically. I'd seen what Brian had been through and was terrified of having to cope with that myself. And, although it sounds crazy now, when I should probably have been thinking about whether I was going to live or die, all I could think about was whether I was going to lose my hair.

'Yes, you will be having chemotherapy,' Mr Whitaker said. 'Your cancer is very aggressive. We are going to throw at it everything that we can.'

Brian and I walked out of the room, still gripping each other's hands. We went down in the lift in total silence. When the doors opened, we stepped out, and I leant back against a wall. Brian put his arms around me. 'This doesn't matter,' he said. 'This isn't what we are about. Cancer isn't us.'

And then we both started to cry, and we clung onto each other for ages. He was right. Brian and I were about laughing and having fun and showbiz and music. We weren't about hospital wards and pills and sickness. But whether we liked it or not, cancer was now a big part of both our lives.

I phoned Coleen as we left the hospital. 'It's cancer,' I said.

'Oh God, I'm so sorry,' she replied.

I couldn't face calling each of my brothers and sisters and telling them the same news, so she offered to ring them all for me.

Two hours after I'd been told I had an aggressive stage-three cancer, I was back on stage. Fortunately I was the Wicked Queen, so I didn't have to smile a lot! Brian hadn't wanted me to go on, but I couldn't see any point in taking the night off. Whether I was working or not, the cancer was still there, and sitting at home weeping over a cup of cocoa wasn't going to get rid of it. Mum and Dad had always taught us that the show must go on, so that's what happened.

I knew I could hold it together, so long as I didn't see Brian at the side of the stage. 'Please don't come to the theatre tonight,' I said. So, for the first time in about a quarter of a century, Brian wasn't there in my dressing room, tidying things up and keeping it just-so while I was on stage. It was the only way I could get through it. No one else at the theatre knew what was happening and, that way, I could almost pretend that it wasn't.

The following night was our last performance of the panto and afterwards there was a big party. It was the last thing I felt like, but Brian and I went along and broke the news to a couple of cast members who we'd grown really close to over the past few weeks. The following day we returned to Blackpool, where we moved in with our friends Graham and Sue. We had been thinking about moving to London for a while, and didn't have a permanent base because I'd been doing so much touring, but staying with Graham and Sue was like home from home.

It was great to be back in Blackpool, and I immediately felt happier being closer to my family. My eldest sister Anne had gone through breast cancer in 2000 and she was very supportive. But I kept thinking how poorly both she and Brian had been during chemotherapy and that was scary. I talked to Anne loads about how she had felt, and she explained to me all the different stages of treatment and how I might feel.

Back in Blackpool, I had another appointment at the hospital. 'Could you just put this gown on, then pop up onto the bed,' said a nurse. Sometimes I felt my entire time in hospital was spent 'popping' from one place to the next!

As I lay down, my right boob slipped down to the side, as most women's boobs do at that angle, but my left boob just stayed exactly where it was. The lump must have been holding it up.

I still couldn't quite believe what was happening. I kept thinking that maybe the doctors had made a terrible mistake and were suddenly going to announce that there was nothing wrong with me after all.

'Do you think I should get a second opinion?' I asked my Macmillan cancer nurse when I called her one evening. She was amazing, always at the end of the phone when I needed her.

'Of course, you could do, Linda,' she said. 'But you would be wasting your time. You have got this cancer and you've just got to focus now on getting rid of it.'

The surgeon said he could carry out a mastectomy the following week, but that seemed way too early. I still needed to get my head around the thought of losing my breast and all the treatment that would follow. He said that waiting another few weeks at this stage wouldn't make much difference, so I was booked in for 21 February. In the meantime, I went back and did two more weeks in *Blood Brothers* in Coventry and Nottingham.

One evening I invited the rest of the cast along to my dressing room after the show. 'Having a party, Linda?' they laughed as they crowded into the room.

'Er, no,' I said. 'Look, I'm only going to tell you this if you promise NOT to be nice to me.' They all nodded, probably thinking I'd gone totally mad. 'I just wanted to let you all know that I'm going to be off work for a while,' I went on. 'I've got breast cancer.'

The room went horribly quiet for a few moments, and then everyone was just great, hugging and kissing me, although still under strict instructions not to say anything too nice that would send me off into floods of tears.

It was a relief getting it all out into the open because then I could make a joke of it. When it was mobbed with people backstage, I'd yell out, 'Mind the way, woman with breast cancer coming through!' Trying to keep laughing was my way of coping. But at times, when I was all alone and thinking about what was happening, it was just horrible. I now knew exactly what Brian meant when he'd said, 'I'm scared.' The last song I had to sing every night in *Blood Brothers* was 'Tell Me It's Not True', which could really get me blubbing, but I always managed to hold it together until I was off stage and back in my dressing room.

Then the story was picked up in the local newspapers, and soon it felt like the whole world knew I was ill. The terribly ironic thing about that was that when the story appeared in a newspaper in Coventry, they used a picture of Bernie by mistake – none of us could have imagined that Bernie really would be fighting breast cancer too, just four years later.

My dressing room began to look like a flower shop! I also got hundreds of cards from both friends and total strangers, wishing me good luck for the operation.

One afternoon we were in the car when Brian's phone rang. 'Can you answer it?' he said. I huffed a bit, annoyed that Brian wasn't using his hands-free. I really didn't fancy talking to anyone just then. 'Hello,' I said, maybe a little bit brusquely.

'Hi, Linda,' said this incredibly smooth American voice. It sounded familiar, but I couldn't quite place it. 'It's Donny Osmond here,' he said. 'I just wanted to wish you good luck and let you know that we are all praying for you.'

I nearly dropped the phone in shock! I'd always loved Donny, ever since my bedroom wall was covered floor to ceiling with his face. I'd even met him a couple of times over the years, on which occasions I'd turned immediately from a confident, professional woman into a giggling teenager. But to hear him on the phone was just amazing.

We had a little chat and after we said goodbye, I couldn't stop shaking for ages. Of course, it was Brian who'd fixed up for Donny to call. He knew how much that would mean to me.

Everyone I met was amazing. But it can be a bit strange when you have cancer. People would stop me in the street and say, 'Ooh, you are incredibly brave.' Everyone seemed to say the same words: 'incredibly brave'. It made me laugh, really, because I wasn't brave at all, let alone incredibly so. I didn't have cancer by choice and I was just doing what the doctors told me to do. I was simply getting on with it, like anyone else would do!

The operation was set for a Tuesday, so the weekend before there was a big family party round at Coleen's house. When we got there, she had pinned an A4 sheet to her front door saying, 'A gathering for the incredibly brave Linda Nolan'. Oh, we did have a laugh!

I was due to check into hospital on the Monday night, but Brian and I hated being apart, so he rang up and asked if I could just go early on the Tuesday morning instead. The doctors agreed, so long as I went to get myself marked for the operation the previous day. So, on the Monday, I lay on a table while they drew big arrows all over my left boob, to show where they were going to slice it open.

Afterwards, Brian and I met up with Coleen and Ray and went for a Harvester meal. I pulled my top down and showed Coleen the arrows. 'Well, I don't think the surgeon will miss that,' Coleen laughed, looking at the thick, black marker–pen lines.

I was terrified about what it would be like to be so phys-ically different. I'd always had big boobs – 38D – and loved low-cut tops and my 'up and at 'em' bras, as Brian called them.

And Brian had always been a boob man; he admitted it himself. How could he possibly still find me attractive in the future?

On the Tuesday morning Brian came with me and held my hand all the way to the doors of the operating theatre. 'This doesn't change anything,' he said before he had to go. 'What we've got isn't about your boobs or your fabulous hair. I love you for you.'

When I woke up, I was in a room all on my own. There was a white sheet lying across my chest. I was still feeling really groggy, but I reached out and lifted up the sheet to see whether it had really happened. Yes, the left side of my body was totally flat, with just a bandage where my boob had been. 'Oh, it's gone then,' I said to myself, quite matter-of-factly.

A couple of minutes later, Brian came in, and just behind him was Coleen. 'Oh, I was expecting you to be swathed in bandages, looking all pale and wistful,' said Coleen, almost sounding disappointed. 'But you look fine.'

Thanks, Col!

Later, when a nurse came in to change my dressings, she asked if I wanted to look at the scar. 'No thanks,' I said, at the same time thinking, 'Why not, you idiot? What are you scared of?'

The cancer had been worse than they had initially thought and they'd also had to remove fourteen cancerous lymph nodes from under my armpit. But I felt relieved. To me, I didn't *have* cancer any more. I'd *had* cancer, but it had been cut away. Now it was just a case of having chemo, to make sure it never came back. There was obviously a long road ahead, but it was a road to recovery. Despite everything, I remained pretty optimistic.

The day of the operation, I started writing a diary. It helped to put down on paper everything I was feeling. I ended my first entry with the words 'Wish Mum and Dad were here.' Mum had always been so good when we were poorly as kids, wrapping us in blankets on the sofa with a glass of Tizer and a comic. But by then Mum was so poorly with Alzheimer's that she didn't even recognize me. Maureen will explain all about that horror in a later chapter.

For the next few days, each of my brothers and sisters turned up to see me, gave me hugs and ate my grapes! It was like they were in some kind of tag team. Anne would bring some grapes, Maureen would eat them. Brian would bring some grapes, Coleen would eat them. And so it went on for days. Denise was away working on a cruise at the time, but she phoned me all the way from Vietnam. It really helped to know that the 'Nolan cavalry', as Brian called it, was right behind me.

Two days after the operation, it was my forty-seventh birthday. But that morning I think the reality of what I'd been through – and what was still to come – really hit me. My phone rang in the ward early in the morning. At the other end, it was Brian, singing 'Happy Birthday' in the style of an opera singer (one of his little jokes!). All of a sudden, I couldn't stop crying – and it wasn't because of his singing! He got straight in the car and jumped every red light on the way to the hospital, to see me as quickly as possible. When he turned up on the ward, his face was deathly white with worry, but he was still clutching all the 'Happy Birthday' balloons he'd bought me. What a sight!

The girls bought me some beautiful underwear and my Macmillan cancer-care nurse showed me how to fit sponge padding into it. Then Brian gave me a really pretty top. They were fabulous gifts because they made me realize I would still be able to wear nice clothes in the future, even if I did only have one boob.

David Essex sent a card and there were bouquets from Status Quo's Francis Rossi, who knew Brian from way back when he was in a band. There was also a massive bunch of flowers from Paul O'Grady, who phoned me in hospital too. Everyone was so kind.

Brian spent every moment he could with me, and soon he had sorted out my hospital room, just like he used to organize my dressing rooms, with cards and pictures Blu-tacked up on the wall and my clothes neatly folded away. He looked pale and worried all the time though, and I was worried that it was exhausting him. But I'm being totally honest when I say that every single time he walked into the room, I'd still be struck by how much I fancied him.

I was in hospital for five days. The night I was discharged we went home to Graham and Sue's and Brian cooked us all a celebratory dinner of lobster followed by beef Wellington. In our bedroom he had laid out all my perfumes, cards and candles, just like he did in my dressing room. That night I was able to sleep cuddled up to Brian again. That worked far better than all those sleeping tablets they gave me in hospital.

At home, I could have a proper look at my boob – or the place where it used to be – for the first time. There was a neat scar about four inches long across my chest. And nothing else. It was totally flat. It looked vile. Before I'd had the operation, the only thing I'd worn in bed was a spray of perfume! But now each night I'd turn away from Brian and when I took my bra off, I'd immediately cover myself up in a baggy T-shirt. I couldn't bear the thought of Brian seeing me naked, but that really hurt him.

'Do you think I won't love you because you've had a breast removed?' he said to me one night.

But it wasn't that. I just felt too embarrassed and ugly to show him the scar. It was weeks later when, one night, we were talking as I got ready for bed and I undid my bra in front of him without even thinking. 'That's amazing,' he said.

'What is?' I asked.

'You're not hiding from me anymore,' he said smiling. I hadn't really been hiding. I just hadn't felt ready to share my scar with anyone.

When we'd arrived at Graham and Sue's house, they were waiting for new sofas to arrive and were having to use sun loungers in the meantime. Coleen decided I needed a bit more comfort, so she bought me my own armchair. In the evenings we'd all sit around together, me like Norma Desmond in *Sunset Boulevard* in my grand armchair and the rest of them on sun loungers. It was hilarious!

Sometimes at night I would wake up and have trouble breathing. I'd be unable to catch my breath and start hyper-ventilating and crying. I knew the chemotherapy was due to start soon and was having panic attacks. I felt so scared. Not of dying, because that wasn't going to happen, but I was scared of how the chemo would make me feel and of losing my hair and the whole bloody thing. Brian would wake up and find me having 'one of my moments'. He'd hug me until I calmed down and finally went back to sleep.

Six weeks after the surgery, I had my first bout of chemotherapy. Brian wanted to come down for the treatment, but I wouldn't let him. 'If you come, Brian, I'll just be a total baby,' I said. 'I'll meet you later. I'll be fine.'

But by the time I met my cancer nurse, I was blubbing. She

asked what I was particularly worried about, and again it came back to my hair. She suggested I should try wearing a cold cap before, during and after the chemo. She explained that it was like an ice-cold swimming cap which freezes the hair follicles and prevents the chemo drugs from killing them. I decided to give it a go.

I hated the chemotherapy, but I loved the idea that each time I went in the drugs were killing a little bit more of the cancer. Cancer and I were not a team – and we were never going to be either!

A couple of nights after that first bout of chemo, I woke up feeling really sick. I started throwing up and was sick twenty-two times before morning. I honestly thought I was going to die. I was never that ill again though, and the hospital thought it must have been a bug.

My chemo took place every three weeks and it had a horrible effect on me. Sometimes I would be vile to Brian. There wasn't any reason for it; I just needed to lash out at someone and he was closest. The only good thing was that he had been through exactly the same thing himself, so was able to understand exactly how I was feeling and why I was being so unreasonable. At times we had terrible rows because I was being so difficult to live with. But beneath all that, we loved each other so much. We loved each other far too much for something like cancer to part us.

Between my chemo sessions, we spent the days pottering around, taking Hudson to the park, doing the crossword and resting.

At the end of May 2006, just over three months after my operation and soon after I'd started having chemo, I went back to work in *Blood Brothers*. If I wasn't working, then Brian wasn't working either, and we needed the money. And we both needed something to do too. We'd never been the type of couple to just sit around, and we were both going a bit stir crazy.

Most of the time I was able to manage at work absolutely fine, but on days six and seven after chemo, I would always feel really rough, as though I had a really bad bout of flu. All my limbs would ache and I'd be barely able to get out of bed, but I'd still summon up the energy to go to the theatre in the evening.

On stage, I sometimes got the feeling people in the audience were whispering about me. Maybe it was my paranoia, but I was sure they'd be saying, 'Oh yes, it's definitely the left boob that's gone, you can tell!' Or maybe they were nudging each other and whispering, 'Poor thing. She does look rough. But she's been *incredibly* brave!'

I came to hate my body. I felt like a freak with only one breast, I was putting on weight because of the amount of drugs I was on and, despite the cold cap, my hair was falling out. My eyebrows and eyelashes went too. To top it all, I wasn't allowed to have my hair coloured, so what hair I did have was looking very grey. It was only later that I discovered my friend Sue would follow me round the house picking up strands of my hair from the carpet and sofas. She knew I'd be devastated if I saw them.

I had been the 'Naughty Nolan' with the risqué photo sessions and low-cut tops, but now I looked like an old woman!

The Blackpool Victoria Hospital didn't do immediate breast reconstructions after mastectomies then, like they do at a lot of hospitals now. I think that was a shame because the longer it went on, the more I hated having just one boob. And while the chicken-fillet prosthesis thing which I was given to slip inside my bra might have looked realistic, it didn't do much to boost my confidence.

Before I'd started on the chemo, Coleen's husband Ray had taken me to meet an old friend of his who made wigs in Leeds. She created the most amazing wig for me and cut it to fit my hair, but I still cried when I saw it on. It was such a visible reminder of what was most likely going to happen to me.

I only ever wore the wig on stage or for photo shoots because I'd kept enough hair to just about manage the rest of the time. When I wore the wig on stage, I was permanently terrified it would fall off. At the beginning of *Blood Brothers*, my character, Mrs Johnstone, does a jive with a teddy boy, and I'd always had problems with my real hair getting caught in his buttons. 'If that happens with a wig and it flies off, it will be the end of me,' I told the rest of the cast. And that time I wasn't joking.

In July 2006, we took *Blood Brothers* to Jersey, but I still had to return to Blackpool every three weeks for chemotherapy. Halfway through my eight sessions of chemo, I'd also started on eighteen sessions of Herceptin, the so-called breast cancer wonder drug that everyone was talking about. Like chemo, I had to have Herceptin pumped into me once every three weeks. It was a boiling summer and I was also suffering hot flushes because the cancer treatment had sent me hurtling into the menopause. Feeling that hot and wearing a wig on stage every night was unbearable. I was also pencilling in my eyebrows because they'd all gone, but then I was sweating so much that the pencil lines ran down my face.

On top of that, a weird side effect of the drugs was that I got terrible blisters on the balls of my feet. They were agony and I was in so much pain, I'd have to sit down in rehearsals.

Every night it was getting harder and harder to get through the show.

'I don't think I can do it anymore, Brian,' I said to him one night.

'But you've been through so much,' he said, hugging me. 'Don't give up because of a little thing like this.' And, of course, Brian, as ever, gave me the strength to keep going.

My moods were all over the place and Brian was normally on the rough end of my temper when it all became too much for me. Once I sent him out to the shops to get stuff for a roast dinner. 'And don't forget the Aunt Bessie's Yorkshire puddings,' I shouted out to him before he left. 'And some jelly!'

But when he returned there were no frozen Aunt Bessie's. Instead, there was a sachet of Yorkshire pudding mix. And the jelly he'd bought was orange flavoured. Normally that's the sort of thing which wouldn't even register with me, but on this occasion I was furious. I was just angry with the world.

'Orange jelly?' I screeched at him. 'Bloody orange jelly? Who buys bloody orange jelly?'

'But I thought you liked oranges at the moment because your taste buds aren't working properly,' he replied, obviously a bit confused at my massive overreaction.

'And how are you going to make Yorkshire puddings in this oven?' I said, pointing at the clapped-out little cooker in our rented flat.

'I'm just going to walk away from this, Lin,' Brian said quietly.

But he'd only got halfway across the room when I lobbed the bag of batter mix right at him. Fortunately, it missed him by a fraction, but it hit a wall, bursting open and spraying batter all over the carpets. I swear, if there had been a knife to hand, I would have thrown that at him too. It was utterly out of character, but the chemotherapy combined with the menopause had turned me into a woman possessed.

I stomped into our bedroom, lay down on the bed and slept for six hours straight. At least now I was able to understand why Brian had been so moody and snappy with me when he was having chemo. Sometimes the treatment just makes you feel angry, and it's the people closest to you who bear the brunt of that.

In August of that year we celebrated our twenty-fifth wedding anniversary. We decided to go to Paris because we'd never been back since our honeymoon. I had my chemo two days early, so we could fit the trip in, but it meant that I spent the first day of the holiday lying in our hotel room, feeling rotten. 'Oh, Paris is lovely on your own,' Brian laughed after going out for a walk.

It only seemed like yesterday that we had been there as newlyweds, necking champagne and dining at the Moulin Rouge. But one thing was just the same: I still fancied the pants off my boy and, oh God, did I love him too.

When we returned home, we moved into a house in Blackpool. The house was only quite small, with a little garden, but we loved it. We were just a few doors down from Denise and I could walk round to Maureen's in no time at all. It was just a couple of hundred yards to the park, so in the mornings Brian and I would take Hudson down there for a walk, then come back and do the crosswords together.

My chemotherapy continued throughout 2007, during which I carried on with *Blood Brothers* across Britain too. And when the chemotherapy finished, I still had to have three weeks of radiotherapy, five days a week. Then, of course, I also had another six months of Herceptin treatments to go to finish my eighteen sessions.

I was exhausted, and Brian was too. His cancer appeared to be under control, although the doctors never said it had gone. He was struggling to walk, and I worried about him night and day. He clearly wasn't well again, although I had no idea exactly how ill he was becoming.

17.

Linda

I Don't Know What to Do

I walked off stage and into my empty dressing room at the end of our last night of *Blood Brothers* in Skegness. In almost twenty-eight years, it had never been like this. Whenever I finished a show, Brian was always there, helping me get changed and collecting together all my belongings. But that night, Saturday 15 September 2007, he hadn't felt well enough to come to meet me at work.

Brian had cut down on his drinking, but his legs had become very swollen and painful, and twice that week I'd got a lift home from the theatre because I didn't want him coming out to fetch me, whatever he might say. The following day was a Sunday, and Brian just about managed to drive us both back to Blackpool for a night at home before I opened in *Blood Brothers* in Manchester on the Monday. I was also due to have my next session of Herceptin earlier in the day. Brian was quiet and distracted in the car and, although he wouldn't admit it, I could tell he was in real pain.

'When I take you in for the Herceptin, I'll just pop into A&E to get myself checked out,' Brian said. He didn't like to make any fuss.

But he was really not well that day. He was struggling to

walk at all and was becoming a bit confused about things. When our friends Graham and Sue popped round, they thought he should go to the hospital straightaway. He was a bit reluctant at first, but eventually he agreed. Graham drove Brian to A&E, where they admitted him overnight.

The next morning, as soon as I'd finished my Herceptin, I went up to the ward to see Brian. The doctors were running tests to see what was the problem, and he was very tired and poorly looking. But I was still convinced that, with a bit of rest, he would be fine by the end of the week. I stayed with him for as long as I could, but then I had to go because Maureen was driving me over to Manchester for my first night in *Blood Brothers* there. I did the show, but went home feeling very sad that Brian wasn't there waiting for me. Then, at about 2 a.m., I woke up feeling freezing cold, then boiling hot. I was being sick, had diarrhoea and felt dreadful. I really thought I was dying. I hung on until about six o'clock, then rang Mo. 'I feel really sick,' I cried down the phone.

Maureen took me straight to the on-call GP, who diagnosed cellulitis, which is a bacterial skin infection that I was prone to because of having lymphedema (caused by having my lymph nodes removed). The doctor put me on a massive dose of antibiotics and I went home to rest. But when I rang the hospital later to ask about visiting Brian, they said there was no way I would be allowed into his ward if I was ill, because of the risk of infection. I was gutted. All day Tuesday and Wednesday, I wasn't allowed near him, but I was still hopeful he'd be home by the weekend.

On the Wednesday, Coleen's Ray and our friend Graham went to visit Brian. When they got back they told me a nurse had said I should speak to Brian's consultant urgently about coming in to visit. 'He's really very poorly,' Ray told me.

I called my Macmillan cancer-care nurse, who spoke to Brian's consultant for me, then said I could come in to visit. But first she wanted me to come to her office. She told me to make sure I had a friend with me. It sounded ominous, but I thought there might be various different reasons why they wouldn't want me to be on my own. Coleen drove me over and sat next to me in the nurse's office.

'Do you know how sick Brian is?' was the nurse's first question.

I knew then what was coming. 'Is he going to die?' I asked quietly.

'Yes,' she said softly.

I started screaming, 'Don't say that! Don't say that!' over and over again. I fell to the floor and remember Coleen on her knees, trying to hold me up. I was physically collapsing. But, at the same time, it was as though it was all happening to somebody else. It was just so wrong. We'd already been through so much. Brian couldn't possibly die.

We were told Brian had liver failure and that his other organs were also beginning to fail. Like I've said, he had drunk a lot in the past, and maybe his liver just couldn't cope anymore. The whole thing was just too much to take in.

I immediately rang Brian's son Lloyd, who was then thirty-three, and his daughter Sarah, thirty-seven, and they both set off for Blackpool straightaway. I also called Brian's best friend, John Parker, who we always just called Parker. He'd been head of promotions at CBS and had hit it off with Brian right from the start. When we got married, he was our best man. Parker was driving south on the M25 when I called him, but he turned his car around at the next junction and drove straight back to Blackpool.

At first I couldn't stop crying, but I was desperate to get back to the ward to see Brian. I tidied myself up and smiled as best as I could as I walked up to his bed. He was still incredibly tired and a little confused, but he was totally conscious. One by one, all my wonderful family turned up at the hospital, and we sat in a waiting room as the hours ticked by. 'I guess this is how it'll be in the future,' someone joked. 'But with fewer and fewer of us waiting outside.'

We drank tea and chatted, anything to avoid the reality that my Brian was dying at the other end of the corridor.

Eventually, we all decided to go home for some sleep. Lloyd and Sarah came back with me, but we'd only been home a couple of hours when the hospital rang to say they were struggling to stabilize Brian and we needed to get back there as soon as possible. Again, I phoned everyone, and soon the whole family was back at the hospital.

When we got to the hospital, a nurse said Brian was bleeding internally and they couldn't stop it. His liver was packing up and he was bleeding from his pores. But Brian, bless him, kept apologizing and trying to stand up.

The doctors said they wanted to put something down his throat, to put a few stitches in his oesophagus to stop the bleeding. I hated the thought of him having to go through more pain when it wasn't going to save him, but the doctors said that without it he would probably bleed to death, and that was a horrible way to go. So I agreed to the operation and stayed with Brian as they prepared him to go down to theatre.

'I'll see you later,' I said, giving him a kiss goodbye. 'I love you.'

'I love you too, Lin,' he replied.

They took my boy away at about 8.30 in the morning. I waited in the canteen, but was feeling so anxious that I started having a panic attack. I couldn't breathe and was sweating. It took ages for me to calm down. Then they phoned an hour later to say he had come through the procedure well and I'd be able to see him in about a quarter of an hour.

Five minutes later they called again and asked me to go straight there. Just as we arrived at his bed, a nurse came through the curtain. 'I'm so sorry,' she said. 'He has just stopped breathing.'

We went into the cubicle, and he was laying there as though he'd just slipped off to sleep. Lloyd and Sarah kissed him while I held his hand. I heard a voice saying, 'I don't know what to do.' It was me.

I lay down on the bed next to him, touching and kissing his face. 'Oh, Brian, Brian, please,' I said over and over again. It was 21 September 2007, and from that day my life would never be the same again.

I asked for a priest to come and give him the last rites. We'd never been hugely religious, but it was very comforting and gave me hope that I might one day see my boy again.

The rest of the day is a blur, but I think I spent it with my brother Brian and his wife Annie. Then I went home with Sarah and Lloyd. They must have heard me crying in the night because they got up and lay down on the bed with me and we talked and laughed for hours about Brian. I told them how proud he'd been of them both and how much he'd loved them and Sarah's little girl, Lucy, who was then eight. He used to call her Lucy Lastick and she called him Granddad Sherbet because he loved those sherbet flying saucers from the sweetshop. The pair of them got on so well and would laugh about anything together. Sarah, Lloyd and I told stories and shared a hundred memories of their dad, until finally we all fell asleep together.

The next few days felt totally unreal, as we arranged the funeral. At least organizing the service gave me something to focus on. The idea was that the funeral was to be Brian Hudson's final performance. It was to be a celebration of his life, with absolutely no black outfits. The pallbearers wore T-shirts, like crew members, and I was in a lilac suit. The coffin was black, with what looked like gaffer tape on the sides and a sign saying This Way Up to make it look like one of the flight cases we used for moving our gear around on the road. All the guests had laminate cards with the words 'Brian Hudson Farewell Gig 07' on them. The family had special VIP ones!

We walked into the church to 'There You'll Be' by Faith Hill. Just one hymn was sung, 'Abide With Me', which made my Brian cry every time he heard it. Then Bernie sang 'Wind Beneath My Wings' like an angel. That had always been mine and Brian's song. He really was my hero. We all left the church to a song by Harmony Grass, which was the band Brian had played in all those years ago.

Afterwards, we went on to the crematorium, where my brother Brian gave a beautiful address, and finally they played 'Always Look on the Bright Side of Life'. Everyone joined in, and amid all those tears there were smiles too, which was wonderful. When the curtains closed around the coffin, my brother Brian did his big, loud American announcer voice and said, 'Ladies and gentlemen, please put your hands together for the fabulous Brian Hudson.' There was a standing ovation for my boy. It was a wonderful send-off.

The days that followed were so hard though. Before the funeral, dozens of cards were arriving every day, but after about ten days, the post stopped and everyone else's lives went back to normal.

My family were amazing. I couldn't bear to be on my own and my sisters took it in turns to stay over with me for the next six weeks. Night after night, one of them would lie on the bed with me while I cried. 'I just don't know what to do,' was what I kept saying. I was utterly lost without Brian. He had done everything for me. I didn't even know how to pay a cheque into the bank, and there I was receiving bills and forms that I couldn't make head nor tail of. I started having panic attacks, where I'd struggle to breathe and start sweating with fear. Thank God for my brothers and sisters, who were always either there with me or at the other end of the phone.

Denise lives just five doors down from me, and she was amazing. She would turn up with a massive laundry bag full of DVDs and say, 'Right, I've got dramas, I've got romantic comedies, I've got thrillers, documentaries and musicals. Which do you fancy?' And we'd sit there together on the sofa, watching a film, just like we'd done when we were kids.

I knew Brian would want me to carry on, and he'd be really proud of me and all that, like people kept saying. But inside I felt like I was dying. I missed him so much. There was a physical ache inside me and the thought that it was never going to go away was horrific. The thought of never seeing, feeling, touching, holding, smelling or laughing with Brian ever again was unbearable.

Many, many times I thought it would be far easier to pile up all the tablets I could find in the house and swallow the lot, so I could be with him again. But how could I do that to Lloyd and Sarah and all my family? I loved them all too much to put them through the pain I was going through. I couldn't eat or sleep and rarely went out. I lost interest in everything.

My first session of Herceptin without Brian was about a fortnight after he died. He'd always come with me before and when I stepped in the door of the treatment room, I totally lost it and started sobbing. On the rare occasions that I went out, I'd cry; I hated leaving our house because that's where I felt closest to Brian. Then I'd cry all the way home again because I knew that when I opened the front door, he wasn't going to be there.

Sometimes I would fall asleep and wake up in a panic because I couldn't remember what he looked like. My clinical psychologist, Dr Jean Brigg, said that was perfectly normal and suggested keeping a picture of him by my bed. I didn't wash my sheets for almost five weeks. I couldn't, because it felt like I would be washing him away.

People would say that time heals, but it didn't really. Three times I rang the Samaritans in the early hours of the morning. I never went as far as lining up a row of tablets, but there was no doubt in my mind that ending it all would be easier than what I was going through.

I'd been having counselling since the orange jelly incident in Jersey, when the side effects of chemotherapy had been really getting to me. My cancer-care nurse had suggested that counselling might help me, and she was right. In my first session after Brian died, I just sat in the chair and cried while Dr Brigg held me. 'I don't know what to do,' I said for the umpteenth time.

Brian and I had been together 24/7 for twenty-eight years. He was my first love, my only love. And now he was gone.

That autumn, Mum was in the final stages of Alzheimer's. I went to the home where she was living and told her that my Brian had died, but she was far too poorly by then to understand what I was saying.

The only thing that kept me going was helping Coleen organize her wedding to Ray. Before Brian died, Coleen and Ray had asked us to be witnesses, and we'd both been so looking forward to it. It was incredibly tough going through that without Brian there next to me, but I did it for Coleen and Ray. And, despite everything, it was a great day. I was just happy that my sister had found someone who made her as happy as Brian had made me.

Then, just before New Year, Mum passed away. We'd known it was coming for months and we wanted her to be at peace, but it was still a terrible blow.

Just before she died, I'd been offered two weeks work in *Blood Brothers*, which was opening in the West End. I felt numb with grief, but I thought that working might blot out some of the pain. I also needed the money. I was on my own now and if I didn't work, then I wouldn't eat. So, two days after Mum's funeral, I was back on stage. I thought I'd be able to manage it OK, but it was very tough.

Maureen drove me down to London and stayed with me for moral support. It was great being back with the cast because many of them had become good friends over the years. Maureen and I stayed at Bernie and Steve's house in Surrey, and Denise came for a while too. Every night one of them would come with me and wait in the dressing room at the Phoenix Theatre while I was on stage. *Blood Brothers* is an emotional play at any time, but doing it then was gruelling.

There's no way I would have managed it without my sisters' support.

A couple of times, I had to go back to Bernie's on the train on my own. Two young girls from the cast would walk me to the Underground station, then I'd get on the tube and stare at my reflection in the window. 'This isn't how it was supposed to be,' I thought.

After that stint in the West End, I rejoined the *Blood Brothers* tour. We travelled to Nottingham, Cardiff, Malvern and Northampton. But it was so lonely, staying in hotels without Brian. I was really struggling.

One night, at the end of May 2008, when we were appearing in Wolverhampton, I woke up with a severe pain in my left arm, which was rapidly swelling up. Seconds later, I was vomiting everywhere. All night I was throwing up, and first thing in the morning I rang the company manager to say I wouldn't be able to go on stage that night. Then I rang my older brother Tommy. 'Come home,' he said, but I felt too sick to even get on the train.

A doctor in Wolverhampton examined me and said I had cellulitis again, the bacterial skin infection caused by having had my lymph nodes removed. The doctor gave me antibiotics, but I was being so sick that I couldn't keep them down for a minute. The doctor said I'd have to go to hospital. In that situation, Brian would always have taken care of everything, but here I was now, in a strange town, feeling utterly alone and really sick. I rang the company manager again and she sent an assistant stage manager called Annie along to get me to the hospital in a taxi. The poor girl was only twenty-three, but she was fantastic. As I sat in the hospital, vomiting over and over again, she rubbed my back and stayed with me for hours.

Maureen was doing a show called *Mum's the Word* with Bernie in Litchfield, so she pulled out that night and drove over to be with me. The doctors put me on intravenous antibiotics and gradually the infection subsided and my arm, which had swollen up like a balloon, returned to normal. I was in hospital for the rest of the week, and Maureen and Bernie drove backwards and forwards between me and their show. Brian would have been pleased to know the Nolan cavalry was with me. But they were both so exhausted that one day Maureen fell asleep on my bed and nearly got a shot of antibiotics from a passing nurse!

When I was discharged, my brothers Tommy and Brian turned up with pillows and blankets in the back of the car and drove me to Brian and Annie's house for lunch, then on to Denise's house. She looked after me fantastically for the next few weeks.

I felt so ill that when Maureen offered to finish the tour for me, I agreed. I was due to rejoin the second part of the tour when it started up again in the autumn, but as the time grew closer, I got more and more anxious. My opening line in *Blood Brothers* was: 'Once I had a husband . . .' It was so painful. I kept telling myself, 'I can do this, I can do this,' but the point was that I didn't want to do it.

I remembered Brian once saying to me that if he died he'd want me to go on stage the same day and do the best show I'd ever done. He was very much a believer in 'the show must go on' and I didn't want to quit *Blood Brothers* because I thought he would have been disappointed. I didn't want anyone to think

I was a quitter. But the thought of touring the country on my own again made me feel sick.

'I don't think I can do it anymore,' I told Dr Brigg.

'Maybe you need to give yourself time to breathe,' she said. 'You have been through cancer and have lost your husband and your mother.'

I was still uncertain about what to do, so I rang my brother Brian. 'What would you say if I said I wasn't going back into *Blood Brothers*?' I asked.

'I'd be delighted,' he said. 'We've all been talking and the rest of us are going to put a bit of money together for you in an account, so you don't need to work for a while. You can take some time out and recover.'

When he said that, it felt like a ten-ton weight had been lifted off my shoulders. I was so relieved that I wouldn't have to go away again and could just stay in our little house in Blackpool.

Grief affects people in different ways. When our Brian lost his wife Linzi, he never returned to their home. He couldn't face it. Our sisters packed up all the furniture and clothes for him. Brian's second wife Annie had also had to cope with terrible pain, when her son from her first marriage died suddenly. Having had to cope with loss themselves, Brian and Annie were a real tower of strength to me.

After my Brian died, I didn't want to be anywhere else but home. Sometimes I would wear one of his T-shirts, and his clothes still hung in the wardrobe. If I buried my face in them deeply, I could still smell him.

Some days I would wake up and think, 'I hate the world.' I'd lie on the sofa all day, crying and unable to move or even speak to anyone. My brothers, sisters and Dr Jean Brigg were amazing, but even they couldn't take the pain away. I'd feel guilty because I'd begun to forget what Brian's voice sounded like, but Dr Brigg told me that was quite normal.

Four months after Brian's death, my doctor put me on anti-depressants, but I'm not sure how much they helped me, as I still felt very low. I was missing Brian, having to cope with all the things he'd taken care of in the past, and I was worried about money too. We didn't really have any savings and I had bills to pay. And I couldn't rely on my brothers and sisters' generosity forever. But for ages I couldn't bear the thought of applying for benefits. I'd been working since I was three years old, and I felt like a loser to have to rely on handouts. But, again, Dr Brigg helped me think it through. 'Benefits are for people like you, who are ill,' she explained.

And so, reluctantly, I applied for help and got enough to live on.

It was the end of 2008 before I returned to hospital for a reconstruction operation to rebuild the breast I'd had removed. I should have had it earlier, but I'd been too low emotionally and the doctors said I needed to be physically and mentally fit to cope with the operation and recovery.

I'd got used to using a prosthesis, but I knew that at some point it would be better to have a reconstruction. I was scared about going into hospital and not having Brian there to help me through it. Maureen was fantastic though. She drove me to Wythenshawe Hospital in Manchester and stayed with me right up until the moment I had to go into the operating theatre. When she left me there, we both cried. It was then that I wanted Brian more than ever.

When I woke up afterwards, Maureen was there next to me. And I was delighted with the outcome of the operation.

The surgeons had taken muscle from my back and put it on my breast with an implant behind it, so it looked very realistic. I had been completely flat on my left side after the mastectomy, so to wake up with a breast again was fantastic.

Again, the Nolan cavalry turned up and looked after me as I recovered.

They had put a port in the side of my breast, so they could put in more saline to make sure it matched the size of my right breast, but my skin had lost its elasticity during radiotherapy and so the breast couldn't be increased in size after all. Instead, a couple of months later, I had to undergo a reduction of my right breast, to make everything equal.

Physically, I felt better than I had in a long time, but emotionally, I was still very fragile. There were still days when I couldn't face getting out of bed. I was lonely, lost and just very, very sad.

18.

Maureen

Goodbye Mum

Within weeks of Dad dying, Mum had become old. When we were kids, she'd had so much energy. She never stopped working, from the moment she got out of bed in the morning until the moment she lay down at night. With eight kids and a husband to look after, as well as a singing job to keep up, she didn't have much choice. But after Dad died, Mum, who was then still only seventy-two, seemed tired and frail and a bit clumsy.

Dad had always taken care of their finances, and she found it hard without him. She lost her confidence and didn't seem to have as much get up and go as she'd once had.

When we went round to see her, she would talk about our dad a lot and get all tearful.

I'd try to cheer her up. 'But you don't have to answer to anyone now, Mum,' I'd say. 'You can do whatever you want.'

But all she really wanted was to still be with Dad. Mum didn't have an easy life at all with our dad, but I don't think she saw it like that. She was happy when we were all at home and she had us kids and Dad to look after. She seemed to thrive on hard work. When we all moved away and Dad died, there was no one to look after anymore. She was the only one left.

It must have seemed very quiet when she looked back to the days when we were all little and the house was filled with noise and people.

Then we noticed that Mum had started to forget things and was becoming confused. She seemed to be constantly losing her handbag. If I went round to her flat, she would be looking everywhere for it. 'I'm sure I left it here,' she would say. It would take her ages until she found it somewhere completely different to where she thought it should be.

She went to stay with Brian and his wife Annie for a while after Dad died, and they noticed some strange things in her behaviour. One day she put a pan of potatoes on the hob, then went out. She would never have done anything like that before.

'I'm a bit worried about her,' Brian said to me.

'Oh, we all do things like that from time to time,' I said. 'And she's not getting any younger.' But, to be honest, I was concerned myself.

After Dad died, Mum moved out of their house because she wanted somewhere smaller and a bit more manageable. She was also suffering from arthritis and thought a flat might be better. But she didn't like the flat, so she moved again. Then that place wasn't right either, so she went into sheltered accommodation. Us kids were all quite pleased about that because it meant there was someone to keep an eye on her day and night, but Mum never really settled there either. There had been so many changes in her life in such a short space of time that it must all have been a bit bewildering for her. I thought maybe that was why she was becoming a bit forgetful.

She still had a very full life. She went to mass most days and once a week she'd go with a group of her friends to the Queen's Hotel in Blackpool, where she'd have lunch and then get up and sing. She might have started to look old, but her voice was still youthful and clear. When she broke into 'Danny Boy' there'd be barely a dry eye in the house. When Mum wasn't out with her friends, or at church, or singing, she had all her children and grandchildren to visit.

Once a year she would travel to the shrine at Lourdes in France with a group of her friends from church. That was one of the highlights of her life. But when the group came back from Lourdes in 2000, two years after Dad's death, a couple of Mum's friends took us to one side and said they were worried about her. Apparently, she'd been losing her hand-bag quite frequently again, and people were having to keep an eye on her all the time, like they would a child, in case she wandered off. More and more things were happening that didn't seem quite right. She started ringing up at three or four o'clock in the morning for a chat.

'Hello, Maureen, are you popping in for a coffee later?' she asked, totally normally, when she called me at three o'clock in the morning once.

'Mum, it's the middle of the night,' I said. 'Are you feeling OK?'

'Oh,' she said hesitating slightly, 'of course I am, love.' Then she seemed to recover herself. 'I was just having a bit of trouble sleeping, so I thought I'd give you a quick ring to see if you were awake.'

I couldn't really understand what was going on, but Mum sounded fine, so I didn't instantly panic. It was only months later that I realized Mum must have lost the ability to tell the time. But at that stage she was still able to cover up her erratic behaviour. She was obviously desperate to hide from us the reality of how ill she was becoming.

'But you're OK?' I said again.

'I told you, I'm fine,' Mum said. 'I'll call you in the morning, love.'

One day a friend called me to say they'd seen Mum standing at the bus stop at five o'clock in the morning. When I asked her about it, she seemed to not have a clue what I was talking about. Then, one evening, my Ritchie was driving home and got stuck in traffic just outside the flat where Mum was living at the time. He was looking out of the side window when he saw her come out of the flat, then go back in, then come out of the door again. 'You know, I don't think she knew where she was or what she was doing,' Ritchie said later, when he told me the story.

At first I told myself that all elderly people get a bit forgetful. But I had a nagging feeling that it was more than that. 'I know she's old, but she's not that old,' I thought. I still couldn't believe there was anything seriously wrong with our mum.

My brothers and sisters all had their own stories about how she'd struggled to remember names, or got muddled up when she was talking to them, but we were really all in a state of denial about her being ill. We'd talk about it between ourselves for hours, swapping stories about the odd things she had done or said, but then we'd wrap up every conversation by saying, 'Oh, for goodness' sake, she's absolutely fine.' Because despite the occasional bouts of forgetfulness, a lot of the time she was still perfectly normal.

Then, a couple of months after Ritchie saw Mum outside her flat, he bumped into her walking along the street. 'Hello, Maureen,' Ritchie said. 'Out shopping?'

Mum looked at him totally blankly. She'd known him for twelve years, and he was the father of her grandson, but she didn't have the slightest clue who he was.

'It's me, Ritchie,' he said. 'Maureen's Ritchie.'

Finally it clicked into place. 'Oh, Ritchie, of course I know who you are,' she joked. But Ritchie was convinced that she really hadn't known at all and was just trying to hide her confusion.

'You're going to have to take her to the doctor's,' Ritchie said when he got home that night. 'She's really not well.'

'OK,' I said. 'I'll speak to the girls.'

Some of us kids were also worried because we'd caught her talking to herself. 'Well, we all do that from time to time,' I joked, still trying to convince myself that it might not be serious. Then some of the girls thought they'd heard Mum talking to Dad. Gradually, very gradually, there were more and more things happening that made us all wonder if maybe there was a bigger problem than we had first realized. None of us said it at first, but I guess we were all thinking it: 'Alzheimer's'. We all knew what a terrible illness that is, and I think we were trying to shield ourselves and each other from the reality of it. Alzhiemer's was also the one thing we knew Mum had dreaded. 'If I get cancer, then I get cancer,' Mum used to say. 'But the worst thing I can imagine is Alzheimer's.' The thought of her saying that would haunt me over the next months and years.

One afternoon, towards the end of 2002, we couldn't pretend any longer. 'I'm taking Mum to her doctor's appointment this week,' I told my brothers and sisters one afternoon, 'and when I'm there, I'm going to mention the forgetfulness.' Everyone agreed it was time to find out what the problem was.

It was really tricky because Mum was still 'with it' enough to know what was going on in the doctor's surgery. After we'd finished discussing whatever it was Mum had needed to go in for, I tried to mouth to the doctor that she'd been getting a bit confused recently.

The doctor was lovely and realized what I was saying. 'So, how have you been feeling lately, Maureen?' she said turning to my mum.

'Absolutely fine,' Mum replied, coming over quite frosty.

'No forgetfulness then?' the doctor went on.

'Absolutely not,' Mum said. And seeing her there in that doctor's surgery, you wouldn't have thought there was a thing wrong with her. Mum and the GP chatted for a while longer and, goodness knows how, but by the end of the conversation the doctor had persuaded Mum to let someone from the Mental Health Trust come to visit her. But, even then, Mum was still adamant there wasn't anything wrong with her. She must have known herself that she was becoming forgetful, but she always refused to admit there was any problem. I imagine she must have been terrified about what was happening to her, but she never said she was scared. All my life I'd never known Mum to be ill. She'd always been so strong – this was the woman who took the bus to hospital when she was in labour! – but now she seemed vulnerable.

When the man from the Mental Health Trust turned up at my house one day, when Mum had come round, she was instantly very suspicious.

'He just wants to ask you a few questions,' I said.

'Why?' she replied.

'Well, you have seemed a little confused recently,' I said.

'Well, I am seventy-four,' she said. 'You'll be confused at my age too.'

Finally she allowed the guy to start asking his questions and although the whole meeting was quite tragic, it was actually hilarious too. 'Mrs Nolan,' he said, 'can you tell me who the Prime Minister is?'

Mum thought for a second, then yelled across at me, 'Maureen, who's the Prime Minister right now?'

'Let's move on,' the guy said. 'Now, Mrs Nolan, which year were you born in?'

Again, Mum thought for a moment, then called over to me. 'And which year was I born in, Maureen?'

It went on like that for ages, until I started giggling. 'Mum,' I said, 'the man wants *you* to answer the questions, not me.'

'Oh!' she said, starting to laugh herself.

Soon all three of us were in hysterics. It was sad though too, because it was becoming startlingly obvious that Mum had lost a lot of her memory. When we got her official diagnosis, they said it was bad, but they weren't at that point sure whether it really was Alzheimer's. Mum was put on some tablets, which the doctors said might slow down her deterioration, but they didn't seem to do much good. Every time I saw her she seemed more confused than the last time. It was also very difficult to make sure she took the tablets, as she couldn't remember to do it on her own.

After a few more tests, the doctors confirmed what we had all feared – Mum was suffering from Alzheimer's. The doctors gave us pamphlets to read about it, which were very helpful, and a great book written by someone who'd had a family member with Alzheimer's. I started to read the book, but when I reached the part where it told you exactly how bad the illness could become, I had to stop. 'Oh God,' I thought, 'I can't read about that. I'll handle it when the time comes.'

Mum was getting more and more confused. A couple of

months after her diagnosis, she nearly burnt her flat down one day by putting a plastic kettle on the stove. She was trying to boil water like in the old days; she'd forgotten you only had to flick a switch nowadays.

By the beginning of 2005, we knew it was no longer safe to leave her on her own in her sheltered accommodation flat, so for a while we took it in turns to have her to stay for a couple of weeks. Mum loved that because she had all her kids and grandkids around her, but it was totally exhausting for whoever was looking after her. It was quickly quite obvious that she couldn't be left on her own even for a moment. You certainly couldn't go out to work because it wasn't safe to leave her in the house on her own.

For a while, she stayed with Coleen during the day and Anne at night, but she was becoming more and more of a risk to herself and others. One day she gave Ciara some tablets and told her they were sweets – she really didn't know what she was doing. Fortunately, Ciara, who was then four, didn't eat them and showed them to her mum, but it could have been terrible. Mum needed to be bathed and helped to go to the toilet because she couldn't do any of those things anymore. It was really hard.

Coleen had her children to look after too, Bernie was living and working down south, Linda was touring in *Blood Brothers* and the rest of us were all working too. Then Anne and I were booked to go to Australia to do a rock and roll show. It was going to mean weeks away from home, but none of us was in a position where we could turn down work; we just weren't rich enough to pack in our careers, we never had been. All us kids would speak to each other for hours on the telephone about whether it was time to consider putting Mum in a home.

None of us wanted to do it, and it made us feel horribly guilty, but more and more it seemed like the only real option.

One day we had a meeting with the GP who'd been our family doctor for years. His auntie had recently had Alzheimer's, so he knew exactly what it was like. 'The kindest thing for everybody concerned, including your mum, might be to find a nice care home that you'll all be happy with,' he said.

That was a turning point for us because it made us believe that being cared for by professionals might be the best thing for Mum too. We got a list of homes in the local area and Anne, Brian and I drove around with Mum, visiting a few of them, until we found one that she liked. She was very confused by then, although she still knew who we all were, and at first she seemed to accept the idea that she would be moving into a home. 'They'll be able to look after you here,' I said to her.

'Yes, it seems very nice,' she said. We were all so relieved.

We went home and, over the next couple of weeks, we packed up Mum's clothes and belongings, ready for the move. Brian and I took her the day she was due to move in. At first Mum must have thought we were just going out for a drive, and she was in a really good mood. Even when we arrived at the home and got her suitcase out of the boot, she was still fine. The staff and other residents at the home were all so lovely and brought us tea and biscuits, and it was all just great. But then, when Brian and I stood up and started to leave, I could see a look of panic flash across Mum's face.

'We've got to go now, Mum,' I said, ordering myself not to cry until we were outside, 'but we'll be back to visit again soon.'

Mum may have been very confused by that stage, but at

that moment I think everything was horribly crystal-clear for her. 'Please don't leave me,' she said, tears starting to pour down her face. 'Maureen, please don't leave me.'

'We've got to, Mum, but we'll be back soon, and you'll only be here for a short while,' I said. I was lying, but it seemed like the kindest thing to say. 'It's lovely here. Everyone is really nice, you've got your own gorgeous room and your own telly.' I was probably trying to convince myself as much as Mum that this was the right thing to do.

'No, please, please don't leave me,' Mum kept saying, again and again and again.

It was torture seeing her sitting there, utterly helpless and looking totally lost. Even though we'd been told this was the best thing for her, a massive part of me just wanted to gather her up like a child and say, 'No, I'm not having this, you're coming home with me.' We were all torn between what we thought was the best thing for Mum and our gut feelings. Some of Mum's friends really disapproved of what we were doing. 'I can't believe she's got six healthy daughters and she's being put in a home,' one woman told our aunty. But looking after Mum by then was a twenty-four hour a day, seven day a week job. None of us could cope. That didn't stop us feeling horribly guilty though.

Denise was amazing with Mum after she went into the home. So were Brian and his wife Annie. I suppose, in some respects, we were all amazing, and someone visited her every day. But Denise was able to bathe Mum and even change her incontinence pads, which some of us others really struggled with. And Annie could sit and talk to her for hours, even though she couldn't really have a conversation at all anymore.

Every time I visited Mum, I found it so upsetting because

on each occasion she would remember less and less. She would repeat the same stories over and over again. Her short-term memory had totally gone, although her long-term memory was still good at first.

'I can't believe my mum and dad haven't been to visit me,' she would say again and again. At first I'd try to explain that they were dead, but after a while I decided that, as she wasn't going to remember anyway, it might be better to tell her what she wanted to hear.

'They'll be coming tomorrow,' I'd say, and she seemed to accept that.

Every Sunday Denise would go and pick Mum up from the home and take her to the Queen's Hotel, where she would go on stage and sing to the lunchtime diners, like she always had done. She still had the most beautiful voice. One of the last bits of her memory to go was her knowledge of songs and lyrics. Even that went in the end though, so Denise would have to sit next to her and quietly prompt her. Once she insisted that she wanted to sing 'Somewhere Over the Rainbow'. Denise tried to persuade her to do something she might find easier to remember, but she wouldn't have it. The compere went on and gave her a big introduction, and then the organist started playing 'Somewhere Over the Rainbow', as instructed. Mum opened her mouth and went straight into the first line of 'Danny Boy'! If it wasn't so sad, it would have been funny.

As the months went by, Mum started becoming more irritable and aggressive, which can happen with Alzheimer's. One day I took her out to a café for lunch and a lovely man on the next table recognized her from her days of singing in the hotels around Blackpool. He was talking to her, but she got really abusive to him. She could swear like a trooper by then, even though she had never done so before. It was awful because Mum was always lovely to everyone and so polite. I explained to the man that Mum now had Alzheimer's and he was fine about it, but it was so upsetting to watch. Mum would have been utterly horrified that she could ever speak to a stranger like that.

Another day, when I arrived at the home, Mum was refusing to get dressed. I said that if she popped her clothes on, I'd take her for a drive down to the beach. 'Oh, I'd love that,' she said. But when one of the carers came to help her put her dress on, she got really angry. She was shouting, 'Get away from me!' and lashing out at the poor woman. It was so totally out of character. But I suppose, by then, our mum's real character had gone for ever. In the end, I picked up Mum's coat and tried to put it over her pyjamas.

'Get away from me, you bitch!' she screamed at me.

It was the most angry I'd ever seen her. I knew she didn't know what she was saying, but it was still horrific. I was shaking and distraught, but just about managed to hold it together until I got outside. Then I cried and cried and cried. It was horrendous.

Then carers at the home told us that other residents were becoming scared of Mum because she was so aggressive. She was on medication to make her less angry, but that was another big guilt thing for us. It's a terrible decision that you have to make. It seemed disgusting that we should keep her sedated and doped up, but if we didn't, she was so angry and upset and frightened that that was horrible too.

Alzheimer's was a living torture for Mum, and for all of us too. It used to devastate me seeing my brothers and sisters so upset and watching them cry. I'd never seen Brian cry before Mum got ill, and it was heartbreaking.

She just didn't 'get' her grandchildren anymore at all. She had loved them all so much, but now they were just an irritation to her. And they all found it hard to cope with her illness too, so that was another thing lost to her. Then, gradually, she began to forget who we were entirely. Brian was the only one who still sparked something in her mind, but I think it was because he looks so much like our dad. When he went in to visit, she would hold his hand and call him Tommy.

With every week that passed, she slipped further from us, so that she became like a zombie, unable to connect with us at all. We would try anything to break through to her and get a smile. We'd point at photos of the family all around her room, show her pictures in magazines, and Denise even went out and got her favourite films on DVD. The nurses showed her videos of The Nolans, but she just stared at them blankly. It became harder and harder to connect with her.

When I went to visit, I'd sing some of the songs we'd grown up with: 'Climb Every Mountain', 'Somewhere Over the Rainbow' and 'Danny Boy'. But because her hearing was going, I had to sing them quite loudly. One day Anne's daughter, Alex, came to visit Mum and had only got in the front door of the home when she heard my voice bellowing through the corridors. 'Oh God, it's Auntie Maureen again,' she said to one of the carers. 'She's so embarrassing!'

After a couple of years, Mum lost her mind almost totally and became more and more like a zombie. I longed for the times when I'd been able to take her out, even when she was confused. Now all she could do was lie in bed. As she became totally unable to move, she suffered terrible bed sores, but there was little the carers could do about them by then. Sometimes we'd arrive to hear her screaming in pain if she was being turned over in the bed. But then, as her body closed down more and more, even the screaming stopped. Somehow that seemed even worse.

Her skin would now bruise at the merest touch, and she was so skinny because she had forgotten how to eat and swallow. For a while, the nurses fed her like a baby, but then her only food became protein drinks taken through a straw. She survived for months on virtually nothing at all.

Once Linda and I were visiting and the nurse had to pull back the bedclothes to check something. When I saw Mum's body, I gasped. She was literally a skeleton covered in the thinnest layer of skin. Linda and I were so upset we had to leave the room.

Then Mum's breathing became really bad and you could hear her struggling for every bit of air. It was horrendous, just horrendous.

I used to cry and cry, saying, 'Please, God, just take her.' I think we all wanted her to be at peace. It didn't matter anymore that she didn't know us. It was just that she must have been in such pain. One night we were visiting and Anne said to her, 'It's OK, Mum, you can go now. You don't have to hang on for us. We'll be alright. You can go and be with Dad.'

But still she hung on. I don't know how she did it for so long, but it was torturous. Towards the end of 2007, the carers at the home told us they now thought Mum could go at any time. One night Linda was called to the home with Auntie Theresa and a priest administered the last rites. But still Mum hung on.

At last, one night, just before Christmas 2007, we got a call from staff at the home to say Mum was very near the end. Bernie, Linda and I went up there and decided to sing for her.

It seemed the most natural thing in the world. Despite everything that was happening, it was quite funny because we kept bickering over whose harmony was whose. If Mum could have heard us, she would have been laughing. We sang for a bit with no reaction from her at all, but then Mum moved her head forward just a fraction and gave the tiniest of smiles. That was wonderful. It was the first real contact we'd had with her in months. She knew we were there. After that, we sang and sang for hours; we just wanted to keep that connection with our mum for as long as we could.

Mum hung on for another week after that. It was the night before New Years' Eve, and I was doing my last night of panto in Durham. I'd just gone to borrow something from a friend's dressing room when my mobile phone rang. It was Bernie. 'I'm sorry, Maureen,' she said quietly. 'Mum's gone.'

I started crying and I couldn't stop.

My brothers and sisters had gone straight to the home to say their goodbyes. I think everyone was relieved she was finally at peace. After the others left, Linda stayed a little longer, held our mum and asked her to give her Brian a little kiss from her. I was desperate to get back home to the others just as quickly as possible. I got straight in my car and drove back. I thought I'd never stop crying.

For the past year, all we'd wanted was for Mum to be at peace, but now it had happened it was awful. I suppose it was because then we could remember the woman she had been before Alzheimer's. She'd been this gorgeous, lovely, cuddly woman who had given so much of her life for us and then had such a horrible end. I felt angry that it had to happen to her. It was so very unfair. As I drove home, I thought about when I was tiny and she'd call me her little Boofy.

'You're my little beauty,' she'd say to me. 'What are you?'

'Your little boofy,' I'd reply. I couldn't say beauty, so Boofy stuck. I always felt so loved by our mum. I think we all did.

We had Mum's funeral at the Sacred Heart Church, where at one time she had gone to mass every day. The church was packed and there were the most beautiful flowers everywhere you looked. Bernie wrote and read the eulogy, just as she'd done at Dad's funeral. It was lovely. At all the family weddings, Mum had sung 'Ave Maria' and it was always a big highlight of the day, so Anne sang it at the funeral service. She sang it so beautifully and there wasn't a dry eye in the church. It was so soon after Linda's Brian's funeral that we were all reeling from that too.

I still miss Mum all the time. I say to people that I meet, 'Treasure the time you've got with your mum because you never know when it might end.' We lost our mum years before she actually died. The worst thing about it was seeing her deteriorate and not being able to do anything to help. It was just such a cruel way for her to end up, when she'd done nothing but care for other people all her life.

Mum and Dad are buried together in Carlton Cemetery in Blackpool, near Bernie's daughter Kate and Brian's wife Linzi.

Our parents might have had their differences when they were alive, and their marriage was certainly no fairytale, but I'm sure they always loved each other and Mum would have wanted to be buried next to her Tommy. I'm glad they're at peace together.

19.

Coleen

The Family Falls Apart

If Dad had still been alive and Mum hadn't been robbed of her mind by Alzheimer's, then I'm sure the fall-out that was about to hit our family would never have happened. Or, at least, it wouldn't have been so bad and caused so much damage. Mum was still alive when it first kicked off in 2006, but by then she was in the home and really didn't know what was going on. Without our parents around, we'd lost the glue that held us all together and, finally, resentments and issues which had been swept under the carpet for years came flooding out.

The fall-out began with the most trivial of rows, which on the face of it had nothing to do with our childhood. But the way the different members of our family reacted to that row had, I believe, everything to do with how we'd been brought up.

I was commuting up and down to London to do *Loose Women* and another, late-night show called *Girl Talk*. I was finding working and keeping on top of the house a struggle and wanted a nanny who could help care for Ciara when Ray wasn't around and who would also pitch in around the house. One night I rang Anne for the telephone number of her daughter Amy's friend, who might be interested in the job.

'Listen, Coleen,' said Anne. 'Would you consider letting me have the job? To be honest, I could do with the cash.'

Anne was going through a difficult divorce with her husband Brian, and money was tight. The only reason I hadn't offered Anne the job first of all was I worried that she might be offended. Anne and I had always been so close, and she virtually brought me up in many ways. When she decided she wanted to write her book about being abused by Dad, I backed her all the way. I thought too much stuff had been swept under the carpet in our family and if writing things down was going to help her cope with what had gone on, then she had to do it. I even helped her find a publisher.

So Anne came to work for us, and at first it was great. Anne was still just as feisty as she had been in the days when she'd been the leader of the girls' gang as a kid. She and Ray – who was usually working from home during the day – would sometimes clash, but after a big clear-the-air row things would soon get back to normal. In fact, they got on really well together. Ray had been helping Anne's daughters, Amy and Alex, because they were interested in getting into show business. But then one of them hadn't gone for an audition she had landed, and he felt disappointed for her. And then, one morning, Anne told Ray the girls had found themselves normal 9–5 jobs.

'Oh,' said Ray. 'You know, they are really talented, but they just can't be arsed, can they?'

And that was it. Everything kicked off.

Anne flipped out, claiming Ray had been pushing them into something they didn't want to do. But it was the girls who'd asked Ray for help in the first place. Anne was ranting and raving at Ray, and at first he thought she was joking and just laughed at her. But when he realized she was deadly serious, he just wandered off and went and sat in his office.

Two minutes later, Anne followed him in there and was screaming about how he and I, and Linda and Brian were all backstabbers. Ray was gobsmacked. We had never stabbed her in the back once! All we'd done was try to support her through her divorce. When Ray told me what she'd said, I was really hurt. I couldn't understand where all this stuff had come from. She just would not calm down, and in the end Ray had to tell Anne to leave.

Later that day, she called me. 'Look, Ray and I have had a row,' she said. 'But I don't want to leave you in the lurch, so if you need someone to look after Ciara, just let me know.'

'OK,' I said. 'I'm sure it'll all blow over.' Little did I know!

I left it for a couple of days because Ray and I were going to the *Loose Women* wrap party at the end of the series in London. We were on our way home on the train when I received a text from Denise inviting me to a girlie night round hers with some of our sisters. I was feeling shattered and still a bit unsure what was going on with Anne, so I just sent a quick text back saying: 'Thanks for the invite, but I'm knackered and just want to wait until things have calmed down a bit. Have a brilliant night. Will speak to you tomorrow.'

A couple of seconds later, my phone bleeped. I picked it up and read the message. It was from Denise, but I could barely believe what she was saying. It was really, really horrible, about Ray and me. And that wasn't the end of it. For the rest of the train journey, I was bombarded with texts from Denise. Some of it was vile. For years, I think Denise had been forgiven pretty bad behaviour like this because we all felt a bit sorry for her. We didn't talk about it, but I think we all had the sense that life had been harder for Denise than for the rest of us. She'd never felt comfortable in the band, even though she was a fabulous singer, and there had always been this feeling that Mum and Dad were harder on her, for reasons we never really understood. But this time I couldn't just ignore what she was saying to me. One text said: 'Don't tell me you are siding with that man and his major sulking when we have all protected him all these years when the men in our family have been slagging him.'

Ray had always felt like an outsider at family gatherings when the men would get together. He never felt they wanted him in their gang! I'd told him he was imagining it but now Denise seemed to be confirming he was right. The messages were getting more vicious, so I texted Denise back and said: 'Let's stop this now because it is getting out of hand.' But it just got worse. She was sending messages about how I'd never liked her and one saying I'd upset her at some ball we'd gone to together. When I worked out what she was talking about, it was something that had happened fifteen years earlier!

All these things which I hadn't even realized were a problem at the time must have got lodged in her brain and were now pouring out. Some of the texts were just horrid. I got back home feeling absolutely devastated, but I was fuming too.

Ray was shaking, he was so upset by it all. All he'd ever meant to say was that he thought Anne's daughters were really gifted and they should try to exploit their talents, and it had led to this. Now he felt like an outsider who had come into the Nolan family and was going to be accused of ripping it apart.

Ray was so upset that he wrote a long, A4-sized letter to every member of the family, explaining exactly what had happened. He said that he'd only said what he did as a compliment to Anne's daughters and apologized for laughing at Anne when she first got mad, thinking that she was joking. Then he offered to meet Anne and Denise at a time and place of their choice, to talk it all out. He hand-delivered the letters, but didn't get a single response. Anne and Denise said nothing, and the others were trying not to get involved. But they were involved because they'd heard Anne's version of events. We actually needed someone to step in and sort the whole thing out. I guess that's what Dad or maybe Mum would have done before, but they weren't there anymore.

Then Auntie Theresa rang up. 'Hi, Coleen,' she said. 'Now, I don't want to get involved in what's going on, but if what Anne says is true, then Ray is really out of order.'

'So you are involved then,' I replied.

'No,' she said. 'No, I'm not.'

'But if you've heard Anne's side of the story, you've got to hear Ray's,' I said.

'I don't want to,' she said.

And that was how it was. If I'd thought Ray had been in the wrong, I'd have told him he was out of order and asked him to apologize. But he really wasn't. And I had to defend him because no one else was going to and he was up against the rest of our family.

Dad had brought us all up saying, 'We have to stick together. Always be careful of outsiders coming in and trying to split us up.' And by outsiders he meant husbands and wives too. None of the Nolan girls had ever stood up for their partners against the family before.

Linda's husband Brian was given a terrible time on occasions, but Linda always accepted it, 'because it's family'. And

Brian never did anything about it because he didn't want to upset Linda, but a few months before he died, he once turned to Ray and said, 'You're doing what I should have done years ago.' The worst example of it all was Anne's husband Brian, who must have hated our dad for what he'd done to his wife but had to pretend everything was okay in front of the family.

Us kids had always made our partners take second place to the family, but I wasn't prepared to do that anymore. Ray wasn't in the wrong, and it just wasn't fair for him to be branded public enemy number one. But, by choosing to side with my husband rather than my sisters, all hell had broken loose.

The other thing Dad brought us up to believe was that 'The Nolans are never wrong.' But this time Anne and Denise Nolan *were* wrong. Everyone gets it wrong sometimes and to think you never do is ridiculous.

For years, any problems in our family had been swept under the carpet. So long as the Nolans were united against the world, then nothing that was happening within our family mattered. Again, Dad's abuse of Anne is a classic example of that.

After Dad died, Anne said she had hated him for years for what he'd done to her, but I never once saw that hatred while he was alive. She always turned up at family dos, she did his shopping and visited him when he got poorly. She could have easily moved away or just distanced herself from her parents if she'd wanted to do that. But instead she pretended as if nothing had ever happened until after he died. And then I think she was overwhelmed with hatred because she'd lost the chance to ever confront him and properly vent her anger. The whole thing was tragic.

I was sick of sweeping stuff under carpets. Also, as the

youngest, I'd had a far more independent childhood than my brothers and sisters. When the girls went down to work in London, I'd stayed in Blackpool and I'd had a totally normal life when I was in my early teens. They'd never had that, and were so much more controlled by Dad than I ever was, which maybe made it harder for them to break away from his 'the Nolans are always right' mantra.

The feud caused massive problems in my relationship with Ray, and there were plenty of times when I truly thought it was going to split us up. We were supposed to be planning our wedding, but it was on, then off, then on, then off a dozen times. 'I really don't think I can go through with it,' Ray said one day. 'I just can't marry into a family where everyone hates me and thinks I'm trying to split them up.'

'But you're not marrying my family, you're marrying me,' I said. He still didn't seem convinced. We had some terrible rows over it all. Ray said he felt like a condemned man on death row who was innocent but no one would listen.

'Just forget it,' I'd say. 'I'm done with it all.'

But he couldn't leave it. It ate away at him and he was getting more and more bitter. He couldn't sleep and I was convinced he was either going to have a nervous break-down or a heart attack. He just couldn't get over the idea that he was being accused of splitting up the famous Nolan family.

Then, one day, Anne rang and asked if she could come round to see us. I said fine, but as soon as she walked in the door, she said, 'I don't want to talk about the argument.'

'Well, how are we going to sort it out then?' I asked.

All my life I'd been the quiet, non-confrontational one, hanging around in the background behind my sisters, but that clearly hadn't been a good thing because all the time there were all these hidden resentments I'd known nothing about until Denise's text messages. This time I wanted us to resolve things properly.

'I don't know why we can't just forget about it all,' said Anne.

'Because you aren't the one who was sent what felt like 20,000 horrible texts and were told everyone hates your husband. How can I take him to a family do when he thinks that?'

'Well, it wouldn't bother me,' said Anne. 'It's family.'

And that was the difference between us. Anne would put the Nolan family above everything, even her husband's feelings, but I was no longer prepared to do that.

'Just because it's family, doesn't make it right,' I said.

We talked for a while and agreed to try to put things behind us and move on, but it was still a bit strained. I still wasn't ready to do that with Denise though, as it had been her who'd sent the most hurtful text messages.

Around that time, I was also struggling with Jake moving away from home. He'd loved performing since he was absolutely tiny, and I knew one day he would want to go into acting. When he saw an advert in *The Stage* magazine for the Sylvia Young Theatre School in London, he was convinced that that was what he wanted to do. We took the train down together, and I waited outside nervously while he auditioned. He was recalled for a second audition the same day and was then offered a place there and then. We were both so excited that we ran out of the school screaming with happiness. But when it finally sunk in that my baby – even though he was then fourteen! – was going to be leaving home, I was distraught. We arranged that he would go and live with Shane and Christie, so I knew he was in good hands, but I missed him terribly.

He still came home every weekend and then we travelled down to London together really early on a Monday morning. When we arrived at Euston, he'd go off to Sylvia Young's and I'd head to the *Loose Women* studio. And the nights I stayed over in London, he'd sleep in my hotel room. So I did still see plenty of him, but it felt weird not having him at home all the time.

As if it wasn't hard enough to cope with one son moving away from home, I also had another about to hit eighteen and become an adult. Time was racing by. We planned a big party for Shane Jnr and all his friends, and he was so excited. I invited the family and included Anne, because we were getting on a bit better, but I couldn't bring myself to invite Denise. I just didn't know what to say to her after all the texts she had sent me.

Anne accepted her invitation, and I was delighted. But then, an hour before the party, she phoned me.

'I'm not going to come,' said Anne. 'I just feel a bit bad for Denise because she wasn't invited.'

'OK,' I said. 'I'll talk to you in the morning.' I had dozens of people about to arrive and couldn't think about it just then.

Anne rang back the next day. 'Do you hate me?' she said.

'I'm not angry for me,' I said. 'But I am angry for Shane Jnr. I really did think we could keep the kids out of all this.'

Again, I swept it under the carpet, and Anne, Auntie Theresa and most of the rest of the family came round to ours that Christmas. I still hadn't spoken to Denise though.

We all got together for our brother Brian's wedding to his lovely long-term girlfriend, Annie, in August 2007. Brian wanted all the girls to sing together and so we did it for him, even though Denise and I still weren't talking. We rehearsed round at Maureen's every day for a week, and would talk about whose harmony was whose, but that was it. On the day of the wedding we all got up and sang for Brian, but Denise and I didn't exchange a word for the rest of the night. It was terribly tragic, but we just got on with it.

The next time we were all together couldn't have been more different from the happy day of that wedding. It was the day we all gathered at the hospital because Linda had called to say her Brian was dying. Linda already had so much to cope with, fighting cancer herself, and it was all so unfair.

Ray and I had finally set a date for our wedding by then. It was to be 3 November 2007, and Brian would have been our witness, with Linda as chief bridesmaid. I couldn't quite believe that it was only two months away but that Brian wasn't going to be there. Ray and Brian were like best mates. When they were together, they laughed all the time, and they could talk for hours on the phone. Brian's death was a terrible time for all of us, but it was just horrific for Linda. The whole family rallied around her, but all she really wanted was Brian – the one thing we couldn't give her.

Linda and Brian were never apart. He did everything for her, which meant that when he died she was almost like a child who'd been abandoned. She had never even really gone to the supermarket because Brian would get up at six every morning and have all the shopping and housework done before she woke up.

A few weeks after Brian died, Linda rang me and said, 'I'm really proud of myself. I've put the Hoover together and I've used it.'

'You should be ashamed of yourself, Linda Hudson,' I joked.

'But I've never had to do it before,' she laughed.

In reality, there really wasn't much for Linda to laugh about then. It was all so hard for her. I don't know where she got her strength from, in that she was still having treatment for cancer herself, her husband had just died and our mum was really sick too. But despite all that, she threw herself into helping me plan our wedding and my hen do.

By then, I had been taken on by a fabulous new agent called Neil Howarth, who had lined up loads of work for me. Within weeks of moving to him, I was on a magazine cover, I had my own column in *Woman* magazine and I landed the Iceland ads. Then he managed to get *Woman* to cover my wedding and found the most idyllic location – Hazlewood Castle in Yorkshire.

The guest list turned out to be very stressful. I invited Anne, but she decided not to come because Denise wasn't invited, and then Auntie Theresa pulled out too. It was so upsetting that two of my sisters and our auntie, who'd been with us all through our childhoods, wasn't going to be there, but I couldn't invite Denise and Auntie Theresa if they weren't speaking to me. And, as much as it hurt me, if Anne chose not to come, then that was her decision.

The morning of my wedding was so wonderful. I was staying in a room at the castle and my full-length ivory dress was hanging in the wardrobe. Everything was as it should be, and totally different to my secret wedding to Shane. The first person to arrive at my room that morning was chief bridesmaid Linda. She charged into the room singing 'Here Comes the Bride', then repeated it over and over again until I was ready to clobber her!

I was just getting ready and putting on my make-up when my mobile phone bleeped. I thought it might be a good luck text from one of my friends, so I picked it up and looked at the screen. It was a message from Shane: 'Always remember you were my wife first,' he joked. 'You were Mrs Roche long before you were Mrs Fensome.'

Roche is Shane's real surname. Perhaps he was thinking he might still be able to tug at my heartstrings on my wedding day to another man. But if that was what he was thinking, he was totally mistaken. Shane was history for me. Ray was my future. I deleted the message and stepped into my wedding dress.

In the morning we exchanged our vows in a civil ceremony inside the castle, which was licensed for weddings. It was just Ray and me, the kids, Linda and Ray's mum, Irene, and it was incredibly emotional. Both Ray and I were crying. We'd been through so much to get to this point, and it felt utterly right. When the registrar pronounced us man and wife, Ciara jumped up and down, she was so excited.

Then, in the afternoon, we had a blessing in front of all our friends and family in a twelfth-century chapel in the castle grounds. It was just amazing. As well as Linda as chief brides-maid, I also had Anne's daughters Amy and Alex and Tommy's daughter Laura as bridesmaids. Then Ciara and Bernie's daughter Erin were flower girls. Shane Jnr was best man and Maureen's son Danny and Tommy's son Tommy were groomsmen. Jake was going to give me away, and he was as proud as punch.

When I walked down the aisle with Jake, it was just magical. I felt so lucky that after everything that had gone before, I'd met someone as fabulous as Ray, and that he and my sons got on so well and we had our gorgeous Ciara. I truly could not have been happier.

My sisters got up and sang 'Let It Be Me' and there wasn't a dry eye in the house. Linda was unbelievable all day long. It must have hurt her so much to be there without Brian, but she never let it show. It was only later, when I looked at a video of my sisters rehearsing their song, that I saw she had totally broken down and cried uncontrollably. But when it came to the actual performance in church, she never missed a beat.

We had thought about maybe bringing Mum out of the home for an hour or so for the service, but in the end we all decided that the upset of leaving her familiar surroundings would be too traumatic for her. And, in all honesty, it would have been really traumatic for us kids too. It did feel very sad that she wasn't there though, and I mentioned her in my speech, and Brian did too.

I really couldn't have asked for a better wedding day. It was just perfect.

By the time we returned from our honeymoon in Cyprus, Mum's condition had got even worse and we knew she was nearing the end. But still she clung on, despite being incredibly poorly. Just after Christmas, on 28 December, I took Ciara in to visit Mum at the home. I touched her hair and kissed her. Two days later, she died in her sleep. I went to the care home with my brothers and sisters to say goodbye. She looked so peaceful, as if she had just fallen asleep. I couldn't cry that day. In fact, all week I didn't shed a single tear. Even though we'd known she was slipping away for months, I think I was actually in shock that she had really gone. And I was relieved for her too, that her suffering was finally over.

It was at Mum's funeral, when they played 'You Raise Me

Up', that I could feel the tears coming, but then I was terrified that if I started crying, I would never stop. So I forced myself to hold it together for a little bit longer.

As the weeks and months after Mum's death dragged by, my sense of loss and sadness only worsened. The further I got from my memories of her with Alzheimer's, the more I was able to remember the way she used to be. And that was the mum that I missed terribly. It took a while, but finally I was able to mourn the mum I'd known before Alzheimer's.

But even the heartbreak of Mum's death did little to heal the rift in our family. We were all there at her funeral, but Denise and Anne still weren't talking to me. By the start of 2008, Ray and I decided we needed to leave Blackpool. Because we all lived so close to each other, I didn't even feel I could go to the park without bumping into Anne or Denise.

We'd been spending a lot of weekends over in Cheshire with our friends Denise Welch and Tim Healy. Denise was a regular on *Loose Women* and we hit it off right from the start. One weekend we got home from theirs and I said to Ray, 'Let's move. We can't stay here anymore because the tension is always there. We just need to put a bit of distance between us and my family.'

We put our house on the market and within a couple of months we'd moved to a lovely new house near Denise and Tim. It was the best thing we ever did. We loved it, and Ciara adored her new school. Jake was still down in London at Sylvia Young's during the week, and then Shane Jnr landed a job as a Bluecoat at Pontin's. I was so proud of him for getting it, but it still broke my heart when he set off for his first season in Somerset. And knowing exactly what young men working on summer seasons get up to didn't calm my nerves either!

I didn't have long to worry about my empty nest though because my agent Neil seemed to have a never-ending round of work lined up for me. I landed a parenting advice column in the *Daily Mirror*, which I loved – I certainly felt I'd been through enough experiences over the years to know what real mums have to cope with! Then I got a call that made me shiver – quite literally! Would I like to take part in the next series of *Dancing on Ice*?

'How hard can it be?' I asked my open-mouthed sisters when I broke the news to them. They didn't answer, but I knew what they were thinking: 'Very'. And it was.

I'll be honest; I wasn't a natural on the ice by any stretch of the imagination. And the training was absolutely gruelling, getting up at 5 a.m. to practise, as well as doing *Loose Women* and all my other work. Then, when the live performances began every Sunday evening from the beginning of January 2009, I was almost constantly terrified. I'd feel physically sick for hours before each show. But, weirdly, I absolutely loved it at the same time. And Ciara was so proud of me that I kept pushing myself for her sake too. The British public must have taken pity on my enthusiasm because they kept voting for me and, week after week, I stayed in.

But then all my enjoyment came to a crashing halt one Saturday night when I got a call from Neil telling me that Anne had given an interview to the *Sunday People*. When I read the article the next day, I was shaking. The headline said: '*Dancing on Ice*'s Coleen Nolan at war with older sister'. In the interview, Anne said she wanted to make peace with us, but all her quotes seemed to show that she still thought Ray was in the wrong. If she did really want to make things up with us, talking about us to a Sunday newspaper was certainly a funny way of going about it.

Now it felt like the whole world knew about our rift – until then no one had said anything publicly. It just made the whole thing seem so raw again, and still there was no end to it in sight.

I battled on with *Dancing on Ice*, even skating with a strapped-up fractured thumb one Sunday. I made it all the way to the semi-final, but then, on my first day of training that week, I was practising a 'flying' manoeuvre in a harness when I twisted awkwardly. My back was agony and I was soon back at Barnet Hospital A&E for the second time in the series.

All week my back was spasming, and I even threw up from the pain, but I was determined to skate that Sunday. I'd only been able to do about an hour's training all week and I could barely move for the pain, but I still went out there, and the crowd was fantastic.

I knew my time in the show was over, but I was just grateful I was able to skate that final time – even if the pain was worse than childbirth!

Dancing on Ice was such a great experience for me because I actually did something that I never thought I'd be able to do – and I enjoyed it too. I think it also sent a message to other forty-something women out there who might have put on a few pounds over the years and had some tough times along the way. I think I showed them that none of that really matters, and it certainly doesn't matter what other people think – if you want something enough, you can still get out there and do it.

20.

Maureen

A Granny and a Newlywed

'How would you feel about being a granny, eh, Mum?' Danny asked me one afternoon as we sat in our front room drinking mugs of tea.

'I'd kill you,' I laughed. The whole idea seemed so far-fetched that I had to laugh. My Danny was only nineteen years old – he still lived at home, I still cooked his tea, and there was no way he could become a father. He had a job, working with Ritchie on the Roy Chubby Brown tours, where he sold merchandise, but in many ways he was still just a kid. We carried on chatting about all sorts of nonsense and I thought no more of the conversation.

Then, a couple of weeks later, Danny was out during the day and he phoned me on my mobile. 'You know what you said about becoming a granny?' he said slowly.

'Yes,' I said, feeling a little bit confused.

'Well, you're going to be one.'

I was totally stunned. I couldn't think of a thing to say. Danny and his girlfriend, Anne-Marie, were in the process of splitting up – surely they couldn't be going to have a baby together? But they were, and it was due in November 2009.

When Ritchie got home, we sat in a bit of a daze as we

tried to take it all in. It sounds a terrible thing to say, because we both now adore our baby granddaughter, but at the time both Ritchie and I cried. Danny seemed so young and we both felt he would lose out on so many opportunities by becoming a dad and having to take on all the responsibilities that go with it. But what could we say? Ritchie and I had barely known each other when I'd fallen pregnant and here we were, still together twenty years later. And even though Danny had been an accident, he was the best thing that had ever happened to me. I couldn't really be cross with him. And even if I had been, that wouldn't have changed the situation. It was just one of those things. We'd always been a really open family and had talked about contraception, but I guess it just took the once without protection and that was that!

It was a shame that Danny and Anne-Marie were breaking up before the baby was born, but they weren't getting on at all at that point. Obviously it was a very difficult situation at times, but gradually it got easier, and Anne-Marie was fabulous at including both him and me in the pregnancy. She even invited us both to one of the antenatal scans. Seeing my first grandchild on the monitor was incredible, and everything finally began to feel real. Suddenly the whole idea of becoming a granny felt very exciting.

But there was more excitement for me around the corner. It was my birthday in June 2009 and to celebrate Ritchie and I went out for something to eat with Linda and Coleen. When the bill came, Ritchie kept pushing it in my direction.

'Oh, right.' I said. 'Got to pay on my own birthday now? Cheers!'

'Yeah, you sort it,' he said, again pushing the little saucer and bill closer to me.

Finally, with a bit of a frown, I picked the bill up from the saucer. There, lying underneath it, was a beautiful diamond ring. I stared at the ring, then looked up at Ritchie, who was grinning madly at me.

'You're kidding, aren't you?' I asked, utterly gobsmacked.

'No,' he said, smiling. 'We've been waiting for too long. Let's get married. Let's do it next year. Let's do it properly.'

So Ritchie had proposed a second time, but this time we were determined to go through with the wedding. Like Ritchie said, we'd waited for long enough.

Around the time of Ritchie's big surprise, I also got another incredible proposal when I was approached to join The Nolans reunion tour.

The thought of touring with my sisters again was the most exciting work offer I'd had in years. Ever since Anne and I had stopped performing together as The Nolans, I'd been working as an actress. I like working, but if I'm honest a big reason I do it is because we need the money. Lots of people think that, because we were in The Nolans, we must be loaded, but the reality is that we saw hardly any of the millions that were made by the group.

I love my house, but it is just a fairly normal, three-bed semi in Blackpool. Ritchie works as a tour manager for Roy Chubby Brown, but we can't afford for either of us to just sit back and put our feet up. The mortgage and the bills have to be paid.

I'd been acting for five years, starting in a show called *Mum's the Word*, which was a series of monologues about motherhood, and then moving on to *Blood Brothers* in the West End. I'd always loved that show, and must have been to see it at least eighteen times before I was in it, so when I was offered the role of Mrs Johnstone, it was like a dream come true. It was hard working in the West End though, when Danny and Ritchie were back home in Blackpool, and I really missed them. Initially it was a six-month contract, but I ended up staying for two years. For one year, I stayed with my cousin Sandra who I adore and who lives near London. Her gorgeous son Jono gave up his bedroom to me for all that time. For another year, I lived with Bernie and Steve. I was so lucky to be able to stay with relatives most of the time because otherwise it can be a very lonely life working in the West End.

After *Blood Brothers* I was in another couple of touring productions. I enjoyed the work, but I'd always dreamt that The Nolans might reform. Then, one day, my phone rang. It was Neil Howarth, a young, energetic guy who was Coleen's agent and was now looking after all of us. 'Hi, Maureen,' he said. 'Now, how do you like the idea of this – The Nolans reunion tour.'

I gasped and actually felt myself starting to shiver. We'd talked about how great it would be for us to reform for years, but to think it was really going to happen was just fantastic. I was thrilled.

But then we heard that Universal, the record company, only wanted to use the four of us who had had the big hits together and who had done the massive tours in Japan. That meant Anne wouldn't be part of the line-up. And Denise had left years earlier, before we'd had any chart success, so she couldn't be involved either. Obviously I was disappointed but I honestly thought Anne and Denise would understand and be OK about it.

I couldn't have been more wrong.

I rang Anne to tell her about the tour and what the record

company had said. I could tell from her voice that Anne was disappointed, and I did feel bad that she wasn't going to be part of it all, but I just didn't know what I could do about it. Universal are a massive company and I didn't feel I could just ring them up and make demands over the line-up.

'I'll need a few days to get my head around this,' Anne said.

'That's fine,' I said. 'I understand that.'

But then Bernie, Linda and I started getting the angry text messages, which were so upsetting. It was so horrible receiving them from two people I'd been so close to all my life. It was awful to have to deal with all that at the same time as rehearsing for the tour, recording a new album and doing all the promotional interviews and photo shoots.

Maybe it was the wrong thing to do, going ahead with the tour even though the record company hadn't invited Anne, but at the time I needed the work and the money, and I really thought Anne wouldn't be interested in doing it anyway, as she had a job outside of show business. I had always tried to keep out of the row between Coleen and our oldest sisters, but Anne and Denise felt that by going on the tour, I was siding with Coleen. They were clearly furious with me. But what could I have done? I didn't want to take sides. I loved all my sisters.

I'm normally pretty laid-back about everything, but the feud hit me really, really hard and upset me a great deal. One day I had a terrible argument with Denise. It was dreadful.

For weeks and weeks, I couldn't think about anything other than the fall-out. I couldn't sleep and was losing weight. I desperately missed seeing Anne and Denise, but I didn't know how to make things better.

The whole thing was totally heartbreaking. I think, in some

ways, it was harder for me than the others because I had been that much closer to Anne and Denise all my life. We were the older ones, and as kids we did absolutely everything together. Even when we got older and moved back to Blackpool, we still lived really close to each other and would meet up or talk on the phone every single day. We'd go to the park together, or the cinema, or have girlie nights in. They'd been a massive part of my life for so long, then suddenly they weren't there.

I just had this terrible feeling of sadness inside me all the time. I didn't feel like I'd fallen out with them, and I would have spoken to them, but it seemed they didn't want to have anything to do with me anymore. I could never have imagined a day when Anne, Denise and I wouldn't be talking to each other. But it seemed that that day had arrived.

It was going round and round in my head all the time until it was making me ill, and in the end I realized I had to disassociate myself from everything that was going on or I'd give myself a nervous breakdown. So I ploughed on with the tour, which was absolutely fantastic, and I loved every minute of it. I just wished it hadn't caused so much upset.

Just days after our closing night, there was even more excitement when Danny and Anne-Marie's daughter was born. She was a beautiful little girl and they named her Ava. It hadn't been how I'd expected to become a granny, but any problems there had been along the way really were totally forgotten the first time I saw Ava. I was utterly swept away. She was gorgeous.

Anne-Marie has been really good about allowing Danny, Ritchie and me to spend time with Ava, and a situation which could have been horrendous has worked out really well. Now I'll babysit her whenever I can and if I'm away touring and only home on a Sunday, Anne-Marie will bring her round when

I'm back, so I get a chance to see her. I want to make sure that Ritchie and I will always be a big part of her life and we do everything we can to be good grandparents.

A couple of months after splitting up with Anne-Marie, Danny started going out with a girl called Maddison, whom he'd gone right through school with. They'd known each other all that time and nothing had ever happened, but then they started going out and, within no time at all, it was obvious they were madly in love.

Even so, nothing had quite prepared me for what was going to happen on Christmas Eve 2009. They went into town to do some last bits of Christmas shopping, had a couple of drinks and then came back to our house because I was having a bit of a party.

After a while, Maddison went upstairs to the landing because she wanted to stand by the window to get some fresh air. She'd been up there a while when Danny shouted: 'Maddison, can you come down? I've got something to tell you.'

'I'll be down in a minute,' Maddison called back.

'You've got to come now,' Danny said again. 'I've got an announcement to make.'

Finally Maddison came down the stairs. Then suddenly I realized that Danny was kneeling down in front of her. He was proposing. He'd bought the ring and everything. Maddison was ecstatic and phoned all her friends and her family. It was amazing.

I was stunned. And, if I'm honest, I was worried too. He still seemed so young to me and everything was moving so fast. Then, in February, Maddison fell pregnant. So that was a big shock again. I don't want my son to sound like one of those boys who goes round getting girls pregnant, because he's not like that; he's a fabulous lad. It was just the way things turned out.

It was all a bit bumpy at first, as Anne-Marie adjusted to the situation. She must have been worried that Ava might get overlooked with a new baby on the way. But now Maddison gets on brilliantly well with Ava and Anne-Marie, and she will even help to look after Ava if necessary. So, considering how awkward it could have been, it all worked out really well.

On 29 October Maddison gave birth to my second grand-daughter, Sienna. The baby had been breach, so Maddison had to have a caesarean section, but the operation went well and Sienna was born a healthy 6lb 1oz. Afterwards, Danny and Maddison brought her home to our house, where they were living before finding their own place.

It was amazing to have a new baby at home again and Ritchie and I adored her. Maddison and Danny doted on their first child, and her older half-sister Ava loved her from the beginning too. Considering how worried I had been about the whole situation, I really couldn't have hoped for a better outcome.

Maddison, Danny and Sienna are now preparing to move into their own place. I know it is the best thing for them, but I'm dreading not having them around. I hate to think how quiet it will be around the house without them here.

I am so proud to have become a grandmother to Ava and Sienna. Sometimes people say to me, 'Oh, isn't it awful being called a granny?' but I think it's wonderful! The word 'granny' doesn't bother me at all. I think it is fantastic to have the opportunity to spend time with young children again – partic-ularly when you don't have to do all the difficult bits! And even though I'm a granny now, I still don't feel old. If I could turn back the clock and go back ten or twenty years, then I probably would, but that's not an option. I'm lucky in that I inherited my mother's good skin, which seems to age quite well. And I do try to keep in shape too. If I feel my clothes are getting a bit tighter, I'll start running a bit more frequently, but I'm not obsessed about working out at all. I'm usually a size ten and I like to stick around that because otherwise I start feeling a bit uncomfortable.

I think one thing that has helped me stay fairly young-looking is that I don't really get stressed about things. My sisters laugh at me and say that I'm so laid–back, I'm horizontal. And it's just not me – Ritchie and Danny are exactly the same. No one ever gets really worked up about anything in our house. Obviously there are some things that I worry about, like how Danny is getting on, Bernie being ill and the fall-out with my sisters. But beyond that, I just don't let little things stress me. And I don't worry so much now about what people think of me or what I ought to be doing to keep other people happy. I think that confidence comes with age.

The only downside with everyone in our house being so laid-back is that sometimes we never quite get round to doing things. Which is why, at the beginning of 2010, I was thinking that our second engagement might end up being just as long as our first. It wasn't at all that I didn't want to marry Ritchie – I really wanted to be his wife – I just couldn't face having to organize a wedding. The thought of all the lists and decision-making made my blood turn cold. Luckily we got a call saying *OK!* magazine were interested in featuring the wedding. They would pay for it and it seemed a good opportunity, so we said yes.

We decided we would like to marry in Spain because we've got a little apartment out there and we've had some great holidays together there. Once we'd made the decision to go ahead with the wedding, there was no more messing about – we had just eight weeks to organize the whole thing. Linda was my chief bridesmaid and she was fantastic, helping me to get everything sorted.

The wedding preparations and organizing my hen do were a great laugh. But there was some sadness too, in that Anne, Denise and Auntie Theresa weren't part of it and wouldn't be at the wedding. I couldn't invite them because by then things were so difficult between us. My only way of coping with that was to try to distance myself from all of it.

But as the wedding day got closer and closer, I really couldn't quite get it into my head that Anne and Denise weren't going to be there. Like I said, I'd been so incredibly close to my older sisters for so long, and I never thought I would get married without them there. The whole situation made me feel so sad, but I didn't see the point in discussing it with anyone because it was difficult for all of us.

Shortly before the wedding, I received a letter from Anne and Denise asking if we could put everything that had happened behind us. I replied that I was about to leave for Spain but that when I returned I would be back in touch. I know some of my other sisters can't forgive some of the things that were said to them, but for me, it was the beginning of a very cautious reunion.

Ritchie and I married on Friday, 13 August 2010. The date might not have been too great, but the wedding was amazing! It took place at eight o'clock in the evening, just as it was cooling down, but there was still a perfect blue sky and that wonderful early evening light that you get in Spain in summer. The wedding was at a golf club and then the reception was outside. More than seventy friends and family came over for it, and we had the most wonderful time. Coleen, Bernie, their daughters Ciara and Erin, Linda and Maddison were bridesmaids, and they looked gorgeous.

And then there was Ritchie. He had been going to wear a stone-coloured linen suit, but then we worried that that was probably what all the men would be wearing – he needed to stand out. It had to be ivory! It might sound a bit John Travolta in *Saturday Night Fever*, but he looked absolutely amazing. My dress was a traditional ivory gown which I'd bought in Blackpool.

It had been eighteen years since we'd first discussed marriage, but even though it had never really been a big deal for me before, when my brother Brian walked me down that aisle, it felt utterly magical. I knew then it was totally the right thing to do. It really was a dream wedding. Afterwards, Ritchie said to me, 'I'd do it all again.'

'Me too,' I replied.

There was hardly any time for a honeymoon though – we had four days further down the coast in Spain with Danny and Maddison before I had to fly back to England to start rehearsing my new play, *The Naked Truth*. I played a pole dancer in the show and even had to have pole dancing lessons to prepare for it. That was certainly a new challenge! I've got hardly any body strength at all, and it nearly killed me. I guess it's a skill that might come in handy though! In the play, my character had breast cancer, which was very poignant. It feels as though our family has learnt way too much about that disease over the past few years.

I was so shocked when Bernie rang me in April 2009 to say she had cancer. After Anne and then Linda, I just couldn't believe it was happening to Bernie now too. But they have been so strong throughout the whole thing. They are an inspiration to women everywhere in the way they have dealt with their illness. I'm so incredibly proud of them.

I am certainly very careful now about regularly checking my breasts for lumps. After Bernie was diagnosed, I decided that if the genetic tests which both she and Linda had done showed their strain of breast cancer was genetic, then I would have a double mastectomy. Fortunately, their tests showed that their cancer wasn't genetic so I guess I'm not really at any greater risk than any other woman. But having had three cases of breast cancer in the family is certainly a wake-up call to the dangers of the disease.

In November 2010 I was invited to Anne's sixtieth birthday party. I was working and couldn't make it, but the next evening we all met round at Denise's and had a great time. Anne sobbed on my shoulder at one point, and it was just wonderful being close to her again. Since then, we have seen each other a few times and Denise has been round to visit Ava and Sienna at our house too. I am absolutely thrilled to be talking to Anne and Denise again and for us to be rebuilding our relationship after everything that went on because of the tour.

But I still don't know whether Anne and Denise will ever fully make things up with Coleen and Linda. The whole situation is terribly sad. When it all first blew up, it was just horrible. It really got me down. And it still upsets me to think that when Anne and I became grandmothers for the first time – Anne's youngest daughter Alex has had a baby son Vinny – we weren't talking to each other. There was so much we had to chat and laugh about then, but we couldn't do it. But now we are able to put that behind us, and I can be friends with all my sisters again.

It is hard being away from home for months on end when I'm touring with a play. But Ritchie's job takes him away a lot too, and we are used to being apart because of our work. I love my work, but I guess if I could wave a magic wand, I'd like to have enough money to be able to just do the plays and tours that I'd love to do and take it easy the rest of the time. I've worked pretty hard non-stop since I was nine. I think I was way too young to be doing that amount of work, but at the time we just got on and did it.

Sometimes I feel frustrated that The Nolans had such a high level of success but none of us has much to show for it. Even now, I hear 'I'm in the Mood for Dancing' on the radio and in shops all the time. It was a huge hit, and we had ten or eleven other consecutive top twenty records, so we were selling an awful lot of music and making a lot of money for someone – but it wasn't ourselves! Looking back, there are people whom we worked with along the way to whom we should have said: 'Hang on a minute. We should be getting some of that money.' But we never did, and a lot of people got rich, while we didn't.

But there's no point in being bitter about it. I just count my blessings and think how fortunate I am to be so happy now. I feel fantastic being married to Ritchie, I've got my fabulous son and his fiancée, and I'm mad about my grand-daughters Ava and Sienna. And, thankfully, it looks as though things have healed with Anne and Denise. Then I've got Tommy, Brian, Linda, Bernie and Coleen, whom I adore too.

Not to mention Auntie Theresa and all my nieces, nephews and now even a great-nephew!

I'm fifty-six years old now and, like my sisters, I've certainly had my highs and lows in life. But I feel very fortunate that I've not had the struggles that Bernie, Linda and Anne have had to deal with. They have all been so strong, and I'm so very proud of them. But I'm proud of all my sisters – and my brothers too.

When I was tiny I felt so special and so secure to be part of something as big and strong as the Nolan family. And I still feel that today.

21.
Linda

Surviving Yet Sad

I stood on stage that first night of The Nolans reunion tour in October 2009 and could feel the tears brimming in my eyes. It was such a bittersweet moment. It was truly wonderful being on stage again, in front of a crowd who were going totally mental for us. But it was so sad that Brian wasn't there to see it. Brian always said that The Nolans were his favourite band and he'd always hoped that we would one day get back together. If he'd still been alive, he would have been even more nervous than us, and he'd have been standing at the side of the stage, crying with happiness that we were reunited. But the reality was that he wasn't there, and that hurt.

I first got a phone call about the tour from Neil Howarth. 'So how do you feel about a Nolans reunion tour?' he asked, buzzing with excitement.

'OK, yeah,' I said. 'That really would be fantastic.'

I almost surprised myself with my enthusiasm. I hadn't worked for more than a year and had been feeling very low. The thought of touring in a play on my own had utterly terrified me, but the prospect of going on the road again with my sisters felt fine. I'd have my security blanket, my family, around me.

Once I'd agreed, I soon found myself in the middle of a whirlwind of activity. For someone who'd barely left the house in the previous few months, it was all very exciting. First we had to record a CD at a studio in Manchester, which was totally full-on. When we were recording back in the 1970s, we would record one track a day, but this time around it was three tracks a day. We then had to film our DVD, make an advert for it and learn all the choreography routines for the tour. And on top of all that, there was a massive promotional schedule in the run-up to the tour. We appeared on *This Morning*, in magazines, newspapers and on countless radio stations. It was exhausting, but so exciting too.

The record company looked after us brilliantly and every day was a whirl of activity. Obviously I still missed Brian dreadfully, particularly as I knew how much he would have enjoyed all the tour preparations. But I finally had something else to think about in my life too. For the first time in a long time, I had a reason to get out of bed in the morning.

At every rehearsal the show's producer would say, 'OK, girls. You'll be stood at the back of the stage, the big Nolans sign will split in half, you'll emerge from behind it and the crowd will go wild.'

Each time he said that, my sisters and I would look at each other in terror. 'What if they don't go wild?' we'd say. 'What if there's no one there?'

'It'll be fine,' the producer said over and over again.

But it was almost thirty years since we'd all been on stage together, and we weren't at all certain that we'd be fine. So that first night in Nottingham, we stood at the back of the stage feeling sick with nerves, then the big Nolans sign split in half and we emerged from behind it. And, yes, the crowd really did go wild. It was just incredible.

Our first song was 'Holding Out for a Hero', which we did alongside these young, gorgeous male dancers. We wore black and white trouser suits with black leather gloves and sunglasses, and at the end of the song we took off our glasses, as if to say: 'It's us!' The crowd went bonkers. The show was directed by Kim Gavin, who has worked on dozens of really big tours, like Take That and Westlife. He had so many fantastic ideas; he was amazing.

'I'm in the Mood for Dancing' was our finale, and before we went out to sing it, we all had to dash backstage to change into black catsuits. There was a short break, but that first night we were rushing to get changed when suddenly all we could hear was the entire audience singing 'I'm in the Mood'.

'Oh my God,' laughed Coleen. 'They're all going mad for us.'

When we went back on stage to sing it ourselves, the noise was mind-blowing.

The tour was amazing, but I still had my down days when I missed Brian terribly. Thankfully though, this was a tour I could manage because my support team was all around me and if I was having a bad day, the girls instinctively understood.

The only other thing which cast a terrible shadow over the tour was the rift between the four of us and Anne and Denise. When Anne and Denise had fallen out with Coleen ages before, I'd tried to keep right out of it. I loved all my sisters and they'd all been incredibly good to me when I was ill and after Brian died. With Denise and Tom only living five doors away, I saw them all the time, and they probably helped saved my life when

I was at my lowest point. We were even due to go on holiday together in the autumn of 2009, along with Auntie Theresa. But while we were still planning the trip, the record company approached Maureen, Bernie, Coleen and me about doing the tour, and that was when everything went wrong.

When the row about the tour line-up first kicked off, I tried to explain to Anne what had happened, and things between us seemed to be OK. But then Denise got involved and it all got really out of hand. She sent me some really vicious text messages, including one calling me a Judas. Denise had left before we even became The Nolans, and so there was no reason why she would be part of a Nolans tour, but she thought it was wrong that the record company hadn't included Anne and I guess she was defending her.

But what could I have done? If I'd pulled out of the tour, there wasn't any guarantee that Anne would have been selected instead of me. And, to be honest, I needed the money. Anne told me she wouldn't have done the tour without me for £100,000. Maybe she wouldn't have, but I was surviving on £75 a week in benefits after Brian died and things were getting desperate. More than that, for the first time in a long time, I felt I had a reason for living.

Then, in one text message, Denise said something about my Brian, and that for me was the point of no return. It felt like I had been stabbed in the heart. Denise had been so good to me after Brian died, but now I was getting the feeling that she'd just done all of that out of pity. She was bringing up things from when Brian and I had lived with her and her partner Tom years before. There had been times when we'd all got on each other's nerves, but I thought that was long forgotten. Obviously not, and the whole thing was raked up again. But Brian wasn't here to defend himself anymore and it hurt so much that they could say those things about him when they knew exactly how painful it had been for me since his death.

I thought about it and realized I wouldn't have accepted that kind of behaviour from a friend, so why was I accepting it from my sisters, who were supposed to love me more than anyone? For my own peace of mind, I just had to stand back from the whole situation. I was finding it hard enough to keep my head above water emotionally as it was. I couldn't cope with any more problems. So if they wanted to send me messages like that, then fine, but I wasn't going to respond.

But when we stopped talking to each other, it was incredibly difficult. Denise still lived down the road from me and, before then, we had seen each other all the time. Nevertheless, I felt there was nothing I could do but accept that from now on our lives would be going down different paths.

Our last night of The Nolans tour was in Belfast, just before Christmas. We were all pretty exhausted by then, but it was so sad that it had come to an end; we'd had a ball.

I think we all had a bit of a come-down after the excitement of the tour, but for me it seemed particularly quiet. I still couldn't face taking on any theatre work and touring on my own, so I spent a lot of time at home alone.

Then, at the beginning of 2010, I had a real dip. The doctor changed my antidepressants and it took me a month to get used to them, and for a while I really struggled. I couldn't see any point in getting out of bed and often I'd still be there at three o'clock in the afternoon. Hudson, my dog, sleeps on the bed with me, and sometimes in the morning he'd lift up his head, as if to say, 'Are we getting up?' But I'd just stroke his head and say, 'No, I'm going to sleep some more.' When I did get up, I would lie on the couch for the rest of the day. I wasn't eating or drinking and I rarely went out.

Dr Brigg kept calling me, so after a while I went back to see her, and gradually I pulled myself back up again. Then, in the spring of 2010, Bernie was diagnosed with breast cancer. She was dreading telling me the news about her cancer herself because she knew how upset I'd be, so she asked Maureen to do it. Maureen picked me up one afternoon to drive into town and she said, 'Linda, there's no easy way to tell you this. Bernie has got breast cancer.'

I couldn't think of anything to say and went totally quiet. 'Oh,' I said.

'It's OK if you want to cry,' said Maureen.

I held it together for a while, then went home, phoned my cancer-care nurse and started crying and crying. It felt like the whole nightmare was starting all over again. I was so scared and worried for Bernie, but when I spoke to her she was so positive. I think she might have been in a state of shock at first, but she asked me loads of questions about what chemo-therapy was like and how she would feel after surgery.

I hope it helped her to have someone to talk to who'd been through chemo, even though the treatment affects everyone differently. With me, I felt terrible on the sixth and seventh days after my chemo; with Bernie, it was twelfth and thir-teenth days. I felt for her so much, particularly because she had to stay strong in front of Erin. But she was amazing throughout the whole treatment, totally incredible.

A couple of months after Bernie's diagnosis, Maureen asked

me to be her matron of honour at her wedding to Ritchie, so then I was running around like a blue-arsed fly getting everything ready for the hen do. We had a garden party at a friend's house and played bingo. We're all bingo mad – just like our mum! The wedding was beautiful and it was wonderful being with my brothers, sisters, nephews and nieces. It was a shame that Anne and Denise weren't there, but I've reached the point now where I accept that our lives have gone in different directions.

As I have started to feel better in myself, I have begun doing voluntary work with a theatre company called TramShed Productions in Blackpool, who help kids from disadvantaged backgrounds. I've loved show business and performing from the very beginning, and it is great to be able to pass that passion onto kids. I find it hugely rewarding.

I have also presented a couple of slots for *The One Show* on BBC1. The first was particularly poignant because it was all to do with genetic testing for breast cancer. It was after Bernie's diagnosis, when all of us were wondering whether we should be screened to see if we have a faulty gene which has caused us to have three cases of breast cancer in the immediate family. For the show, I met women who'd had the test – which just involves having a sample of blood taken – and I talked to them about the decisions they had made based on their results. If you do carry the gene, there is about a 40 per cent chance of developing breast cancer and a 60 per cent chance of getting ovarian cancer. A lot of women with the faulty gene immediately opt for a double mastectomy and hysterectomy. Then, in front of the camera, I underwent the test myself. It took months to get the results of these tests, but thankfully when they arrived they were negative.

I loved doing the television filming and I also do occasional promotional work, which I enjoy, but I still don't feel strong enough to go on tour on my own.

During the summer of 2010, I received a phone call from my agent asking if I would like to do panto at Christmas. I'd been offered the part of the Wicked Queen in *Snow White* at Worthing. That felt ever such a long way from home. As ever, I rang my brothers and sisters to ask their advice. 'That's fantastic!' they all said.

'Is it?' I asked. I really wasn't sure.

I was excited at the idea of going back into a show, but was dreading being on my own every night in an apartment, hundreds of miles from home. Brian's best friend, Parker, lives fairly near to Worthing and he promised to look after me during my stay. And, of course, my brothers and sisters said they'd travel down to visit too. The only day off I would have would be Christmas Day, and we arranged that I would go to Bernie and Steve's house in Weybridge for the day and that Maureen and Ritchie would drive down there too.

I was still worried that I'd have too much time on my own to think, and I knew how dangerous that could be for me. Despite all my concerns, I agreed to take the part. It was a small step forward for me.

'We think you'll be perfect,' my nephews and nieces joked. 'You won't even need make-up to be the Wicked Queen.' They are so cheeky!

I still spend time a lot of my time with my brothers and sisters, but things aren't any better with Denise and Anne. Our brothers would love everything to go back to how it used to be, but I don't think I can do that now. Too many hurtful things were said. I don't think I would be here now without the love and support I had from all my brothers and sisters after Brian died, and I truly wish Denise and Anne nothing but the best in life. But I still can't imagine a day when I could put behind me what was said about Brian and be able to sit around a dinner table with them again.

I see Brian's children as much as possible. Last summer his daughter Sarah, her husband Gary and their little girl Lucy came up to Blackpool for a week and we had a fantastic time. Lucy and I talk about her granddad a lot. We laugh about things he used to do, like the time he was looking after her and fell asleep. When he woke up, she'd written a massive sign saying, 'World's best babysitter', with an arrow pointing at him!

A couple of times since he has died, Lucy says she has seen her granddad. Once Lucy and I were talking and she said, 'Granddad stands behind you sometimes. You can't see him, but I can. He is looking after you.' Sometimes I wonder about that. I'd love to think it is true.

I also go down to London to visit Brian's son Lloyd and his girlfriend Kam whenever I can. Both Lloyd and Sarah are very like their dad in the way they look and their personalities. They've got his sense of humour and, as a friend once said, 'While those two are around, Brian will never be dead.' They are fabulous to me and send me cards every Mother's Day, which means so much.

I suppose one of my only regrets in life is not having had children of my own, but I guess it was just never meant to be. For so long, all Brian and I ever needed was each other. Having two wonderful step-children is a real gift.

I have lots of friends all over the country who I can phone for a chat if I'm feeling a bit down. And there is also Dr Brigg, who has kept me going through some of the hardest times. She is amazing.

In August last year I had to go to Paris for a work commitment. I went on my own, which was quite a big deal for me, but it was only when I got off the aeroplane and was in the back of a cab that I worked out that it was exactly thirty years ago to the day that I'd been there with Brian on our honeymoon. All of a sudden I got really sad. But then I said to myself, 'No, I shouldn't be sad because that was a beautiful time. We had such a magical time here together.' Of course, it isn't easy to just stop yourself from feeling sad, and it was a very melancholy trip, but it was lovely to see all the sights that I'd visited with Brian.

For ages I couldn't move any of Brian's clothes or belongings out of the house, and it was almost three years after his death that I began to sort out his things, although a lot of his clothes still hang in the wardrobe and sometimes I spray his aftershave on myself so I can smell him around me. I also felt strong enough to redecorate the lounge, change the carpet and move furniture around. That was a really big thing for me. But I still have a little table in there with a card on it that he sent me on the first anniversary of my surgery. On the front it says, 'I dropped a tear in the ocean, when they find it I'll stop loving you.'

I do appreciate life, particularly after what I have been through and what I've seen Bernie and Anne go through. But, in all honesty, I hate my life without Brian. I find it hard to look into the future and think what it will be like, because without Brian I can't imagine being happy. People say it is better to have loved and lost than never to have loved at all, and sometimes I think that is true. But I just wish I could have met Brian sooner, so that I could have loved him longer.

Some nights I wake up and reach out for him before I remember that he's not there. Then I remember that my life is never going to be the way it once was. I've lost my husband, my best friend, my soul mate, my lover, everything. When Brian died I couldn't think about the next hour; just breathing in and out was hard enough. But now, three years down the line, I know I can get through a day, a week, a month, a year without him. I have survived, and I will continue to survive. But life is so much less without Brian.

22.

Coleen

New Challenges, New Plans

After *Dancing on Ice* and The Nolans tour, I was looking forward to spending most of 2010 sat in front of the telly with a mug of tea. But that wasn't to be. I was worked off my feet, filming another fitness DVD, appearing on *Loose Women*, presenting a *Dancing on Ice* Friday show and filing my weekly columns. Not to mention writing this book! Then, one day, I received an amazing call from my agent, Neil. 'How do you feel about going back to *This Morning*?' he asked.

I hesitated. I love Phillip Schofield and Holly Willoughby, and they're a great team together, but I'd been so hurt and upset by what had happened the last time I was on the show that I was a bit reluctant to put myself back in front of the firing line all over again.

'Don't worry,' Neil said. 'That was years ago. This time it's going to be entirely different.'

I was certainly a very different person to the one I'd been when I first went on the show nine years earlier. I had the confidence I'd built up from appearing on *Loose Women* and *Dancing on Ice* and I wasn't a frazzled new mum either. On top of that, I'd matured as a person and just felt generally surer of myself. Not in a 'look at me' way, but in the way that I think most women feel more content when they hit their forties.

Having said all that, I was still shaking with nerves when I turned up for my first day at the studios at the beginning of September 2010. My job was to host the Hub every Monday and Tuesday, which was the section of the show where viewers sent in their comments about the topics being discussed. Everyone was so lovely that I soon felt as though I'd been there forever and all my bad experiences on *This Morning* in the past were a dim and distant memory.

I also continued to appear on *Loose Women* twice a week. We have such a laugh on the show, although I still haven't quite learnt not to just say the first thing that comes into my head when I'm on air!

'Can you please stop saying all these things about me on the show?' Ray said to me recently. What upsets him is that I'll make some off-the-cuff remark and then it is reported in the women's weekly magazines, totally out of context. One week there was a front-page story in a magazine headlined: 'Ray's Ultimatum'. The article said that he was threatening to leave me unless I lost weight!

'Have you got any idea how that makes me look?' he said.

'Have you got any idea how that makes *me* look?' I replied. 'Like a total dork!'

The problem was that there wasn't much I could do about the magazines taking a jokey comment from me and spinning it into some shock-horror drama.

'Can you just be more careful what you say in future?' Ray snapped.

'But it's what I get paid to do,' I retaliated.

We had a good few rows about it, but deep down I could

see his point. The problem is, I find it really hard to control what I'm saying and not be totally honest. If I go on *Loose Women* and they say, 'How's Ray?' and we've just had a row, I'll say, 'Don't talk to me about Ray!' The words just come tumbling out of my mouth. Poor Ray.

I did say to the producers recently that I'd had enough of talking about Shane on the show. I was just a bit bored of it. He was an important part of my life, but that is ancient history now – I've been with Ray for ten years! But it is very hard on that show because if we are talking about exes or infidelity (which quite often we are!), I can hardly just sit there with my gob shut for ten minutes until the subject moves on.

Sometimes Shane says to Jake or Shane Jnr: 'It's a good job your mum was married to me; she wouldn't have anything to talk about otherwise!' But I think he'd secretly hate it if I didn't talk about him!

Shane and I still speak on the phone if there is anything we need to discuss about the boys, and we get on pretty well. At the end of September 2010 we were all together for Jake's eighteenth birthday party at a big hotel in Manchester, and had the most fantastic night. Whatever may have happened between Shane and me, our two wonderful boys came out of that marriage, so I can never regret it.

I love being a working mum, but I try to do everything I can to be with Ciara as much as possible. But as all women out there who do the same know all too well, it ain't half hard work at times! In a normal week, I put Ciara to bed on a Sunday evening, then get the train down to London and stay over to do *This Morning* on a Monday and Tuesday. I'm back home in time to pick Ciara up from school on a Tuesday afternoon. Then, on Wednesday morning, I'm on the train again first thing to return to London for *Loose Women* and am back again by teatime. Then it's the same return trip all over again on the Thursday.

Some people think I'm mad, hurtling up and down between Manchester and London all the time, but it's only just over two hours on the train nowadays, and once I'm sat there with a cup of tea and a magazine, the time flies by. I'd rather do that than be stuck in a hotel room in London on my own all week. I couldn't bear being away from Ciara and Ray. However much I enjoy my work, I hate being away from my family. I don't care where I'm supposed to be or who I'm supposed to be with, if there is a school play, or a sports day, or a harvest festival, I'll move heaven and earth to be there. I can remember all too clearly what it's like as a kid when your mum and dad don't turn up for things like that. It's just horrible.

Around the same time as I returned to *This Morning*, I was also approached to become the new agony aunt at the *Daily Mirror*. I cannot tell you how proud I was about that. I've always loved the *Daily Mirror* and used to read it in the days when Marge Proops wrote an advice column. She was a legend at helping people to sort out their problems, and the thought of following in her footsteps was quite awe-inspiring. I don't claim to have the answer to everyone's problems at all, but I do feel that I've been through plenty of things, good and bad, over the years. I've had a husband who cheated on me and made the mistake of having an affair myself; I've been through divorce and the challenges of introducing a stepdad into the family; I'm a working mum trying to juggle a million different things; I've had two sisters with breast cancer and my mum had Alzheimer's. But I'm not saying I'm extraordinary to have been through all that – in many ways, I'm simply normal. What I hope I give to all the hundreds of readers who've started writing to me is the belief that they're not the only people in the world who are struggling. And however bad things might seem to them at the time, they will get better – they always do.

No, I certainly don't want people to think that everything in my life is rosy all the time, because it just isn't. In fact, at the start of 2010, Ray and I had the first big blip in our marriage.

He had landed some really good work, playing with Rick Astley on his nationwide tour and then supporting Peter Kaye at the MEN arena in Manchester. He was playing massive venues that were sold out night after night, and it was all his dreams come true.

It has been hard for Ray over the years, when I've been the main breadwinner and the one in the spotlight and he has had to stay at home with Ciara. Ray is a very traditional man and would far rather it were the other way round. He still thinks a man should support his wife and family. So when he got this great opportunity to get out there and play his music again for the first time in ten years, he grabbed it with both hands.

Ray is incredibly focused when he is working, and I think that when he became really wrapped up in his work I just felt a bit squeezed out. Up until then, I had been very spoilt because I was used to having Ray all to myself and not having to share his attention with anything else. But suddenly I felt like he was out all the time and when he was at home he was thinking about something else. It's not like he was coming in at three in the morning or anything – he was usually home by mid-evening – but when he did come in, I could tell his mind was somewhere else.

We started rowing more and more often, and I could feel

myself panicking. It felt as though something was going badly wrong in my marriage, but I didn't know how to stop it. And some of the rows were getting way out of hand, with both of us saying hurtful and nasty things that we'd never said before. And while in the past a good row had helped us clear the air, now each argument was followed by long silences and simmering resentment.

'What is your problem?' Ray said one night. 'Do you think I'm seeing someone else? Do you think if I was I would be coming home at half eight in the evening?'

I couldn't answer him. I didn't think he was seeing someone else, but for the first time since we'd been together, I did feel vulnerable. All those terrible feelings of insecurity that I'd had during the years with Shane came flooding back.

On the tour, there were two really attractive backing singers. I've worked in the industry long enough to know how things can happen on tours, and my mind went into overdrive. All I wanted was for Ray to give me a hug and show he understood why I'd be worried and lay my concerns to rest. But he felt he was being unfairly accused of something, and that made him angry. So, of course, he just pushed me further away. And while I wanted to talk about what was going on between us, he just wanted to get on with his work.

'I am not Shane Richie!' he yelled at me one night during a really bad row when I'd been questioning him about what he'd been up to.

And that, of course, was it. I was punishing him for all the insecurities I'd had buried within me since my first marriage. I'd never thought I had been scarred by what had happened with Shane, but that episode with Ray proved to me that I had been.

'I know you're not Shane,' I said to Ray later. 'But I was just scared it was all starting again.'

That night, for the first time in ages, we talked for hours and hours about how we had been feeling. I explained to Ray that I'd felt squeezed out by his work and the only thing I could compare that with was how it had been when Shane was cheating on me. Wrongly, I'd made the same assumptions.

Ray told me that he'd been so angry that I hadn't been supporting him when he was really enjoying his work for the first time in ages, and that anger was what had made him push me away even further.

Like so many couples, we had just stopped communicating, and once that happens, things can go horribly wrong quite quickly. The whole thing was a real shock to me because it was the first time we'd had a major wobble in ten years together. But thankfully, in the end, we were able to talk, and we could put things right again. We have both learned from it. Ray is being more attentive and I'm being more supportive of his needs too. I guess that's the thing with marriage; you can never rest on your laurels and think you've got it sussed. You really do have to keep working at it every single day.

Ray likes to get problems sorted with a good old row rather than let things fester for months on end, and I've learnt the benefit of that. Even when terrible things were going on in my marriage to Shane, we never rowed. But Ray has taught me to confront problems rather than hide from them. I think Ray loves that he has brought that aspect out in me – although it does mean he gets the occasional ear-bashing now! But once we've had the row, we are both able to move on. It's so much healthier.

I think that, in general, I'm probably a better wife for Ray than I was for Shane. I'm older, more confident and less needy. I've survived as a single parent, and I've built up a career, which means Ray knows I'm with him because I want to be, not because I'm scared of being on my own. And the dynamics of this relationship are so different. It is a real 50/50 partnership.

I'm always complaining that Ray is not romantic, but he is solid and always there for me. And that is worth far more than bunches of red roses and soppy messages.

The other two gorgeous men in my life – Shane Jnr and Jake – are still my rocks too. Shane Jnr is now working as a singer and flies out to Turkey once every few weeks to perform gigs in some of the big hotels. On New Year's Eve 2010, he performed in front of thousands of people at a big hotel in Egypt. And, bizarrely, just like his dad, he also did a tour of *Boogie Nights*, performing at Pontins centres all over the country. He even played Roddy, just like Shane! Shane Jnr and Jake have a band together too. They write their own music and do covers of songs by groups like Kings of Leon and The Killers. When they both got up on stage and sang at Jake's eighteenth birthday, I felt so proud of them. They're great boys.

Jake has done fabulously well since leaving the Sylvia Young Theatre School. His biggest break so far has been landing the role of Isaac Nuttal in *Emmerdale*. People might think his mum and dad have pulled strings for him in the industry, but we really haven't – he did the whole thing by himself and was absolutely fantastic. When he called me to say he'd got the part, I was making my bed. It had been a few weeks since his audition and we were all thinking that he couldn't have got the part. It was only a few weeks before we were all supposed to be flying to Spain for Maureen's wedding, and I was just waiting to see whether Jake would be coming with us or filming.

'Hiya, Mum,' said his voice on the other end of the phone. 'Just thought I should let you know you can go ahead and book those tickets for Auntie Maureen's wedding,' he said.

I could feel my heart sink as I realized he must have been turned down for the part.

'But don't book me one,' he went on, 'because I'm going to be in *Emmerdale*.'

I just fell on the bed. I was so happy for him. Ray came in to see what was going on and when I told him he started jumping around the bedroom. We were all just so delighted. Jake has now signed with a big London acting agent, and I'm really hopeful he'll get some great parts in the future. Maybe he'll even go to Hollywood to try his luck out there. He really is incredibly talented, but above all he's still my baby.

Ciara is now nine and just a delight to be around. Of course, it's not easy bringing up girls these days – there are so many pressures on them about what they wear and where they go, not to mention wanting to talk to their friends over the internet and on their mobile phones all the time. I try to be fair, but I keep a very close eye on her. I do think little girls are growing up far too young nowadays. One of the best things we have started doing together recently is visiting a stables near our home. Ciara is mad about horses and so, after a lot of umming and ahing, Ray and I decided to buy her a pony called Whitney. She looks after her brilliantly and we both often go up there after school to clean out the stables and take Whitney for a ride. I was mad about horses when I was the same age as Ciara, and I love it that we've got a hobby we can share. Hopefully it'll carry on for years to come.

I did have a drama at the stables back in September 2010, when I noticed that a pony called Ade had got his collar caught on a stable door lock. I had just reached over to free the collar when he bolted backwards, crushing my fingers between his collar and the lock. The pain was horrific and when I heard this disgusting crunching noise I knew my fingers were broken.

I was taken straight to casualty at Wythenshawe hospital, where an X-ray showed the middle finger of my right hand had come totally away from my hand. Another finger was fractured too. I was wearing a platinum and diamond ring which Ray had given me when I was in *Dancing on Ice*, but because my fingers were swelling up, there was a race against time to cut the ring off. The nurse was trying to cut it away with this contraption like a blunt tin opener, but in the end my friend from the stables had to do it. He is a big guy and he needed all his strength to cut it off. The pain was terrible, even though I was on gas and air and high-dose painkillers.

The doctor sent me home with my arm strapped up, saying he hoped the bones would fuse back together. But three days later my hand still looked like a balloon and the pain was still awful. I went back to the hospital and the doctor said that I would need an operation to fit a titanium plate to mend the bones. It was a three-hour operation and I was unable to use my hand for weeks afterwards.

Relations with Anne and Denise are still the same. I'm still angry and hurt about what they have said in interviews and on the internet about the four of us who did the reunion tour. At one time Anne said she no longer thought of us as her sisters, and although in the past I could never have imagined feeling that way, now I feel it is for the best if I take the same approach. We clearly can't get along together anymore, so maybe it is best to have nothing to do with each other. I know Bernie and Maureen are now back in touch with Anne and Denise, and that is absolutely fine. But I think the wounds are too deep for Linda and me. The rows left too many scars.

When The Nolans reunion tour was announced, I knew I'd get blamed for Anne not being part of the line-up. I was determined to do everything I could to get her included, so I rang a lady called Angela, who works at Universal and was involved in organizing the tour. 'Please don't leave Anne out just because you think we might not be able to work together,' I said. 'We are both professional and there would be no problem at all. We managed it for our brother's wedding, and we could do it again.'

Angela said that Universal were determined they just wanted four of us – and that would be the four who were big in Japan. But, sure enough, I was still blamed for Anne being missed out. Both Anne and Denise gave interviews to newspapers and magazines and posted stuff on the internet which was really hurtful. I felt so angry, particularly as a lot of their attacks were still targeted at Ray. They obviously felt like he was some outsider who'd come in and ripped apart The Nolan family. They couldn't see that he was the man who, after years of upset, had made me truly happy. And I think what has finally ripped apart our family was their refusal to accept they had done something wrong.

The whole thing really upset Ray again. When he read what Denise and Anne had said, he was shaking and couldn't stop himself from crying. I seriously thought it was going to give him a heart attack. For days neither of us slept; night after night, we'd lie in bed with it all churning in our minds.

When Bernie, Linda and Maureen started getting all the nasty text messages too, in the run-up to the tour, I think they realized for the first time what Ray and I had been going through for years. The girls were really upset at first and used to cry about the messages, but then they got angry, really angry. It was like a massive black cloud hanging over all of us as we prepared for the tour.

Then, one day, I got an email from a fan saying, 'Your sisters' statements on their websites are disgraceful. We're delighted the four girls are back together.'

And somehow that one message lifted me out of the gloom. We all got on with it and gave the tour every ounce of energy that we had – which is quite a lot, believe me! It was funny though, because on that tour I immediately slotted back into my role of baby of the family again. I didn't speak in interviews and hung around in the background when we were all together. I might have been forty-four, but I was the baby sister once more. The tour was just fabulous though – we all had a total ball!

It was strange going to Maureen's wedding and Anne and Denise not being there. I think it was particularly hard for Maureen because they had always been so close. The feud really hurt her, and Maureen is so lovely and always sees the good in everyone. We call her Mary Poppins! But despite that, the wedding was totally fabulous. Maureen looked amazing and we all had a wonderful time. I was so happy for her that things had worked out so well with Ritchie in the end, because it certainly wasn't easy for her in the early days, when they first got together.

Our brothers Tommy and Brian have pretty much kept out of all the problems in the family, although I know they'd love us all to get along together again. Tommy was always quite independent and he has his own life and his own friends, which I think is very healthy. Brian is fabulous and great fun to be with. He is carved out of the same block as Dad though, and firmly believes that family should come first, so he probably does think I've done the wrong thing in falling out with Anne and Denise. But he keeps out of it.

I still feel that what has happened is largely to do with the way we were brought up and brainwashed into thinking that family always had to come first and the Nolans were always right. For too long, problems were swept under the carpet rather than dealt with properly.

I blame Dad for a lot of that stuff. I think he caused a lot of the insecurities in Denise which have eaten away at her over the years. Denise absolutely idolized our dad, but he could be harder on the older girls than he was on the younger ones like me, and I think he's the reason Denise had insecurities about her looks. I also think she felt Mum never had much time for her either. All her life she tried to win their attention. I think it was because she was trying to please Dad that she always upheld his obsession with family coming first.

I think Dad had an incredible hold over all us kids, although it was far worse for the older girls. Obviously there was his sexual interest in Anne, and he was clearly sick in the head regarding that. But he was obsessed with all his daughters, absolutely obsessed. I guess that's why he tried to control us all so much.

And we idolized him. When Anne first told me what Dad had done to her, I cried. And you know what? I was crying partly because he hadn't done it to me. I thought: 'He can't have loved me as much as Anne.' And however tragic that might sound, the feeling does stay with you: 'Why not me?' Normally, if I heard about a man abusing a child, I'd think: 'That's disgusting, he should be strung up!' But when it was my own dad, my emotions were so confused. I hated what he'd done, but I couldn't stop loving him.

Ray once said to me, 'If your dad had been alive when Ciara was born, there is no way I'd have allowed him to see her. Your family might have been happy to pretend for years that everything was normal, but I wouldn't be. He wouldn't have been allowed in this house.'

'But he was my dad,' I tried to explain. 'And if he hadn't been allowed in this house, then I wouldn't have been able to be with you.'

'Well,' said Ray, 'he would still not have been allowed near my daughter. I would have informed Social Services.'

What Dad did to Anne was totally wrong. And I also think it is pretty disgusting that he dragged eight kids around to pubs and clubs until the early hours on a school night. Then, of course, there was his drinking and violence, although I was a lot younger than my brothers and sisters when all that stopped. But despite all that, I loved him. There are still times when I miss him and think: 'Oh, I wish Dad were here now and I could tell him all about this.' When I was splitting up with Shane, Mum was always too busy to really listen, but Dad would be on the phone for hours with me. He was like a counsellor.

So although I think my dad is behind a lot of the problems that have now come out in our family, I still love him and I miss him.

As for Mum, I miss her now more than ever. When she first died, it was almost a relief. Her final years had been so awful that I was pleased she was finally at peace. But now I only remember her as she was before she had Alzhiemer's, and I miss her so very much.

When Bernie was diagnosed with breast cancer in April 2010, it was a horrible shock for all of us. Bernie was always so full of energy and fun that I'd never think to connect her with illness. On our tour, long after I'd gone to bed with a cuppa and a biscuit, Bernie would still be partying with the band and anyone else who could keep up with her.

Bernie, as ever, went into her cancer treatment fighting – and carried on fighting throughout. We were all so proud of her, although maybe a bit more worried than any of us dared to show. We'd seen Anne and Linda go through the treatment before, and it was horrific knowing that Bernie was going to have to go through the same thing.

I still worry about Linda too. It is three years since Brian died, but she still finds it very tough to cope without him. I don't think she will ever move on from Brian, which in some ways is a terrible shame, because she is such a lively, vibrant person with so much love to give. But she loved him so much that, for her, the thought of moving on is too much to bear.

When she says things like she hates her life, it makes me feel very sad. Sometimes I get frustrated with her and say, 'But, Linda, you've survived cancer and had a great life; you have so much to be thankful for.' But for a long time all she has been able to feel is the sadness. Gradually she is starting to redecorate the house and rebuild her life, but it will take her a long time.

Bernie is on the road to recovery, Linda is rebuilding her

life and Maureen is finally a newlywed, at fifty-six! I guess we've all had tough times along the way, but we're survivors. And I'm sure it is the love and support we've given each other over the years that has enabled us to survive the bad times. There are many things that I would never have got through without my sisters and brothers beside me.

Goodness knows what the future holds for me, although I'm guessing it will be eventful if the past few years are anything to go by! But so long as I have my family, Ray and my three fabulous kids with me, I know it will most definitely be OK.

23.
Bernie

Cancer's a Scary Word

I looked down at my boobs as I fastened up my bra one morning. 'That's a bit weird,' I thought to myself. My left breast looked a bit different. I couldn't quite work out what was unusual about it – maybe it was a slightly different shape or a fraction bigger. I couldn't be certain what the change was, but I was sure there was one.

I ran my hands over the breast, but there was nothing there. And I'd had a mammogram the previous year, so I was fairly confident that there weren't any problems. But, still, something wasn't quite right.

'Steve, do you think my boob looks different?' I asked when he walked into the bedroom.

'Er, not sure,' he replied.

I decided maybe I was imagining things and put the whole issue out of my mind. I had plenty of other stuff to think about. It was the end of 2009, and Coleen's agent Neil Howarth had called me to ask if I was interested in taking part in a new show that was coming on in the New Year. It was called *Popstar to Operastar* and would feature a group of pop and rock singers turning their hand to more traditional music.

'So, would you like to be considered for it?' Neil asked.

'I'd love to,' I replied.

Since leaving *The Bill* at the end of 2005, I'd been in a couple of touring theatre productions, which I loved but were hard work. First of all, I appeared in a six-month tour of *Mum's the Word*, which was a collection of monologues about motherhood. Then I did twelve months in *Flashdance*. That was a fabulous show, but a whole year of travelling up and down the country was gruelling. I'd commute home whenever I could, and Steve and Erin would come up to join me for weekends or during the school holidays when I couldn't get back.

It was while I was in *Flashdance* that Maureen rung me one day and told me about the plan for a Nolans reunion tour. I was thrilled at the idea. We were struggling for money a bit by then and I hadn't got any work lined up for when *Flashdance* came to an end. An arena tour and an album was too good an opportunity to turn down.

Working with my sisters again took a bit of adjustment at first, and it wasn't all a barrel of laughs! At one point I walked out when we were rehearsing. The four of us were staying at Coleen's house for the weekend and were rehearsing in her lounge. I like to have a laugh as much as the rest of them, but I can also be very pedantic about music and harmony, and when I'm working I take it very seriously. I'm not saying they don't, but I can be particularly fussy.

I just felt it wasn't the right place for us to rehearse, and we had so much to do. We had a major tour coming up, Coleen hadn't been live on stage for seventeen years, Linda had been really ill and Maureen is very nervous anyway. I felt we really needed to knuckle down.

I was also a bit irritated that there seemed to be an attitude again that we should just let the management and record company make all the decisions about what we did. 'Don't rock the boat' seemed to be the mantra, but I felt we had to have some say about what we were doing.

I was given the Katy Perry song 'I Kissed a Girl' as my solo on the tour, but I really hated it musically. I think the others thought I should just get on with it, but in the end I managed to get it changed to 'So What?' by Pink. I was also dead set against us singing 'I Will Survive', but I was outvoted on that and we did it. The audiences actually loved it, and I'm prepared to accept that was the right decision.

But one night during that weekend of rehearsing, the four of us went out for dinner and had a massive row. I think the tensions had been building for a while and it all burst out. I felt I was being ganged up on, although I can see now that maybe I'd been getting on their nerves that day.

'Nothing is ever good enough for you, is it?' Coleen said at one point.

I was really hurt by that at the time, although thinking about it now, I know we all say things in the heat of the moment, especially in families, when you know you all love each other.

But the next morning I just got up, packed my bag and told the others I was catching the train home. When I came downstairs, Maureen was in the kitchen.

'What are you doing?' she asked.

'I'm going home, where I feel respected and loved,' I said.

It was an awful atmosphere, but I felt I had to get away. Just as the cab arrived, Maureen started crying and came over and hugged me.

I had a lovely couple of days at home and after that I finally felt ready to go back and carry on with the rehearsals. The argument was never mentioned again and after that we got on really well. I think working together after all those years was harder for us to adjust to than we had thought it would be. We get on brilliantly as sisters and the only thing we have ever rowed about is work, and that's because we've all got different ideas about the best way to do things. But gradually we got back into working together effectively again.

Once the tour started, we were all having such a great time that all the problems were forgotten about. In fact, there was a bit of an anticlimax when the tour finished, which was why I was so pleased when Neil called me with news about *Popstar to Operastar*. It was going to be a ITV1 primetime show on a Friday evening, and sounded fantastic. The only problem for me was that the job had come through Coleen's agent, who had organized the tour. It meant I was going to have to leave my old agent, Tony, whom I'd worked with since I was in The Nolans. He was a great guy, and I adored him and his family, but I felt I had to move on.

The first step for *Popstar to Operster* was to go along for an audition, where I sang 'Stop!' again. Then I was asked to sing a short burst of an operatic song. It was very nerve-wracking because I'd never sung like that before. Mum had trained as an opera singer and she had always said to me when I was younger: 'You could sing opera, you know.' But I'd never done it. And Mum had never listened to opera when we were children; it was always Sinatra on the record player at home. When I got older, my passion was Motown, not opera.

I had to wait for a couple of weeks before the call came to tell me I'd been selected for the show. Then I was hurled headlong into an endless round of rehearsals with vocal coaches.

Any spare moment I had, I spent singing around the house. It drove Steve and Erin mad!

With all that going on, I honestly didn't think any more about my left boob and why it was looking a little different. It really did go out of my mind.

I loved *Popstar to Operastar* from day one. There was just so much to learn. Opera singing is a whole different technique – the way you place your voice, breathe and move your jaw. It's a lot more technical than pop music, but I had two fantastic coaches, Mary King and Claire Moore.

There were eight celebrities competing in the show, including Kym Marsh from *Corrie*, Jimmy Osmond and Danny Jones from McFly, and we all had a great time together, even though one of us got voted out by the public each week.

Almost every week I won the public vote, which was amazing, and I was incredibly grateful. I did work hard at it though. After my weekly lesson with the show's mentors, Katherine Jenkins and Rolando Villazon, I'd go home and try to put everything they'd told me into practice. It was tough going though, because not only did I have to sing in a style totally differently to anything I'd ever done before, it was often in a different language too! And some weeks I also had to wear a massive great costume. One week I sang in French and another I sang in Italian, but that didn't bother me too much. I'd just go over the lyrics again and again in my head until they'd sunk in.

It was about halfway through the series that, one night at home, I noticed that my left breast was looking even more different and the skin underneath it was dimpling. Again, I thought it seemed odd, so I checked for a lump or anything that felt unusual, but it all seemed perfectly normal to me. I put it out of my mind and got back to concentrating on *Popstar to Operastar*.

I was delighted to make it through to the final, and when I lost to Darius by half a percentage point, it was gutting but also pleasing that I'd come so close. I still get people coming up to me in the street now, saying, 'You were robbed!' I had a ball on that show, although I have to admit that I haven't listened to a note of opera since!

With the show over, I finally had time to breathe. And it was only then that I seriously started to think about the changes in my left boob. In just a couple of weeks the dimpling had become far more obvious and my nipple seemed to be pointing slightly off to the side. I'd read in the past that an inverted nipple could be a sign of breast cancer, but I'd never heard that dimpling or a nipple pointing outwards could be a sign too. And as I still couldn't feel a lump or anything strange, it really didn't occur to me that it might be breast cancer. Even when I had an appointment with my GP about a problem with my back, I still didn't instantly think I should tell him about my breast too. In fact, it only occurred to me to mention it just was I was leaving the surgery. I'm always really conscious about that rule they have that you're only allowed to mention one complaint per appointment, so I thought I'd probably just not bother.

I was almost at the door when I casually said, 'Oh, and my boob looks a bit of a different shape at the moment too. But I can't feel a lump. It's probably nothing.'

'Well, let's take a look then,' my GP said.

I sat back down and he examined me carefully. 'Oh, I can feel a lump,' he said.

'Oh God,' I thought. I'd been so convinced that there

couldn't be a problem because I didn't have a lump, but I can't have been checking myself correctly. I felt sick. But even then, I still didn't think it would be cancer. How could it be? I was still in my forties. I was fit, healthy and everyone always said I was brimming with energy and life.

I went home and told Steve. He was shocked too, but at that point we really, honestly didn't worry too much about it. I was utterly convinced it would be a cyst or something like that, which would be sorted out in a couple of weeks. I never thought it would be cancerous.

The following week, on 12 April, I had an appointment at a breast-screening centre in Guildford. Steve came with me and waited outside while I went in for a mammogram. I'd had them done before, and afterwards you usually just go and sit in the waiting room until a nurse comes out, tells you everything is fine and sends you home. So I could tell something was wrong when we had to wait for so long after the mammogram. When the nurse came out, she said, 'We'd just like to see you in the screening room again.'

This wasn't what was supposed to happen at all. I was beginning to feel a bit shaky, but I tried my hardest to remain positive. The nurse sat opposite me and explained that they weren't happy with the results of the mammogram and they'd like to do an ultrasound test too.

'OK,' I said. The test was over quite quickly and a few minutes later a doctor was sitting in front of me.

This really, really wasn't what was supposed to be happening.

'Mrs Doneathy,' the doctor said. 'We've found a lot of calcium in your breast, which is a sign of cancer to come, so we will have to do something about that.' Then he paused.

'But we have also found three areas where we think there might be cancer already.'

'Oh my God. Oh my God. Oh my God,' I thought. Except I wasn't really thinking, I was just in shock. My heart was pounding; I could hear the sound of it in my head.

The doctor then explained that they needed to carry out a biopsy immediately. The sample of tissue from my breast would be sent away and in about a week we'd get results back which would tell us for certain whether I had cancer.

The biopsy was horribly painful, but I knew I didn't have a choice now. I was already on a ride that I couldn't get off.

'Mrs Doneathy,' the doctor said quietly, 'we'll let you know for certain next week. But it does look like cancer to me and we don't really make mistakes here about that sort of thing.'

I nodded, not quite trusting myself to speak.

'Would you like us to tell your husband, or would you prefer to do it?' one of the nurses asked me.

'You'd better do it,' I replied. They'd be better at explaining the medical stuff than me, and I was still too shocked to put into words what I'd just been told. I went to the door and poked my head round. 'Steve, can you come in here a sec?' I said.

The moment he looked up at me, he knew. His face went deathly pale and he walked into the room without saying a thing.

'We think we have found cancer in your wife's left breast,' the nurse explained slowly. Steve stared straight ahead, his face completely white. He looked like someone who had gone into shock after a terrible accident. He still managed to ask questions though. I can't remember what. I was just sitting there, letting it all go on around me.

I didn't cry. Not then. At that point, none of it seemed real. It couldn't be real.

We walked out of the hospital and got into our car. 'We'd better go and pick up Erin then,' I said.

'Yeah, we should,' said Steve. There were no tears, no screaming. Nothing. Just total shock.

'We won't tell her,' I said. 'Not before her birthday. It wouldn't be fair.'

'OK,' said Steve.

Erin had gone round to play at a friend's house that afternoon. I'd told her that I had an appointment at a Well Woman clinic. I'm good mates with Erin's friend's mum, and I'd told her where I was really going. 'How did it go?' she mouthed to me across the hall as Erin put on her coat and shoes. I just shook my head.

Neither Steve nor I cried that night, but we were both very quiet. Steve's mum had died three years earlier. She'd had breast cancer then got secondary cancer in her liver and hadn't been able to fight it any longer. I knew that was exactly what Steve would be thinking about.

The following morning, when we woke up, Steve just cried and cried as I held him. 'It's going to be OK,' I told him. And, for the most part, I really did believe that.

That day I was due on stage in Lincoln for the second week of a tour of *Mum's the Word*. It was the school Easter holidays, so Steve and Erin were due to go up with me. I couldn't ring in sick the day before the show opened, and I didn't feel sick anyway. I felt perfectly fine, which was what made the whole thing so difficult to get my head round.

It was another fortnight until Erin's eleventh birthday and

I didn't want her to worry about me, so Steve and I did everything we could to act normally in front of her. But, while I'd always been quite comfortable about her seeing me with no clothes on, I started covering up my boob if she walked into the room. I didn't want her to see the terrible bruising that the biopsy had left.

On 19 April, Steve and I went back for the results of the biopsy. The doctor brought out my notes and looked at us seriously. 'Yes, I'm sorry to say this, but you have definitely got cancer and you will need to have a mastectomy,' he said.

However much I'd told myself that this was going to be the outcome of my results, I was still so shocked. Right up until that moment, I'd clung on to the hope that maybe, just maybe, the whole thing had been a terrible mistake. But the doctor still hadn't finished. 'Even if you didn't have the lumps in your breast, you have got so much calcium there, which is a sign of cancer to come, that we would have had to do a mastectomy anyway,' he said. 'I'm sorry.'

I felt utterly battered by the time we left the hospital and got back to the car. Then, for the first time, I cried about it all. For about five minutes, I just lost it. I totally lost it.

'I can't believe I've done this to Erin,' I sobbed.

'What are you talking about?' said Steve.

'I can't believe I'm making her go through all this. For a year, at least, everything is going to be about cancer. She'll have to see me ill. Every time she looks around, people will be talking about it. It's going to be terrible for her.'

I cried and cried, and Steve cried too. I had no idea what the future was going to be like, but it certainly seemed pretty scary. But, after a few minutes, I gave myself a shake and stopped the crying. I'd got it all out of my system, and that was it. I'd had my mini-meltdown and now it was time to get on with getting rid of this disease.

'Right,' I said. 'We've just got to get on with this now. We've just got to do it.'

And, apart from one low moment during my chemo, that was the only time I cried. From then on, I made a conscious decision not to waste a single ounce of energy on being upset. I needed all my strength to fight this cancer. I was determined to beat it.

I got home, called the producers of *Mum's the Word* and told them I wouldn't be able to come back because I'd been diagnosed with breast cancer. They were lovely and told me they'd keep the role open for me, but to take off just as long as I needed.

It was still another week until Erin's birthday, so we tried to keep it from her a bit longer, but she could obviously sense something was up. One morning she came into the kitchen and said, 'Look, I can tell something is wrong because Daddy is being so nice to you. What's going on?'

Steve had taken the diagnosis really badly and was very upset. He'd been running around after me for days, asking me if I was OK, making cups of tea and generally trying to look after me. We looked at each other and knew it was time to tell Erin the truth.

'OK, Erin, sit down and we'll tell you,' I said. She sat down and I just told her the facts as calmly and accurately as I could. 'Right, I've got breast cancer,' I said. 'But it's fine. Auntie Anne and Auntie Linda have had it and they're both fine. And I'm going to be fine too. It's all going to be OK.'

Erin just sat looking at me for a couple of seconds. Then she said, 'Are you going to die?'

'No,' I said. 'Definitely not. Just look at Auntie Anne and Auntie Linda. I'm going to be fine, like them.'

I guess having had cancer in the family before did help because Erin had been able to see people she loved come through it. For some kids who hadn't had that experience, it might have been a whole lot more scary. Erin asked, 'Is it big?'

'No, it's not,' I replied.

'OK,' she said. 'I don't want to know any more.' Then just a single tear ran down her face.

'It's OK if you cry,' I said. But she didn't. Erin is very composed and mature in that way. She can be a drama queen, like all eleven-year-olds, when it comes to the most ridiculous things, but when big things happen she has an amazing ability to cope.

After I'd told Erin, I then had to tell the rest of the family, which was equally painful. Maureen just broke down on the phone when I told her. 'I'll call you back, I'll call you back,' she said. She rang back when she'd managed to calm down a bit, but she was still really upset.

Then I rang my brother Brian, who was devastated, and then Linda. Because Linda had been through it all herself, she was able to ask questions about the illness with some knowledge, and I was able to ask her things too. What was chemotherapy like? How bad was the mastectomy? It was great having her to compare notes with throughout the treatment.

At that time I still wasn't talking to Anne after the fall-out over The Nolans reunion tour. It was such a shame that we couldn't speak because she'd been through breast cancer too and had had a lumpectomy. But we exchanged a few texts, and I was pleased about that.

I think Coleen took the news worse than anyone. Maureen had said she'd break the news to her, so I was expecting a phone call soon afterwards, but I didn't hear anything for days. I was beginning to get a bit annoyed when I found out that Coleen had taken it so badly that she hadn't been able to speak to anyone for a while. When she did ring, she was still devastated.

I think everyone was shocked that this time it was happening to me. Out of the whole family, I'd always been the one who was so healthy and full of life. I was the one always running around and partying. And even on the tour, it was me who had to climb on a table and be lifted off by the dancers!

Sometimes I would think: 'Why me?' But then I'd think: 'Why not me? Who the fuck do I think I am? This can happen to anyone.'

I think all us sisters were very worried because with three of us having had breast cancer, we couldn't help but wonder whether it was genetic. If so, would we all be at risk, as well as Erin, Anne's daughters Alex and Amy and Coleen's little Ciara?

The newspapers got hold of the story, so I decided to get the facts straight by doing an interview with the *News of the World*. I couldn't believe it when they put my story on the front page. Maybe some of my straight-talking shocked people, but it was how I felt. 'Cancer's a scary word, but it can bugger off,' I told the paper. 'I don't care – just get this s*** out of me.'

I got a massive response to that article and received hundreds of letters, cards and text messages from people I knew and from total strangers too. I think that made me realize how cancer affects virtually everyone's lives and, being in the public eye, it was really important to try to send out a positive message that might help other people going through a similar situation.

'I'm going to kick this cancer's arse,' I said on one television interview.

But I wasn't just saying that stuff for effect. It was honestly how I felt. And the angrier and bolshier I became about the illness, the better I felt. Getting angry at the cancer gave me a new energy to beat it. I was utterly determined that it wasn't going to beat me.

The next step for me was to meet with a surgeon, who explained the strain of cancer that I had. He said that it was a particularly aggressive form and had already spread to some of my lymph nodes. He recommended that I should begin chemotherapy immediately, to start blasting it, then have the mastectomy later.

Maybe I should have crumbled with the news that the cancer had already spread, but that only made me angrier and more determined to beat it. I didn't tell Erin the cancer was aggressive; I didn't want her to have even more to worry about. I was just desperate to get on with my chemo. I wanted to start zapping this stuff inside me as quickly as possible.

Because if this was a fight, there was only going to be one winner – me!

24.
Bernie

The Future

Steve and I sat side by side, sharing the packet of sandwiches I'd brought with us and filling in a crossword. At first glance it could have looked as though Steve and I were enjoying a relaxing day out together. But the reality was quite different. For while we puzzled over ten across and six down, a highly poisonous cocktail of drugs was being pumped into my body – this was my first session of chemotherapy.

I'd been desperate to get going with the chemo. The sooner I could get those drugs in my body so they could start zapping the cancer, the better. My first chemo session at the Royal Surrey County Hospital in Guildford was on 13 May – just a month after I'd had the mammogram which detected the lumps and calcium in my breast. I had all my treatment on the NHS and I thought the speed with which they got on with things was brilliant.

My family had all been incredibly supportive. Linda phoned or texted me every single day and the others were always on the phone too. I even started speaking to Anne again, which was great, and I exchanged text messages with Denise and Auntie Theresa too, which I was pleased about. When things go wrong it is so good to have a close family who really care.

That really helped, particularly as for the first few weeks Steve felt very down about it all. He couldn't stop thinking about how his mum had suffered.

'I just can't cope with the idea of losing you,' Steve would say.

'But I'm not going anywhere,' I kept telling him. He couldn't accept it though.

Then, one day, we received an email from a woman who'd read about my diagnosis in the newspapers. Her message said: 'Dear Bernie. I'd just like you to know that exactly ten years ago today I was also diagnosed with breast cancer. I had a mastectomy and a reconstruction, but now I am absolutely fine. You may have a tough year ahead, but you will be OK. Cancer is out of my life now. My life is totally normal.'

I showed Steve that email and it had an incredible effect on him. It was as though he suddenly believed what I was saying – that it was possible to have cancer and live a normal life again afterwards. It was like something just switched in his head and from that moment on he believed, like I did, that I was going to be OK. That day, we went out for lunch at a Carluccio's restaurant near our house and there was a totally different atmosphere between us. Steve stopped panicking, and from then on he was absolutely brilliant.

Everyone was quite worried about how I'd cope with my first chemo session, particularly as I'd always been scared of needles. But with the amount of injections and treatments I had to have that summer, needles were soon the least of my worries! I'd be lying if I said I wasn't apprehensive about chemotherapy, but I wasn't scared. I was just a bit nervous about how I might feel afterwards. I knew how sick Linda had been after her first session, and also how upsetting she'd found losing her hair.

But I couldn't dwell on any of that bad stuff. I just had to focus on getting this cancer out of my body. Steve was insistent on coming with me for my chemotherapy, and it was great that he did because it was nice to have a bit of company. Sitting watching a load of drugs getting pumped out of a bag and round your body for eight hours must be pretty boring if you haven't got anyone to chat with.

For the first couple of hours of that first session, everything went absolutely fine. My chemotherapy was made up of a mixture of drugs including Herceptin, Carboplatin, a new drug that was being trialled called Pertuzumab and Docetaxel. The doctors were really hopeful that Pertuzumab could help a lot of women with breast cancer in the future and so I was more than happy to go on the trial if it could help their research.

I had my first three drugs, including the trial drug, and everything was going absolutely fine. I felt totally normal in fact. And as they started pumping my final drug, Docetaxel, into me, Steve and I settled down to watch the George Clooney DVD, *Up in the Air* on our laptop.

The drug had only been going into me for two minutes when I felt horribly unwell. 'I don't feel right, Steve,' I said. I was struggling to catch my breath and I could feel my face getting redder, hotter and bigger by the second. It felt as though my entire body was swelling up and I could feel my airways closing. It was utterly terrifying. 'I can't breathe, Steve,' I managed to say. He looked at me in total terror.

There was a nurse in the room with us and she rushed over, pulled the drip out of my arm and slammed an emergency button. Within seconds, all hell broke loose in there, with medics running in all directions. I was choking for breath and truly thought that this was it – I was dying.

With so many doctors and nurses around me, Steve had been pushed to the doorway. I looked up and saw him standing there, looking completely bewildered. 'Oh my God,' he said. 'Oh my God.' Just a couple of minutes earlier we'd been watching George Clooney. Now he thought I was dying.

A nurse injected me with a massive dose of the anti-allergy drug Piriton, and almost immediately I could feel my body starting to return to normal and I was able to breathe better. Within fifteen minutes, I was completely back to normal. But it had been a terrifying incident. It seems I'd had a bad allergic reaction to the Docetaxel and I certainly wouldn't be able to have any more of it. But as soon as my breathing was back to normal, I just wanted to get straight back on with my chemo.

'We think you've had enough for today,' my nurse said, smiling.

'But I didn't have all the Docetaxel,' I said. 'I don't want to miss out on any drugs.'

I was upset because I felt I hadn't had enough chemo and I'd be missing an opportunity to blast the cancer.

'Don't worry,' the nurse said. 'You've had plenty of drugs for one session.'

Two weeks after that first session, I had to return to the hospital for an ultrasound test to see how successful the treatment had been. My three tumours were only quite small, but they were very aggressive, so it was vital that the chemo started attacking them as quickly as possible.

When the doctors gave me the ultrasound results, they were delighted. The biggest of my three lumps had shrunk from 5.2cms to 3.3cms – that was about two-thirds of the size.

It was a fantastic result and really made me believe that, at this rate, we'd soon get those tumours blasted into history.

Because of my bad reaction to Docetaxel, I had to be taken off the trial of Pertuzumab because for a trial to work certain drugs have to be taken in a particular order. So from then on I carried on with my chemo with a different cocktail of drugs: Herceptin, Carboplatin and Taxel, which was a slightly different version of the Docataxel that had given me the allergic reaction. In total, I had six sessions of chemotherapy, one every three weeks. For the next couple of sessions, they made me lie on a bed while the drugs went into me, just in case I had another allergic reaction, but fortunately I never did.

Each time I arrived at the hospital for a session of chemo, I felt like I was taking another great punch at this bastard cancer. This was me fighting back. 'Chemo is our friend,' I'd say, laughing with the nurses. And it was. Chemotherapy is the thing that keeps you alive. It's your weapon against something that is trying to kill you. So rather than dread it, I actually looked forward to it.

When the bag holding the chemo drug was empty, a machine started bleeping to alert the nurses. But whenever they came to change my bag, I'd say: 'Looks like there's a drop more in that bag to me, can't you squeeze it out?'

After a couple of sessions, I didn't even need to say it. 'We know, we know,' the nurses would say, 'you want every last drop.'

And I did. I wanted every last drop of every available drug to blast this cancer. Yeah, chemotherapy can make you feel really crappy, it makes your hair fall out and gave me horrendous mouth ulcers, but I loved it. It was keeping me alive.

Like Linda, I also wore a cold cap when I was having chemo,

to try to prevent my hair falling out. I'd always loved my hair and was constantly trying new looks with it, and the thought of losing it all did make me feel a bit funny. I hoped the cold cap would prevent it falling out, but after just a couple of sessions I could feel it thinning and I noticed blonde strands all over the house. It was a horrible, visible sign of how my body was coming under attack.

Because breast cancer is outside your body, the actual disease never makes you feel ill. I felt absolutely fine, apart from the side effects of chemo. And, even then, I was quite lucky that I didn't get half as ill as some other people who really suffer with it. The main side effect for me was tiredness. And not just the tiredness you get if you've had a few late nights. This was an overwhelming sense of exhaustion, and when it came on there was absolutely nothing I could do apart from go straight home and go to sleep. But apart from the tiredness, I was able to carry on leading a fairly normal life. The doctors told me not to just sit around at home waiting for the chemo side effects to kick in, so we carried on doing normal things – taking our dog for a walk, doing the shopping and popping out for lunch.

Steve was fantastic and looked after me wonderfully. He cooked all my meals and I didn't have to lift a finger. And Erin was great in that she kept my mind off what was going on. All kids are essentially quite selfish, and as long as their lives are unaffected by something, they just carry on in the same way. But that was good for me to be around. From the moment I told Erin that I wasn't going to die, she just took all the cancer and chemo totally in her stride.

When I told her I was starting chemo, she said, 'Does this mean we're not going to Auntie Maureen's wedding in Spain?'

Steve was really mad with her about that, but I tried to

explain to him that Erin was reacting exactly the same as any other kid her age would. Their first thought is almost always 'How is this situation going to affect me?' At that time, we still weren't sure whether we would make it to Maureen's wedding, although I desperately hoped that we would.

After my second round of chemo, I came down with the most horrific mouth ulcers. I counted them in the mirror and there were twenty-five in there. They were agony. For more than a week I couldn't eat, I could barely drink and I couldn't talk. If I did manage to speak a few words, I sounded like the Elephant Man. Erin bought me a notepad and said, 'Just write on this, Mummy.'

I'd never realized before how much of my life revolved around food and drink, but for two weeks I couldn't even go out for a coffee. All I could do was sit around and think about the pain in my mouth. Then I started worrying that I wasn't getting the right nutrition to help the chemo work. I was living off milkshakes and energy drinks, which I sipped through a straw. It was the only time I vomited during chemotherapy too.

It even hurt to swallow and at night I would dribble until my lips were covered in sores. I cried once at that point, and it was the only time during my treatment that I felt really down. But as soon as they started to get better after a couple of weeks, I threw all my energy straight back into fighting cancer.

By the end of June, before my third session of chemo had even started, I was left with just small tufts of hair and bald patches here and there. The cold cap obviously hadn't worked for me. My hair made me look sicker than I felt, and I was sure people would be saying, 'Oh, look at the state of that poor woman over there.' So I just thought, 'Sod it. I'm shaving the lot off.'

My biggest worry was that I didn't have a clue what my head would look like totally bald. Some people have beautifully shaped heads, but others can look really odd. Steve got his hair clippers out and gently shaved off my remaining tufts of hair. I didn't feel particularly upset by that then; I was just a bit nervous about what I was going to look like.

When Steve had finished, I looked in the mirror. 'Oh, that's not too bad,' I thought. It was a shock seeing myself completely bald, but at least I had a decent-shaped head. And I even discovered a birth mark on the back of my scalp which I would never have known existed!

Getting rid of my hair felt very liberating because I felt like I was taking control of what was happening. But I also found it more traumatic than I had expected. At first I felt very exposed and not very attractive and I was nervous about going out without a scarf over my head, but gradually I got a bit braver about it.

A reporter from *News of the World* phoned and said the paper was interested in following up the story of my treatment. Would I agree to have my photograph taken completely bald? I wasn't sure at first. I was still coming to terms with having no hair myself and the thought of exposing myself to the entire country was very scary.

But the more I thought about it, the more I thought, 'Why not? It's nothing to be ashamed about. Going bald shows that the chemo is working. I should be proud of it.'

So I agreed, and my bald head appeared in newspapers in front rooms all over the country. And, with good make-up, I didn't look too bad.

It was harder when I lost my eyelashes and eyebrows though. Then I looked a right bugger! First thing in the morning, I'd look in the mirror and see someone who looked like they'd been rescued from a prisoner of war camp. But I took the bit between the teeth and went out and spent a fortune on false eyelashes and the best eyebrow pencils I could find.

Then, every morning, before I came downstairs and Erin saw me, I would put on my falsies and pencil in my eyebrows. And it instantly made me feel better. Even on the days when I really didn't feel like doing all that and putting on my make-up, I still did it. False eyelashes can be a right pain and Steve and I had a real laugh over my attempts to draw on eyebrows. At first I'd spend whole days walking around with a permanently surprised expression on my face, but gradually I got better at it.

At first I wore a wig a lot when I went out, but although it was a lovely wig, I didn't feel quite comfortable in it.

Towards the end of my treatment, in September, I was invited to the TV Choice Awards at the Dorchester Hotel in London. I was a bit worried about walking up a red carpet with a bald head, so I decided to wear my wig. On the evening, I was just about to get in the car to go to the do when I looked at myself in the mirror. I had a fabulous long dress on, full make-up and my blonde wig, but something just didn't feel right.

'I can't do it,' I thought. 'I can't go out there in this wig and hide my head from people when I've been saying I'm proud that my bald head shows I'm beating cancer.'

I pulled the wig off and threw it into the corner of the room. I was going to be bald and proud.

Maureen's wedding was planned for 13 August and throughout my treatment I'd kept on hoping that I'd be able to make it for the big day. As it got closer, I asked the doctors if they could delay one of my chemo sessions for a week so I could fly out to be there. They agreed, and I was so chuffed to see our Maureen finally marry Ritchie. My mouth ulcers were still painful at that point, but I had a wonderful time, and it was lovely spending time with my brothers and sisters.

There was more good news that month when I received results of the tests which had been done to discover whether my strain of breast cancer was genetic. It wasn't. Thank God. It meant that Erin wasn't at any more risk than anyone else of getting the disease in the future. Linda's cancer was also found to be non-genetic. It seems it may just have been a terrible coincidence that out of six sisters, three of us had been struck down with it. That day I cried again, but this time it was with happiness, knowing that I wasn't going to pass cancer on to Erin. To celebrate, we cracked open a bottle of champagne.

My last session of chemotherapy took place on Friday, 1 October and that night we hit the champagne again. I felt like I could see the light at the end of the tunnel. But I still had one last major hurdle to get over – the mastectomy and breast reconstruction. Normally women have a mastectomy first, then chemotherapy, but because my cancer was so aggressive and had already spread to my lymph nodes, they'd done it the other way round.

My operation was scheduled for Friday, 8 October. I understand some women find the thought of losing a breast really difficult, but I'd never been particularly bothered about my boobs, so I found that less traumatic than losing my hair. And Steve had no qualms about it either. 'I don't care if you've got no boobs,' he said. 'And I'm not just saying that, I mean it. I love *you*.'

I even asked the surgeon if I could have both breasts removed at the same time, just in case the cancer ever came back on the other side, but he felt that was unnecessary at that time, and he warned me that it would be a very long operation and the recovery would be far harder if I had a double mastectomy. As it was, I was facing a five-hour operation, during which they would remove my left breast, carry out an immediate reconstruction and take away thirteen lymph nodes. For a while I did feel a bit scared about it all.

At my next meeting with my surgeon, I told him I was getting nervous. He talked me through everything he would be doing in the operation, in the hope that it would calm me down. But halfway through, I had to stop him. 'Hang on, hang on,' I said. 'That's enough detail for me. Just wake me up when it's over!'

By the time I got home, I'd regained my more usual positive approach to it all.

'How do you feel about the op?' Linda asked me one night on the phone.

'I'm actually quite excited,' I said. 'I want to get on with it, get it over and done with and then I can move on.'

It felt to me like being pregnant. 'Like a baby, it's in there, it's got to come out and it's going to hurt,' I said to Steve. 'But, like being in labour, it is giving new life.'

On the morning of the op, Steve and I dropped Erin with a friend who'd offered to take her to school. 'See ya, Mum,' she yelled as she got out of the car. 'Good luck.'

I had butterflies in my tummy when we got to the hospital, and Steve was very quiet.

'I just wish I could take all this away for you,' he said as I lay on the trolley in my hospital gown. 'I wish it was happening to me.'

'I'll be fine,' I said. 'I'll be absolutely fine. And when I wake, I'll have new boobs – well, one anyway!'

Then the nurse came and told Steve he'd have to go and wait outside because they were ready to take me into the operating theatre. He gave me a kiss and walked away. As the hospital porters pushed my bed down the corridor, I saw Steve walking away. He wasn't crying, but he looked so, so sad. 'I'll see you later,' I called out.

They took me into a small room next to the operating theatre. Out of the window, I could see a huge painting of a sunflower on a wall. It was such a simple thing, but it filled me with real joy. 'Isn't that lovely,' I thought. 'But I'm going to be able to see flowers for real when I get out of here. I'm going to be fine.' It might sound strange, but at that moment I felt so lucky that I was alive and that I was going to survive.

After the operation, I woke up in a recovery room, but I was still feeling a bit dozy when they wheeled me back to the ward. They pushed me around a corner and there, sitting all on his own outside the ward, was Steve. He must have been waiting there for hours.

'Alright, babe?' I said. His face lit up.

'Are you OK?' he said.

'Yeah, I'm good,' I said. 'Really good.'

At that point, I was still so drugged up on morphine that I couldn't feel any pain. That evening, I was in my hospital bed, eating Minstrels, watching the telly and texting my mates. Linda had come down and taken Erin to London for the weekend. They went shopping and to the theatre and cinema and had a great time.

On the day after the operation, I was able to sit up enough to look down at my new boob.

'Oh my God, what is it going to look like?' I thought just before I pulled open my hospital gown. The doctors had shown me pictures of mastectomies and reconstructions before I had my op, and the women's breasts all looked black and blue with bruising. But mine was nothing like that. In fact, it looked pretty much the same as my old breast. Obviously there was a scar, but they'd put my skin back around the implant, and somehow the surgeon had even managed to get the same sagginess in my left boob as in my right one! So they matched perfectly. He'd even put my nipple back in the same place.

By the time Erin came in to visit on the Monday, I was sitting up and looking much better, so I was pleased about that. I didn't want her worrying about me.

In the days after the operation, it was quite painful though, particularly as they'd had to dig quite deep into my back to get muscle to reconstruct my breast. But each day I felt stronger and on the Thursday after the op, I was allowed home. For a couple of days, I lay on the couch while Steve ran around like the perfect nurse. Linda was also there to help out and look after Erin.

On the Sunday after I got home, it was my fiftieth birthday. I'd always liked to celebrate big birthdays with a party, and my fortieth had been a massive do, but there was no way I was up to a party this time. Maureen had said she would be coming down that weekend, but had to leave on the Sunday morning.

I knew it was going to be a quiet day, and I was a bit upset about that, but I tried not to think about it. But then, on the Friday evening, my brother Brian and his wife Annie turned up. And the next day Maureen and her husband Ritchie and my friend Rick arrived. 'And of course I'm not leaving on your birthday,' Maureen laughed.

They'd planned it all along that there would be a few of us around on my fiftieth, to make it special. On my birthday, I opened my lovely presents and then we got all wrapped up and went and had a few drinks in the garden of a pub down by the River Thames – except there was no alcohol for me! It was one of those gorgeous, bright autumn days and it was just wonderful to be sitting there, breathing in the fresh air and feeling alive.

Afterwards, we went home and a couple more of my friends came round and Steve cooked a huge dinner. After the meal, Steve came into the room carrying a huge cake and everyone sang 'Happy Birthday'. I didn't cry, but it was pretty emotional. It had been a rough old year, but I'd made it. I was alive.

After the surgery, I still had to have a few more sessions of Herceptin once every three weeks, but my surgeon said the cancer had gone and my prognosis was good. That feeling of being clear of cancer was just incredible. I really had won. I really had got that stuff out of me. I felt like the luckiest woman alive.

By the beginning of November, my hair had begun to grow back and I was feeling much stronger after the operation. I'll have to have a mammogram and blood test every year for ten years, just to check everything is OK, but I can't see any point in worrying about that now.

The Future

Looking back over 2010, it seems incredible that I was diagnosed with cancer, underwent all that treatment and got clear of it. It all happened so fast; it was like a whirlwind.

By the end of 2010, I was ready to go back to work. Before I had my operation, I was offered a role in the touring stage show of *Calendar Girls*. They'd said they would hold the part open for me for as long as I wanted, and I'd said I'd be ready to start in January 2011. But, of course, in that show there is the really famous nude scene where members of the Women's Institute take their clothes off to shoot a nude calendar. I'm sure some people must have thought I was mad to agree to strip off on stage three months after having a mastectomy. But my character is only seen naked by the audience from the back, so all they would be able to see is the scar where my muscle was taken. Yeah, I guess the other actresses would see the scar on my boob, but so what?

I think it is good to send out a message that there is nothing wrong with scars. I'll definitely wear backless dresses in the future, and people will be able to see my scar. Those scars are part of me now, and I can't see any reason why I should hide them away.

I've tried to tackle the cancer, chemotherapy and all its side effects head on ever since it was diagnosed. And I'm sure having a very positive attitude made everything far more manageable. Certainly, feeling anger was very powerful for me. It gave me the strength to go into battle with the cancer and to refuse to ever give up.

Life has to go on. For me, there was never any question about that, and I was adamant I would do whatever it took to beat that bastard cancer. And I did.

My brothers, sisters, friends, Erin and especially Steve were all amazing. I'd always known Steve was an incredible bloke, but when I was ill, I saw it more clearly than ever. He did absolutely everything for me, and I can't imagine anyone could have looked after me better. And while we've always been very close, I feel that the cancer has strengthened our bond even more. It made it crystal clear to me that all I ever wanted was to be here, alive, with Steve and Erin.

And now I'm feeling better, I can look forward again. I'd love to do another Nolans tour and it would be great to get more telly work too. I've been working since I was so tiny that I could never imagine giving it up. Work has always been very important to me.

I'm back in contact with Anne, Denise and Auntie Theresa now, which I'm really pleased about. In November 2010 I went up to Blackpool for Anne's sixtieth birthday and we had a great time.

I speak to all my sisters and brothers regularly, and it is a wonderful feeling to know that they are always there for me if I need them.

Even though it was a bit delayed, I planned a massive fiftieth birthday party for myself in 2011. I felt I had so much to celebrate. Yeah, I've had some tough times along the way, but so have my sisters and brothers, and so have a lot of other people. But I don't think it is so much what happens to you in life that matters, as how you deal with it. And we've fought, and we've survived.

Now I have a wonderful family, a gorgeous daughter and an amazing husband. I feel incredibly lucky. So, let's party!

Picture acknowledgements

All pictures courtesy of the authors with the following exceptions:

Page 3 top: © BBC; page 4 top: Mirrorpix; page 4 bottom: Sig Fujita;
page 5 bottom: Alastair H.M. Patrick; page 6 top right: Shirley Hill;
page 6 bottom left: John Paul Brooke/Scope; page 7 bottom: © *Hello!*;
page 9: Paul Mitchell/*Woman* magazine/IPC+Syndication;
page 10 top: Nicky Johnston; page 10 bottom: Ken McKay/Rex Features;
page 12 bottom left: CAMERA PRESS/Nicky Johnston;
page 15 bottom: Nicky Johnston/*The News of the World*/
nisyndication.com; page 16: Nicky Johnston/© Universal 2011.
All rights reserved.

Also available from
THE NOLANS

The Nolans
I'm in the Mood Again – CD

The Nolans
The Ultimate Girls' Night!

The Nolans Live
I'm in the Mood Again Tour

Includes, The Nolans' smash hit album,
Live DVD from the sensational show,
Bonus collectors' artcards, The Nolans'
Biography – The Story of the Nolans

extracts reading groups
competitions books new
discounts extracts
competitions
new
events books
extracts
new reading groups
interviews
events extracts
discounts
new books events
events new
discounts extracts discounts
www.panmacmillan.com
extracts events reading groups
competitions books extracts new